Sales and Distribution Controlling with SAP® NetWeaver BI

SAP® Essentials

Expert SAP knowledge for your day-to-day work

Whether you wish to expand your SAP knowledge, deepen it, or master a use case, SAP Essentials provide you with targeted expert knowledge that helps support you in your day-to-day work. To the point, detailed, and ready to use.

SAP PRESS is a joint initiative of SAP and Galileo Press. The know-how offered by SAP specialists combined with the expertise of the Galileo Press publishing house offers the reader expert books in the field. SAP PRESS features first-hand information and expert advice, and provides useful skills for professional decision-making.

SAP PRESS offers a variety of books on technical and business related topics for the SAP user. For further information, please visit our website: *www.sap-press.com.*

D. Rajen Iyer
Effective SAP SD
2007, 365 pp.
978-1-59229-101-4

Norbert Effer, Jean-Marie R. Fiechter, Jens Rohlf
SAP BW Data Modeling
2005, 437 pp.
978-1-59229-043-7

Peter Scott
SAP BEx Tools
2009, ~200 pp.
978-1-59229-279-0

John Jordan
Product Cost Controlling
2008, 572 pp.
978-1-59229-167-0

Susanne Hess, Stefanie Lenz, Jochen Scheibler

Sales and Distribution Controlling with SAP® NetWeaver BI

Galileo Press

Bonn • Boston

ISBN 978-1-59229-266-0

© 2009 by Galileo Press Inc., Boston (MA)

1st Edition 2009

German Edition first published 2008 by Galileo Press, Bonn, Germany.

Galileo Press is named after the Italian physicist, mathematician and philosopher Galileo Galilei (1564–1642). He is known as one of the founders of modern science and an advocate of our contemporary, heliocentric worldview. His words *Eppur si muove* (And yet it moves) have become legendary. The Galileo Press logo depicts Jupiter orbited by the four Galilean moons, which were discovered by Galileo in 1610.

Editor   Patricia Kremer

English Edition Editor   Meg Dunkerley

Translation   Lemoine International, Inc., Salt Lake City, UT

Copyeditor   Julie McNamee

Cover Design   Jill Winitzer

Photo Credit   Getty Images/Jason Edwards

Layout Design   Vera Brauner

Production Editor   Kelly O'Callaghan

Typesetting   Publishers' Design and Production Services, Inc.

Printed and bound in Canada

Contents

Acknowledgments

This book was made possible by the support of several staff members of the PIKON International Consulting Group (*www.pikon.com*). PIKON is a consultancy company that specializes in ERP, Business Intelligence, and Business Integration.

We would like to thank all of the staff in the Business Intelligence department for their dedication and unfailing support. Without them, this book would not have been published. Specifically, thanks are due to Stefan Kerl and André Klos for their help with the manuscript; Oliver Dworschak for his support with structuring and describing the web applications; and Zoltan Both, Heiko Breitenstein, Yuanyuan Gao, Cornelia Köhler, Andrea Steidle, and Andrew Barker for their work on modeling and completing the system examples.

We would also like to thank Rauno Müller for his valuable suggestions and his critical appraisal of Chapter 4.

Lena Holz and Tobias Hock also deserve our thanks for their thorough proofreading of the manuscripts.

Thanks are likewise due to our editors, Patricia Kremer and Meg Dunkerley. Working with them was always pleasant and productive, and their useful ideas and their support in the writing process were of great assistance to us. We would also like to thank the English copyeditor, Julie McNamee and the English translator, Lemoine International.

Given all of the wonderful help we received, we, the authors, are entirely responsible for any outstanding errors.

Susanne Hess, Stefanie Lenz, and **Jochen Scheibler**

1 Introduction

Effectively controlling sales and distribution processes is a challenge for many companies. Sales and distribution controlling has three main phases: first, the analysis of processes in the source system; second, the definition of meaningful key figures; and finally, the creation of target group-specific reports.

Having a process-oriented sales and distribution controlling system — more accurately described as a system for measuring, evaluating, and, ultimately, steering process-oriented sales activities — is centrally important in many companies. Because a large quantity of raw data is created throughout the entire sales and distribution process in SAP® ERP, this data must first be converted into a meaningful, analyzable form using the appropriate tools. The basis for this conversion involves defining appropriate key figures. These figures can then be analyzed to generate information for the various target groups. In the next phase, the key figures are calculated on the basis of the raw data, and then compiled and summarized to make them systematic, target-oriented, and user-oriented. As part of this phase, reports are predefined, which at a later stage provide users with flexible analysis options via a central point of access. *SAP NetWeaver Business Intelligence* (SAP NetWeaver BI) provides users with a tool that is ideally suited to preparation and representing the required information.

1.1 Goals and Basic Principles

This book introduces you to the basic functions of SAP NetWeaver BI, Release 7.0 by showing you how this tool works and how you can use it to create a target-oriented reporting concept in your company.

Then, we create a sample scenario that illustrates potential ways of implementing effective sales and distribution controlling using SAP NetWeaver BI. This is followed by a description of the steps you need to take, starting with data extraction in the source systems, moving on to creating the required objects, and finishing with data flow logic and the transformations in SAP Business Information Warehouse (SAP BW), which is a component of SAP NetWeaver BI.

Next, we look at the creation of raw data in the sales process, and show you the dependencies between the various steps in the process. As part of this section, we introduce a range of sample key figures that can play a significant role in sales and distribution controlling.

We explain step-by-step how you can create these key figures in SAP NetWeaver BI and represent them in reports. Because there are often many ways of doing this, depending on the individual situation and exact requirements, we look in particular detail at this topic to give you a good overview of the various options. We finish off the scenario by showing you how to represent cross-component information for a specific central object, such as *Material* or *Customer*.

Note that the key figures used in this book represent a sample scenario only and make no claim to be exhaustive. The implementation options, too, are intended to be useful examples only. Without doubt, there are other key figures that are just as informative, depending on your company's specific area of specialization, specific target groups, and your own personal interests. For the purpose of this book, we've decided to restrict ourselves to some important, representative figures to show you how to implement your own key figures in SAP NetWeaver BI.

1.2   Sales in SAP ERP with the Sales and Distribution Component

The aim of enterprise resource planning (ERP) systems is to support the entire business value chain using appropriate software functions. Figure 1.1 shows the typical value chain of a production-based company.

The customer makes an inquiry, in response to which he receives a quotation. If the customer accepts the quotation, he places a sales order. The requirements of the sales order are then used in *material requirements planning* (MRP). In the MRP-function, new production and procurement proposals are triggered on the basis of information such as the following:

- Stocks
- Planned goods issues (other sales orders)
- Planned goods receipts (from procurement or production)

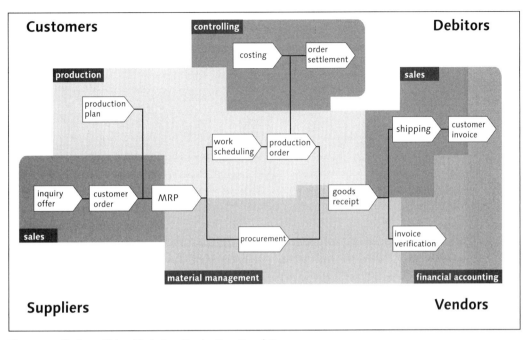

Figure 1.1 Business Value Chain in a Production-Based Company

In purchasing, orders for the required raw materials trigger goods receipts. Production itself is controlled by planned orders and production orders. In a parallel process, the controlling determines costs and uses the production confirmations to identify any deviations between planned costs and actual costs. The production process ends with the completion of finished products, which are stored and, ultimately, delivered to the customer. The customer then receives an invoice for the order in question and makes the payment.

ERP systems support each individual process step by means of corresponding transactions, which are executed by users. The central benefit of ERP systems is that the various areas of the business are integrated with each other. This integration means, for example, that a credit limit specified in financial accounting (FI) can be checked as early as the order creation stage. For another example, the availability check in the sales order can access stocks and planned goods receipts in production and procurement. The goods issue posting process reduces the physical stocks in materials management (MM) as well as the value-based stocks in financial accounting. The invoice created in the sales process is used as the basis for form printing, and turnover posting takes place at the same time in FI. All of these integration functions have helped make ERP systems in general and SAP systems in particular, indispensable components of modern business.

The *sales and distribution* (SD) component supports the sales process in the following phases:

1. Quotation
2. Order
3. Shipment/delivery
4. Billing

ERP systems provide integrated sales functions for all of these phases. The sales processes themselves are subdivided into several variants. In the standard order processing process, the quotation data is transferred to the order and a delivery document is created with reference to the order. This delivery document is then the basis of the billing process. Other sales and distribution processes include the following:

▶ **Third-party business processing**
The products sold in the order are delivered by a third-party supplier directly to the end customer.

▶ **Consignment process**
The products are moved to consignment stores but remain the property of the supplier. Only after the stock is withdrawn by the customer in accordance with demand it is posted on a value basis and billed.

▶ **Returns process**
This process reflects return deliveries made by the customer.

▶ **Outline agreement**
This process administrates longer-term supply relationships.

▶ **Credit memo and debit memo**
Credit memos are used to credit an item to a customer, and debit memos are used to create subsequent debits.

▶ **Cross-company process**
This process makes it possible for products to be purchased from the stocks of affiliated companies (if these companies use the same SAP ERP system).

The list of process variants could be continued for a long time, so only the most important ones are included here.

In Chapter 4, Key Figures in the Sales and Distribution Process, we illustrate where the source data in the SD component comes from, on the basis of SAP ERP Release 6.0. This is the data that is used to create evaluations in the SAP NetWeaver BI system. As elsewhere, it hardly needs stating here that the quality of the evaluations can be only as good as the quality of the source data. Clearly, to create useful, meaningful evaluations in SAP NetWeaver BI, you must be prepared to come to grips with how the source data arises and how it's structured.

1.3 Overview of SAP NetWeaver BI

A BI system is used to provide target group-specific reports on the basis of systematic information storage and processing. The aim is to support and facilitate the process of operational and strategic decision making in the context of the company's goals.

1.3.1 SAP NetWeaver BI and Its Components

SAP NetWeaver BI provides a data warehousing infrastructure called the *SAP Business Information Warehouse* (SAP BW). SAP BW enables modeling any kind of structures, to store large quantities of both historical and current data in an optimized form, and to prepare this data for reporting purposes.

> **Terminology Definition: SAP BW and SAP NetWeaver BI**
>
> We use the term *SAP Business Information Warehouse* (SAP BW) to refer to the data warehousing component within *SAP NetWeaver Business Intelligence* (SAP NetWeaver BI). In other words, SAP BW is a part of SAP NetWeaver BI. Up to Release 3.5, the SAP data warehousing product was called SAP BW; in Release 7.0, it was renamed SAP NetWeaver BI.

There are two approaches to reporting in SAP NetWeaver BI. One uses the *Business Explorer Analyzer* (BEx Analyzer) and is based on Microsoft Excel. The other consists of portal-based reporting via the web using the SAP NetWeaver platform. It's also possible to create a geographical representation of values, for example, to represent current sales figures, grouped by country, on a graphical map. The Business Explorer Maps tool is used for geographical functions.

You can provide users with the evaluations they require in a number of ways. For example, you can bundle evaluations for special user groups in the form of menus;

gather user group-specific reports together in a portal; or send links and full HTML pages containing reporting results via email. The *Business Explorer Broadcaster* tool is used for this purpose.

SAP NetWeaver BI also provides comprehensive tools for system administration tasks, such as periodically supplying the system with data, and user administration with authorization management. Periodically supplying the system with data and other frequently used functions can be combined in the system using *process chains* and then scheduled as background jobs on a recurring basis. A monitoring function for loading processes is also available.

In addition to the role-based authorization concept with which we're familiar from SAP ERP, SAP NetWeaver BI also contains *analysis authorizations*. These authorizations control access to specific characteristics and their instances. In many cases, these are characteristics that are related to organizational units, such as the sales organization or the sales and distribution channel. For reporting purposes, the user in question is restricted to the instance of the characteristic to which he requires authorization and thus sees only one part of the data.

The final part of the SAP NetWeaver BI data warehouse solution is *Integrated Planning (IP)*, which, as the name suggests, is an integrated tool for enterprise planning. This tool is used to model planning applications in which users can manually enter and save planning data. It can also be used to define planning functions that enable automated data creation and modification.

Because reporting and planning use the same tools, it's possible to develop integrated analytic solutions that contain both planning and analysis functions.

1.3.2 Benefits and Advantages of a Data Warehouse

You may wonder why a company would create and manage a special, dedicated data warehouse when the data already exists elsewhere. The reasons will be explored with justification here.

Required data is present in various locations. This data is sure to consist of data that is stored in *online transaction processing* systems *(OLTP)*, and there may also be data that was simply created manually and is stored in separate files, for example. Data in external databases is also a possible data source.

Of course, it's possible to have reporting in an OLTP system. However, in many cases, standard reporting concepts can use data from a single area only, for example, billing document data. With such systems, if you need enterprise-wide reporting—for example, if you want to combine invoicing data with information from accounts receivable accounting—these reports have to be programmed specially.

Also, every evaluation that is started in the OLTP system places additional strain on the *performance* of the system. In short, OLTP systems are designed and optimized for daily operations (for creating data) but not for reporting.

The advantage of SAP BW is that it's a dedicated system, optimized for reporting purposes. Evaluations that would place an unnecessary strain on an OLTP system are transferred to SAP BW, which can carry out fast and flexible analyses.

SAP BW gathers together data from a variety of sources and makes it unified. For example, you can load data from OLTP systems to SAP BW, connect to external databases from within SAP BW, and use flat files as data providers. The data is then stored in SAP BW in shared storage locations using a *modeling concept* that is adapted to the scenario. The data can be added to, corrected, and consolidated within the data flow.

Using SAP BW means that there is no need for special programming to be carried out in the OLTP system or for data to be laboriously compiled by hand. Both these tasks require a lot of time and effort and are highly error-prone.

SAP BW is capable of combining data from different sources, including data from different modules of the SAP ERP system, which means that cross-system and cross-module reports can be created in a straightforward manner.

SAP BW provides decision makers with comprehensive, bundled data that is tailored to their individual requirements in a central, easy-to-access location. This meaningful data enables important business questions to be answered at a glance and targeted decisions to be made. Fast, automated, flexible data reporting can increase transparency, lend additional security to decision making, and minimize risks.

The *online analytical processing functions (OLAP)* in SAP BW enable the user to access the data they need and represents this data in an optimal form. Flexible navigation options in evaluations mean that the data can be represented in any of several different views, in accordance with the user's requirements. A report view that is specially created this way can be saved in a work folder and is available for new reports using updated data later on.

Also, data warehouses make it very easy for users to create new reports on the basis of existing data structures, without the need to involve programmers or the company's IT department.

1.4   Summary

In this introductory chapter, we've described the background you need to be aware of when dealing with the subject of process-oriented sales controlling. Two systems are involved: the source SAP ERP system, which provides the source data that you need; and SAP NetWeaver BI, which further processes and saves the data, and compiles it for the purposes of target group-specific reports.

The next chapter describes the basics of the SAP NetWeaver BI system. You'll learn about the standard components of a SAP BW system, the procedures that exist for extracting data from the source systems, and the main basic functions and navigation options involved in reporting.

2 SAP NetWeaver BI

This chapter introduces you to SAP NetWeaver Business Intelligence (SAP NetWeaver BI) by first describing the basic principles of modeling in the SAP Business Information Warehouse (SAP BW) as well as the basic elements of data retrieval. Finally, the chapter describes the reporting options in Microsoft Excel and through the web.

2.1 The Basic Principles of Modeling in SAP NetWeaver BI

The following sections provide an overview of the various SAP NetWeaver BI components, that is, the system's data structures and the corresponding modeling or the definition of the basic objects in SAP BW. The description includes characteristics and key figures, as well as the DataStores that can integrate extracted and generated data.

You also define rules that must be adhered to when aggregating, correcting, changing, consolidating, and updating extracted data. This is part of the *extract, transform, and load* (ETL) concept, which describes the areas of data extraction, data transformation, and data loading. The ETL concept also comprises the phases in which the data is extracted from the source systems and transferred into a SAP BW target structure according to specific transformation rules.

Another basic area of SAP NetWeaver BI is *reporting*. The goal and purpose of every SAP BW system is to store particular data in a format optimized for reporting. Based on this data, the evaluations are defined and made available to the users. The users have numerous navigation options to easily generate the required view for their data. They can also create new evaluations on the basis of existing data structures.

Reporting can either be carried out in a web-based portal or by means of a Microsoft Excel-based tool called *Business Explorer Analyzer*. Sections 2.3, Reporting Options in Microsoft Excel, and 2.4, Web Reporting, provide more information on reporting.

2.1.1 Data Structures in a Data Warehouse

In this context, we must first distinguish between the basic objects in SAP BW, that is, the *InfoObjects* and the *InfoProviders* that are necessary to store data. InfoObjects are the basic meta objects — the smallest units in SAP BW — which are *key figures* and *characteristics*.

Key figures are data fields that represent values or quantities. Examples of key figures are amounts, such as sales order value or billing values; quantities, such as the *delivered quantity*; or numbers, such as the *number of orders*. The defining feature of a key figure is its aggregation behavior, which describes how a key figure is to be aggregated. Usually, the individual data records are summed; however, you can also use exception aggregations, for example, *Last Value via an Aggregation Reference Characteristic*. The *Last Value via the Month Characteristic* option can be used for balance key figures because you can only create a correct balance in the course of time.

Characteristics further specify the key figures and define which view is supposed to be evaluated in reporting. They are the criteria that can be used to analyze the data. For example, the *sales order value* key figure can be analyzed per customer or per material. In this case, *customer* and *material* are the characteristics.

Characteristics can also have *texts*, *attributes*, and *hierarchies*. Texts are the descriptions of the characteristic attributes, for example, the name of the customer. Attributes are information that logically belongs to the characteristic. For the example of the *customer* characteristic, attributes could be the corresponding location, the sales district, the customer group, and so on. The hierarchy refers to the hierarchical structure of the characteristic's attributes, which are related to one another. For example, the *customer* characteristic can have a customer hierarchy that groups all customers of the enterprise by their location in the different countries.

Key figures and characteristics are summarized here:

- **Key figures**
  - Data fields that represent values and quantities (amounts, quantities, numbers)
  - Particular aggregation behavior
  - Example: sales order value, delivered quantity, number of billing documents

▶ **Characteristics**

    ▶ Business reference objects for the key figures

    ▶ Can have texts, attributes, and hierarchies

    ▶ Example: customer

The *DataStore* is a further important component in the data structure area. SAP BW includes various objects that can store data. Here, you must differentiate among the following data storage levels:

1. PSA Tables

2. DSOs

3. InfoCubes

PSA (*Persistent Staging Area*) tables are the lowest storage level. These flat tables depend on the source system and contain the fields that are provided by the source system. The data is stored unmodified and hasn't been transformed in SAP BW yet. However, you can't use the data within these tables for reporting. The data is only available as a kind of interim state for further updates within SAP BW. It may also be useful to analyze the data in the PSA tables for checking and testing purposes.

The DSOs (*DataStore objects*) make up the next data storage level, which are also flat tables. However, in contrast to the PSA tables, they can be used for reporting. DSOs contain the already mentioned InfoObjects as characteristics and key figures. DSOs are used in SAP BW for two reasons:

▶ **Storage of detailed data**
They enable you to store detailed data, usually at document level. If necessary, you can use this data for reporting. However, this is more of an exception because evaluations are usually based on aggregated data. For example, if you want to analyze particular facts in a special case, you can access the detailed data (document level) by navigating to the data of a DSO.

▶ **Consolidation and enrichment of data**
DSOs allow for a consolidation and enrichment of data across multiple levels. In this context, the lowest level usually includes data at document level. This data can be consolidated in several transformation steps and enriched with additional information. The resulting data is stored in additional DSOs, that is, the data is available at all stages in SAP BW and can be used for detailed or aggregated reporting as required.

Finally, you can store the data in *InfoCubes*, which are based on a multi-dimensional data model that enables optimum access to the data for reporting. An InfoCube also consists of various InfoObjects. Several dimension tables link the characteristics to the key figures that are defined in the fact table. This distribution of the characteristic combinations into various smaller dimension tables enables performance-optimized access to the data. In reporting, the characteristics contained in an InfoCube are used to access the attributes, texts, or hierarchies of this characteristic that are separately stored in master data, text, or hierarchy tables. Figure 2.1 shows an example of an InfoCube database schema.

Like DSOs and InfoObjects, InfoCubes are referred to as *InfoProviders* in the SAP BW system because they provide information for reporting.

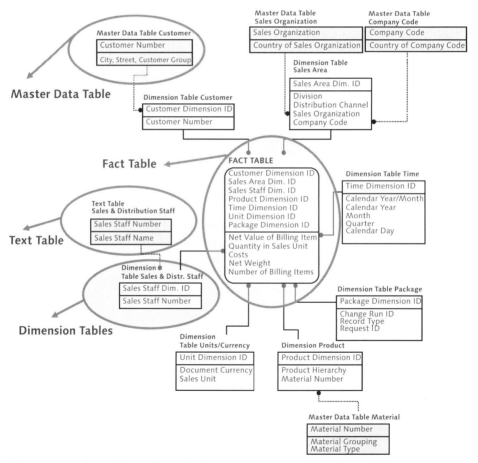

Figure 2.1 Database Schema of an InfoCube

In addition to the InfoCubes and DSOs, you can define *MultiProviders* in SAP BW. A MultiProvider links the data of multiple InfoProviders to allow cross-company reporting. You can use a MultiProvider, for example, to link the billing documents to the open items of a customer to evaluate this information together in reporting.

MultiProviders don't store data; instead, the data is read from the underlying Info-Cubes, DSOs, and InfoObjects for evaluations. MultiProviders only provide the structure that is used to link the data.

2.1.2 Extract, Transform, and Load (ETL)

Now that you're familiar with the data structures of SAP BW objects, you have to bring them to life, that is, fill them with data.

A critical prerequisite for extracting data from a source system is the *DataSource*. It contains all characteristics and key figures that are supposed to be extracted and filled via specific *extraction logic*. You'll find further information in Section 2.2, The Basic Principles of Data Retrieval. To load sales order values and quantities into the SAP BW system, for example, you need a DataSource in the source system. Irrespective of whether a Business Content DataSource is available or whether you must define your own DataSource, this DataSource is made known in SAP BW through *replication*, which means the information on the delivered characteristics and key figures is provided in the source system and in SAP BW.

In the next step, you define the link between the information from the source system and the SAP BW objects. You must specify which characteristics and key figures of the DataSource correspond to the InfoObjects in the DataStores of the SAP BW system. This mapping is defined in *transformation rules*, which link a Data-Source to a data target, such as DSOs or InfoCubes.

There are various options to map information in accordance with these transformation rules:

- ▶ **1:1 mapping**
  A characteristic from the source system is mapped to an InfoObject in SAP BW without logic. This is the simplest transformation rule.
- ▶ **Mapping fixed values**
  Fixed values are mapped to the InfoObjects, for example, for which no information from the source system can be delivered.

▶ **Creating a routine**
A routine enables you to use your own ABAP source code to map complex transformation logic. Routines are provided both for the individual InfoObjects that are contained in the data target and globally for the entire transformation (start, end, and expert routine), for example, to enable cross-company calculations.

The transformation rules enable you to clean up, enrich, consolidate, or aggregate the data delivered from the source system. Consequently, the data can be stored in SAP BW in the best possible way according to your specific requirements.

In some cases, you may have to transform data across multiple stages, for example, when complex formatting and aggregations are required in addition to the actual logic or when data from different source systems is supposed to be standardized first and then processed using the same logic. To map such requirements, there are two different methods:

▶ **Storage via interim steps**
To store data in *interim steps* means to use several DSOs in which data is respectively stored after a transformation step and then updated with the next transformation. This option can be used, for example, if you require stored data after specific transformation steps.

▶ **Interposing an InfoSource**
If you don't have to temporarily store data, you can also interpose an *InfoSource*. An InfoSource is a structure that consists of InfoObjects and can't store data itself. It only provides the option to link two transformations to each other. First, the data is transformed from the source object (DataSource or DSO) to the InfoSource, and then transformed from the InfoSource to the target object (DSO or InfoCube).

To trigger and control the loading of data from the source system into the SAP BW system, two additional object categories are needed:

▶ InfoPackages
▶ Data transfer processes (DTPs)

InfoPackages are used to request data from a source system and store it in the PSA tables in SAP BW. You can start the data extraction immediately or schedule it in the background, periodically if required. In the InfoPackage, you can use specific criteria to filter the data that you want to request. For this purpose, you're provided with the fields that were selected as *selection fields* in the DataSource of the source system. For example, if the Sales Organization field is a selection field, you can restrict the InfoPackage to a specific sales organization to load only this data into the SAP BW system. The system stores the imported data in the corresponding PSA table. From there, you can update and store the data in further DataProviders within the SAP BW system.

Data transfer processes (DTPs) control the update of the data. Via DTPs, data originally stored in the PSA table are updated into the data targets. For this process, you need an active transformation rule for the respective data target. If you must update data from a DSO or an InfoCube into additional data targets, both an active transformation rule and a DTP are required here as well.

The system can supply only one data target with data for each DTP. If various data targets must be supplied from one source, you will need to create multiple DTPs. You can load the data online via DTPs or by means of *process chains* by scheduling the process periodically in the background.

A *process chain* bundles several process steps and can include the entire data flow from the source system to the update of the data in the InfoCubes of SAP BW. A process chain can comprise various loading steps through InfoPackages, DTPs, or post-processing of the data targets, for example, setting up database indices and statistics or compressing data to ensure optimal performance.

You can execute process chains online with a direct start or initiate them in the background. Usually, they are periodically scheduled, for example, to supply the SAP BW system each night with the most up-to-date data from the source systems.

The data flow from the source system to the data targets in SAP BW is illustrated in Figure 2.2.

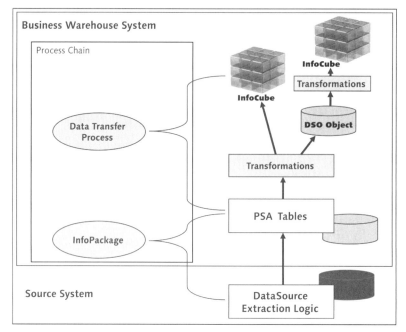

Figure 2.2 Data Flow from the Source System to the Data Targets in SAP BW

This section described the data flow from the source systems to the DataStores in SAP BW. The process and background of data retrieval in the source system were only outlined here, but the following section provides detailed information on these aspects.

2.2 The Basic Principles of Data Retrieval

As already mentioned, SAP BW objects have to be supplied with data. The data supply begins with extracting the data from a source.

The DataSource is the central object in the data supply process because it provides the data for the extraction. The DataSource has a specific structure that is defined by the *extract structure* and is identical in the source and in SAP BW. An *extractor* selects and formats the data in the source system and transfers the data from the source to the input storage location of the SAP BW system, the PSA tables. The data is stored in the format in which it was determined by the extractor in the source and transferred into the SAP BW system through the DataSource. Data formatting as it's carried out in transformations isn't possible here.

Depending on the data type, the system distinguishes among DataSources for master data, transaction data, texts, and hierarchies. Whereas master data, texts, and hierarchies refer to InfoObjects, transaction data is updated in DSOs or InfoCubes. SAP BW supports connecting various sources, as shown in Figure 2.3.

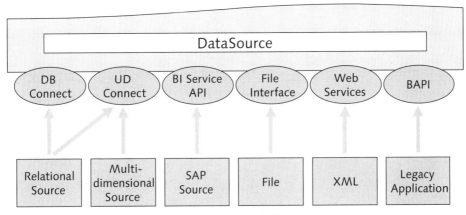

Figure 2.3 Data Sources and Their Connections to SAP BW

Figure 2.3 illustrates that data can be extracted from SAP systems as well as from relational or multidimensional database systems, flat files (e.g., CSV or ASCII), XML, or other applications in SAP BW. The extraction from the sources is implemented in different technical ways; that is, you must connect the different sources to SAP BW using the appropriate method.

2.2.1   Extraction from SAP Source Systems

When retrieving data from SAP systems, the different types of DataSources you'll be working with are as follows:

▶ Business Content DataSources

▶ Customer-specific DataSources

▶ Generic DataSources

Business Content DataSources are implemented by SAP and can be used to extract data after the DataSources have been transferred from the content version to the active version. Individual DataSources comprise specific technical areas or objects. For example, the 0CUSTOMER_ATTR DataSource extracts general customer master data, such as address, name, account group, and so on from the SAP ERP system, and the 0CUSTOMER_TEXT DataSource extracts the customer name as a text. Such DataSources are supplied by extractors that are hard-coded for one DataSource, respectively. Depending on the application, Business Content DataSources are provided for master data, transaction data, texts, and hierarchies. The logistics extractors for transaction data, for example, 2LIS_11_VAHDR for SD sales order header data, represent a special case in this context. Such DataSources must first be managed via Transaction LBWE (*LO Data Extraction: Customizing Cockpit*).

Figure 2.4 shows the LO Data Extraction: Customizing Cockpit in which all settings for these DataSources are implemented centrally. In addition to defining the extract structure (specifying fields for a field selection), you must also select and activate the update type for the application data. Only after the update has been activated, relevant information is updated in specific tables when logistics documents are generated or changed. During the extraction process, the data is read from these tables and transferred to SAP BW. The DataSources that are available for sales and distribution are directly based on the SD documents. In contrast to the document extraction, you can also extract SD information from the Sales Information System (SIS). Section 2.2.2, Document Extraction versus Extraction from SIS, describes the differences between these two options in detail.

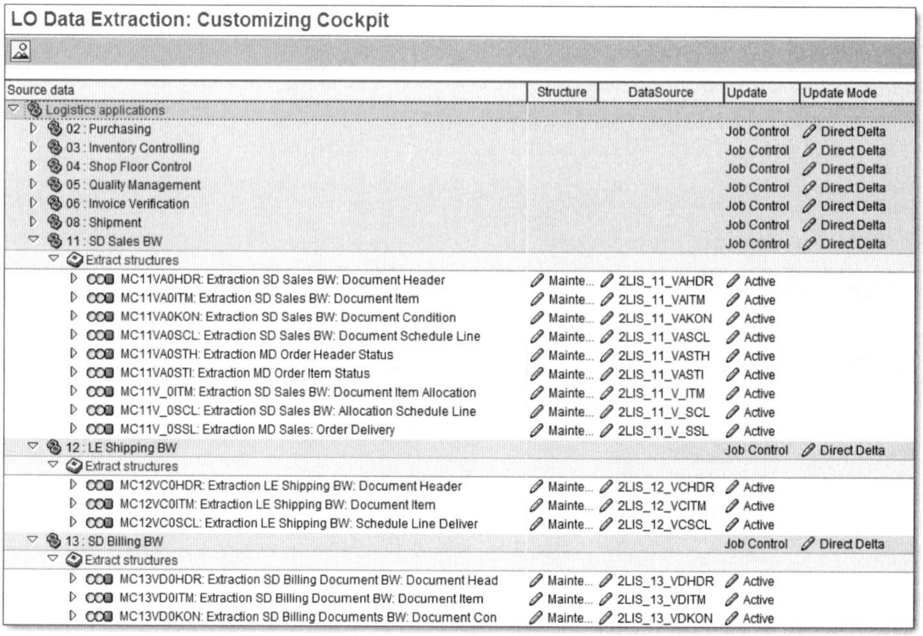

Figure 2.4 Administration of DataSources Through the Customizing Cockpit

For application areas that need to be customized in the SAP ERP software, such as InfoStructures of the *Logistics Information System* (LIS) or the Profitability Analysis (CO-PA), you can generate *customer-specific DataSources*, which are supplied by generic extractors. At runtime, the name of the DataSource reveals what data is supposed to be determined and from which sources.

Generic DataSources are used when the technical requirements can't be met by the Business Content DataSources. Generic DataSources are supplied by individually created customer-specific extractors. You distinguish between the following data determination methods:

▶ **Table/view**
A generic DataSource that is based on a table or view extracts the data from the specified database table or database view. In this context, you can't integrate technical logic; that is, the data is extracted as it's stored in the database. This is an easy way to retrieve additional data from SAP systems.

▶ **SAP Query**
The option to load data from an SAP query (strictly speaking, from the InfoSet) into SAP BW is another way to easily create a generic DataSource. The SAP Query application is used to create reports that aren't contained in the SAP ERP standard version. These queries are based on *InfoSets*, which represent a customer-specific grouping of table fields. However, it only makes sense to create SAP queries in exceptional cases to supply a generic DataSource. This option is usually only used if the SAP query is already provided and the data is supposed to be additionally available in SAP BW. Customers that often use SAP queries in SAP ERP can benefit from this to a large extent.

▶ **Function module**
Finally, you can create a generic DataSource using a function module. This is the most flexible but also the most complex way to create your own extractor. The function module must have a particular structure to extract the data in SAP BW (you can find some examples in the RSAX function group). When the general structure of such a function module has been considered, you can define the logic of the data determination within the function module as you wish. This enables you to format data already in the source system according to the functional requirements.

2.2.2 Document Extraction versus Extraction from SIS

As described in Section 4.4, Excursus: Orders on Hand and Incoming Orders via the SIS, in detail, you can determine SD information from documents as well as via the information structures of SIS. For this purpose, SAP ERP provides predefined structures but also allows you to use your own structures. For reporting with SAP NetWeaver BI, you can extract this data (as stored in the corresponding information structure). To do this, you must generate a DataSource via Transaction LBW0 based on an information structure (see Figure 2.5).

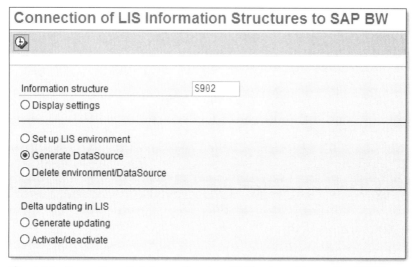

Figure 2.5   Generating a DataSource Based on SIS Structures (Transaction LBW0)

Figure 2.5 shows the transaction for the generation (and maintenance) of Data-Sources, based on information structures. Table 2.1 lists the basic differences between the two options to load SD information into SAP BW.

Keyword	Extraction from SIS	Document Extraction
Degree of detail	Aggregated	Detailed
Data volume	Low	High
Sophistication of the technology	Obsolete	Up-to-date
Future viability	No further developments by SAP	Will be enhanced
Availability of SAP standard DataSources	Few	Many
Changes at document level	Not visible	Visible

Table 2.1 Differences Between the Extraction from SIS and the Document Extraction

The comparison in Table 2.1 clarifies the disadvantages of the extraction from SIS versus the extraction based on the documents. The latter is the more up-to-date and future-proof method to assure a detailed and flexible reporting.

2.2.3 Delta Capability of DataSources

When a DataSource is delta capable, it means that only new and changed data records are delivered after the last loading process. The advantage of the delta capability consists of the reduction of the number of data records per loading process. The special aspects that must be considered when loading delta-capable DataSources are described in more detail in Section 2.2.5, The Extraction Process. The delta capability of an extraction can be implemented in two ways:

▶ Using a field in the data record
▶ Filling a queue

For the first option, a field in the data record is used to determine the new or changed data records. These are usually numbers or date and time stamps.

Another way to ensure the delta capability is to fill a queue (a kind of clipboard), which is filled from the corresponding application. However, this requires that the application supports the process. In this case, the respective data record is written to the queue when a document is created or changed. This data record can then be transferred to the SAP BW system. When filling a queue, the system distinguishes between *delta direct* and *queued delta*. In the first case, the data is immediately written to the queue. In the second case, you must regularly schedule a job that writes the data to the queue. This option is recommended for higher data volumes. A delta queue is usually only used in conjunction with Business Content DataSources, for example, for logistics documents.

You can also implement generic DataSources with delta capability. For this purpose, a field from the extract structure is selected as the *delta field* — just like in the first alternative. However, you must ensure that this field indicates whether the record is new or has been changed. When an extractor is used based on a function module, this field is supposed to check whether the data record is to be extracted.

2.2.4   Extension of DataSources

You can extend almost all active DataSources by adding and filling in further fields. For this purpose, the extract structure is extended by additional fields using an *append structure*. An append structure is attached to an existing structure (or table) and consequently extends it by its fields. You must then fill these fields during the extraction, that is, implement the filling of the additional fields in the corresponding SAP exits via ABAP.

A structure must be extended when an existing DataSource delivers only a part of the required information so that further information needs to be added.

2.2.5   The Extraction Process

If a DataSource was created in the source system or transferred from the Business Content, it's made known in SAP BW through replication. To load data from the source system, you must create an InfoPackage as described in Section 2.1.2, Extract, Transform, and Load (ETL). This InfoPackage defines and initiates the loading process.

If you use the delta procedure for a DataSource, you must initialize the delta for the first loading process, which is controlled by the InfoPackage. When the initialization is successful, you can start a loading process via the delta. In this case, SAP BW stores the relevant value for the delta procedure after each loading process and transfers this value to the source system during the next extraction process.

> **Example of Transferring the Relevant Delta Value**
>
> If the delta procedure is based on a date field, the date of the last loading process is transferred during the extraction. Consequently, the DataSource determines only the data records in the source system that have been created or changed after this date.

In addition to loading via the delta, you can also use full uploads. Here, for each extraction, the system determines all data records for the selection made and transfers them to SAP BW. When the loading process is successful, you can update the data from the PSA into the InfoProviders. The *monitor* in SAP BW displays the status of a loading process. If errors occur during the extraction, the monitor indicates the cause of the errors.

2.3   Reporting Options in Microsoft Excel

A goal of SAP NetWeaver BI is to provide users with evaluations that they can use to obtain necessary information of all kinds. This is ensured by flexible analysis options.

For this purpose, SAP NetWeaver BI provides two different methods:

▶ Business Explorer

▶ Web reporting

We'll describe the options of the *Business Explorer* (BEx) here in detail; the web reporting options are discussed later in Section 2.4, Web Reporting. The BEx tool consists of the following two elements:

▶ **Business Explorer Query Designer**
  This is the tool to define the evaluations (the queries), that is, the structure and content of the evaluations.

▶ **Business Explorer Analyzer**
  This tool executes the queries in Excel. Evaluations that are carried out with this tool can be stored locally and processed with Excel. You can also use all evaluation and design options provided by Excel.

Because many users already have experience with Excel, they usually won't have any problems with the BEx tool.

2.3.1 Defining Queries in the BEx Query Designer

You start the Query Designer via the following menu path: START • PROGRAMS • BUSINESS EXPLORER • QUERY DESIGNER. When creating a new query, you must first select an InfoProvider to define the evaluation upon. The left area of the screen contains all characteristics and key figures that were included in the InfoProvider. Figure 2.6 shows the initial view of the Query Designer.

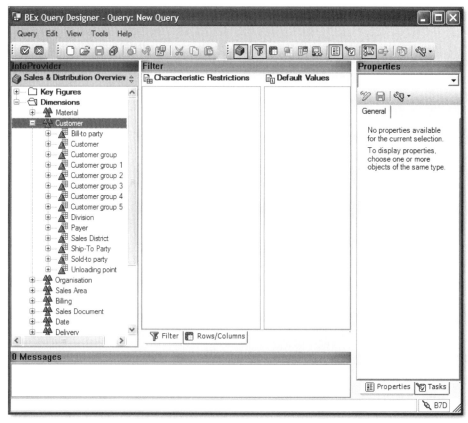

Figure 2.6   Initial View of the BEx Query Designer

The Query Designer consists of the following areas:

▶ Selection of key figures and characteristics (left area of the screen)

▶ Area for CHARACTERISTIC RESTRICTIONS (AREA FOR FILTER VALUES) (shown on the FILTER tab)

- Area for DEFAULT VALUES (shown on the FILTER tab)
- Area for FREE CHARACTERISTICS (shown on the ROWS/COLUMNS tab)
- ROWS area (shown on the ROWS/COLUMNS tab)
- COLUMNS area (shown on the ROWS/COLUMNS tab)
- PROPERTIES pane (right area of the screen)
- Output area in the MESSAGES pane (bottom area of the screen)

You can filter the evaluation by fixed attributes of characteristics using CHARACTERISTIC RESTRICTIONS, for example, to include only the data of a specific sales organization in an evaluation. When the evaluation is carried out, you can no longer change this restriction.

The DEFAULT VALUES option also enables you to filter by particular characteristic attributes. However, these can be changed in the executed query, if required. If the query is filtered by data of a specific distribution channel, for example, you can remove this filter in the executed query and analyze all distribution channels.

Free characteristics aren't displayed in the first drilldown of the report; that is, they aren't included in the rows or columns of the report definition. However, you can use these characteristics to navigate — perform possible analysis steps within the evaluation — in the executed query. This is described later in this chapter.

In the Query Designer, you select the characteristics and key figures that you require for the evaluation to be defined and move them to the respective areas via drag and drop. This enables you to easily specify and save the definition, layout, and content of the evaluation.

In the PROPERTIES pane on the right side, you can detail the characteristics of the query elements. You can, for example, determine the number of decimal places, define the scaling of key figures, or set the display option of a characteristic as a key or description. You can also specify the properties of other elements, such as variables or the query itself. The bottom area for MESSAGES in the Query Designer displays information, warnings, and error messages.

Figures 2.7 and 2.8 show the result of a complete query definition. Figure 2.7 shows possible filter and default values.

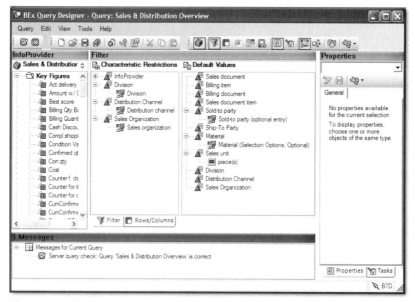

Figure 2.7 Filter Pane in the Query Designer

Figure 2.8 displays the initial view of the query's characteristics and key figures.

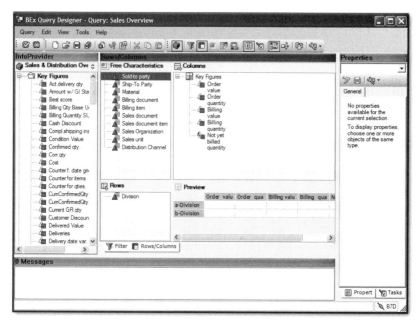

Figure 2.8 Row, Column, and Free Characteristics in the Query Designer

2.3.2 Executing Queries with the BEx Analyzer

You start the BEx Analyzer via the following menu path: START • PROGRAMS • BUSINESS EXPLORER • ANALYZER. Excel opens with additional toolbars:

► BEx Analysis Toolbox

► BEx Design Toolbox

You can use these additional toolbars to control the execution of queries, the navigation in reports, and the creation and design of your own workbooks. The BEx ANALYSIS TOOLBOX is used to execute queries (see Figure 2.9).

Figure 2.9   Toolbar of the BEx Analysis Toolbox

You open a query that you want to start via the leftmost button, OPEN. This calls a selection screen in which you can select specific attributes for defined characteristics. Figure 2.10 shows an example of a selection screen.

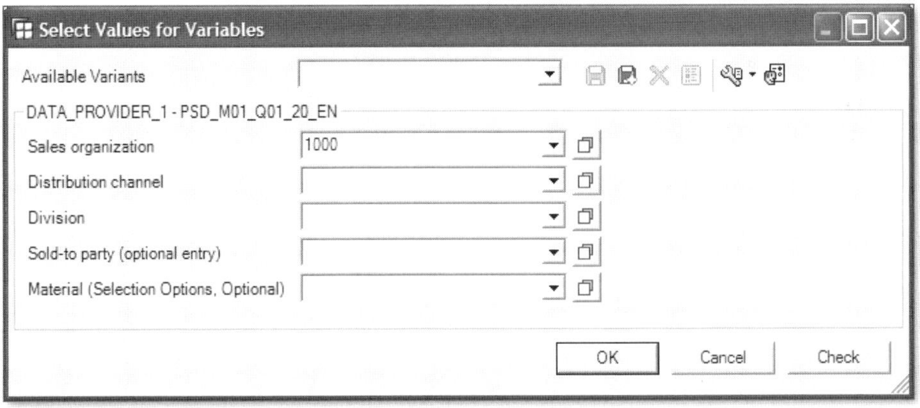

Figure 2.10   Selection Screen of the BEx Analyzer

After you select the required attributes and confirm the specification by clicking OK, the system outputs the result of the query. The layout of the report corresponds to the settings from the query definition. Figure 2.11 shows an example of a query's initial view.

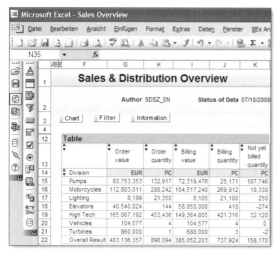

Figure 2.11   Initial View of the BEx Analyzer Query Result

You can then further navigate in the executed report, for example, by filtering the data by specific characteristic attributes, changing the order of the characteristics, or including additional drilldowns of other available characteristics.

To navigate in evaluations, you can use the *context menu* by right-clicking in the result area. The content of this menu depends on the context; that is, it depends on where you click. Figure 2.12 shows such a context menu.

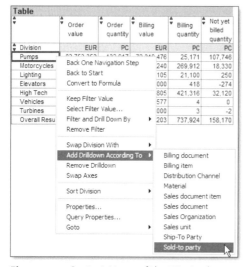

Figure 2.12   Context Menu of the BEx Analyzer

There is an additional option to navigate in the report. This option is provided in the FILTER pane, which you can display using the FILTER button. As you can see in Figure 2.13, it opens in the left area of the screen.

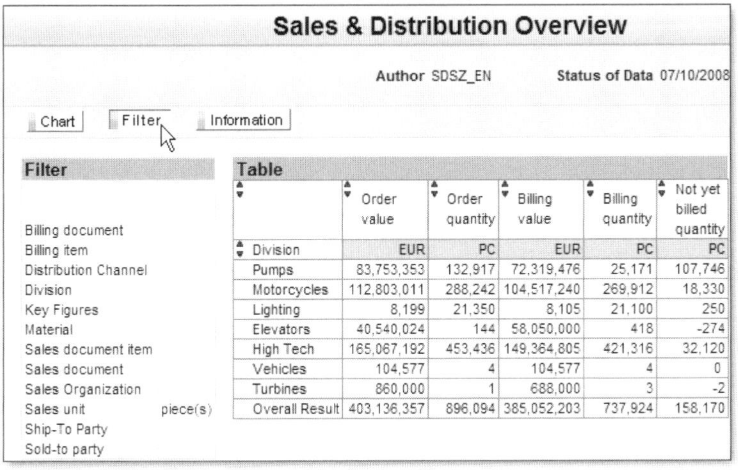

Figure 2.13 Filter Pane of the BEx Analyzer

You can also navigate within this FILTER pane by right-clicking on the respective field in the filter pane. The options provided are shown in Figure 2.14.

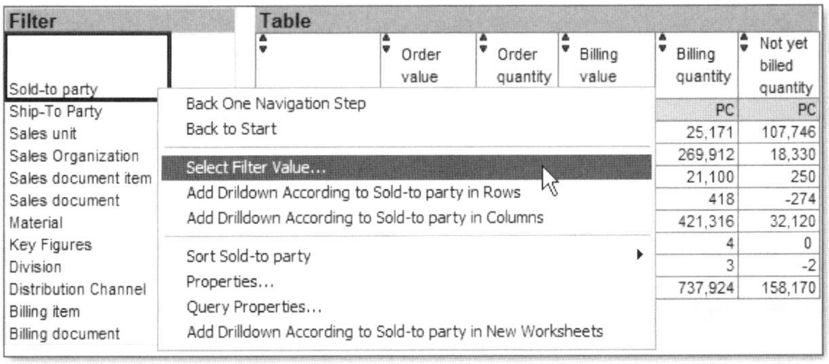

Figure 2.14 Navigation Filter Pane of the BEx Analyzer

You can also navigate via drag and drop. You must click on a characteristic in the filter pane and move it into the result area to add a drilldown according to this characteristic or replace it by another characteristic. The following sections discuss the navigation options provided in the context menu shown earlier in Figure 2.12.

According to the query definition, our example contains the Division characteristic in the first drilldown as well as the Order value, Order quantity, Billing value, Billing quantity, and Not yet billed quantity key figures (refer to Figure 2.11).

Modifying the Drilldown

To add an additional drilldown to our evaluation, for example, by sold-to party, click on a cell of a characteristic, and select the Add Drilldown According To • Sold-To Party option in the context menu. This adds an additional column with all sold-to parties that are contained in the selected data volume (see Figure 2.15).

Table			Order value	Order quantity	Billing value	Billing quantity	Not yet billed quantity
Division	Sold-to party		EUR	PC	EUR	PC	PC
Pumps	1000	Becker Berlin	8,875,447	3,891	4,219,824	1,633	2,258
	1025	Karl Miller LLC.	168,000	2	168,000	2	0
	1032	Institute for Envirc	13,100,416	4,244	12,143,218	3,939	305
	1125	Meier European Le	167,324	0			0
	1171	Hitech Ltd.	78,000	30	26,000	10	20
	1200	Minerva Energieve	284,023	97	284,023	97	0
	1320	Becker Koeln	7,784,242	2,488	7,440,962	2,363	125
	1321	Becker Stuttgart	20,408,019	6,641	19,792,791	6,440	201
	1350	NSM Pumpentech(	2,812	1	2,812	1	0
	1390	Technik und Syste	46,248	14	46,248	14	0
	1400	A.I.T. LLC.	523,848	190	523,052	186	4
	1410	PILAR am Neckar	616,618	220	616,618	220	0
	1700	Electricité, Gaz et	796	4			4
	2000	Carbor Ltd.	18,397,872	6,032	16,301,184	5,342	690
	4999	Hallmann Enginee	58,664	18	30,664	10	8

Figure 2.15 Adding the Drilldown via the BEx Analyzer

To remove this additional drilldown from the query, select the Remove Drilldown option in the context menu of the characteristic that you would like to remove.

To undo a navigation step or return to the initial drilldown according to the query definition, you can choose either Back One Navigation Step or Back to Start from the context menu shown in Figures 2.12 and 2.14.

Selecting or Keeping a Filter Value

If you want to define specific characteristic attributes as filter values, you must choose the Select Filter Value option from the context menu of the corresponding characteristic. This opens a window in which you can specify individual characteristic attributes as well as characteristic intervals. Figure 2.16 shows an example of such a window.

Figure 2.16 Selecting the Filter Value via the BEx Analyzer

The result is a display that is filtered by the selected attributes. Figure 2.17 shows a sample result after the data was filtered by sold-to parties with the numbers between 1000 and 1100. The filter block in the left area of the screen displays the filter content.

Filter		Table			Order value	Order quantity	Billing value	Billing quantity	Not yet billed quantity
Billing document									
Billing item		Division	Sold-to party		EUR	PC	EUR	PC	PC
Distribution Channel		Pumps	1000	Becker Berlin	8,875,447	3,891	4,219,824	1,633	2,258
Division			1025	Karl Miller LLC.	168,000	2	168,000	2	0
Key Figures			1032	Institute for Envird	13,100,416	4,244	12,143,218	3,939	305
Material			Result		22,143,863	8,137	16,531,042	5,574	2,563
Sales document item		Motorcycles	1000	Becker Berlin	153,943	13	14,497	1	12
Sales document			Result		153,943	13	14,497	1	12
Sales Organization		Lighting	1001	Lamp Market Llc	1,899	5,040	1,899	5,040	0
Sales unit	piece(s)		1002	Omega Soft-Hard	2,265	5,760	2,265	5,760	0
Ship-To Party			1033	Karsson High Tec	2,600	6,900	2,506	6,650	250
Sold-to party	1000 Be		Result		6,764	17,700	6,670	17,450	250
		Elevators	1000	Becker Berlin	940,024	12	0	0	12
			Result		940,024	12	0	0	12
		High Tech	1000	Becker Berlin	416,448	1,126	170,739	721	405
			1002	Omega Soft-Hard	271,229	320	271,229	320	0
			1018	Miller's Drugstore	85,900	100	40,373	47	53
			1032	Institute for Envird	11,442	81	10,402	10	71
			1033	Karsson High Tec	21,243,160	22,049	19,466,013	20,160	1,889
			1034	ERL Freiburg	10,402	80	10,402	10	70
			Result		22,038,580	23,756	19,969,157	21,268	2,488
		Vehicles	1012	Autohaus Franzl (	104,577	4	104,577	4	0
			Result		104,577	4	104,577	4	0
		Overall Result			45,387,752	49,622	36,625,944	44,297	5,325

Figure 2.17 Result of the Select Filter Value BEx Analyzer Option

Instead of manually selecting a filter value, you can also keep a displayed value as a filter value via the KEEP FILTER VALUE option in the context menu. As before, the cursor must be positioned on the value that is supposed to be kept for this purpose. In the result of our example, the output is filtered by the selected sold-to party 1000, as you can see in Figure 2.18.

Table

Division	Sold-to party		Order value	Order quantity	Billing value	Billing quantity	Not yet billed quantity
			EUR	PC	EUR	PC	PC
Pumps	1000	Becker Berlin	8,875,447	3,891	4,219,824	1,633	2,258
Motorcycles	1000	Becker Berlin	153,943	13	14,497	1	12
Elevators	1000	Becker Berlin	940,024	12	0	0	12
High Tech	1000	Becker Berlin	416,448	1,126	170,739	721	405
Overall Result			10,385,862	5,042	4,405,060	2,355	2,687

Figure 2.18 Result of the Keep Filter Value BEx Analyzer Option

As an extension, you can also keep a filter value in a navigation step and generate an additional drilldown by an additional characteristic at the same time. To do this, select the FILTER AND DRILL DOWN BY entry in the context menu as shown in Figure 2.19.

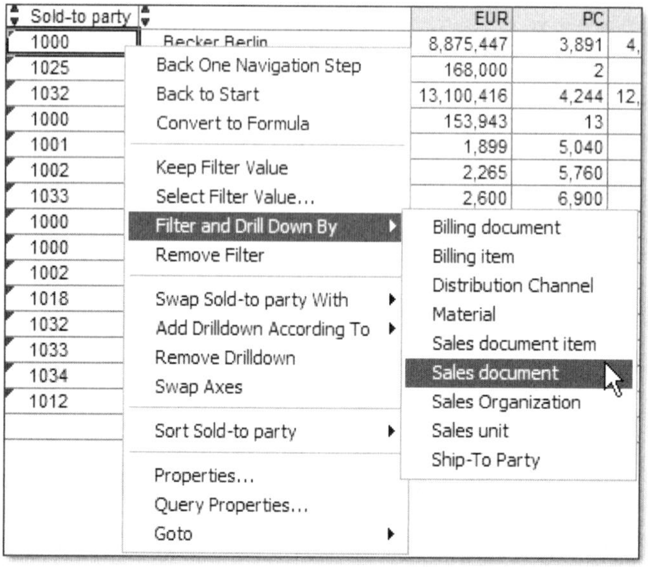

Figure 2.19 Filter and Drill Down with the BEx Analyzer

In our example, the data is filtered by sold-to party 1000, and a drilldown by sales document is added. The result of the performed navigation step is shown in Figure 2.20.

Filter		Table						
				Order value	Order quantity	Billing value	Billing quantity	Not yet billed quantity
Billing document		Division	Sales document	EUR	PC	EUR	PC	PC
Billing item		Pumps	5045	1,472,521	520	1,472,521	520	0
Distribution Channel			5104	244,142	85	244,142	85	0
Division			5673	706,104	265	706,104	265	0
Key Figures			5678	648,737	243	648,737	243	0
Material			6559	536,089	174	536,089	174	0
Sales document item			11769	500	5	301	4	1
Sales document			11770	398	2	398	2	0
Sales Organization			11789	199	1	199	1	0
Sales unit	piece(s)		11790	2,799	2	2,799	2	0
Ship-To Party			11791	2,799	2	2,799	2	0
Sold-to party	1000 Bec		11792	2,799	2	199	1	1

Figure 2.20 Result of the Filter and Drill Down BEx Analyzer Option

Now, the evaluation is filtered by sold-to party 1000, and the drilldown by sold-to party disappears. The filter block displays the filtered value. In addition, a drilldown by sales document was generated that displays all sales documents of sold-to party 1000 in detail.

Swapping Characteristics or Axes

Sometimes, you may need to change the order of the characteristics displayed or swap a displayed characteristic with a freely available characteristic. For this purpose, you can use the SWAP ... WITH option. In our example, by using the SWAP SALES DOCUMENT WITH MATERIAL option, the system removes the drilldown by SALES DOCUMENT and replaces it with a drilldown by MATERIAL. Figure 2.21 displays the corresponding result.

Table								
			Order value	Order quantity	Billing value	Billing quantity	Not yet billed quantity
Division	Material		EUR	PC	EUR	PC	PC
Pumps	100-100	Casing	74,360	389	27,286	146	243
	100-200	Fly wheel	12,418	159			159
	P-100	Pump PRECISION 100	6,245,772	2,505	1,347,372	522	1,983
	P-101	Pump PRECISION 101	396,017	143	396,017	143	0
	P-102	Pump PRECISION 102	228,611	75	225,726	74	1
	P-103	Pump PRECISION 103	99,702	30	99,702	30	0
	P-104	Pump PRECISION 104	344,955	104	184,432	54	50
	P-109	Pump cast steel IDESN	1,728,295	596	1,728,295	596	0
	P-402	Pump standard IDESN(	200,680	63	200,680	63	0

Figure 2.21 Result of the Swap Characteristics BEx Analyzer Option

You can swap two already displayed characteristics in the same way. In the view shown in Figure 2.21, for example, if you want to evaluate which materials were sold in which divisions, you must only swap the positions of the characteristics and use the MATERIAL on the left as the first characteristic.

You can also swap the axes of the evaluation and map the key figures in the rows and the characteristics in the columns, for example. This navigation option isn't always useful because there are usually a lot of characteristic values and only a few key figures. However, for specific requirements, it's quite helpful option. For this purpose, select the SWAP AXES option in the context menu to get the result shown in Figure 2.22.

Table							
	Division	Pumps					
	Material	100-100	100-200	P-100		P-101	P-102
		Casing	Fly wheel	Pump PRECISION 100		Pump PRECISION 101	Pump PRECISION 102
Order value	EUR	74,360	12,418	6,245,772		396,017	228,611
Order quantity	PC	389	159	2,505		143	75
Billing value	EUR	27,286		1,347,372		396,017	225,726
Billing quantity	PC	146		522		143	74
Not yet billed quantity	PC	243	159	1,983		0	1

Figure 2.22   Result of the Swap Axes BEx Analyzer Option

Sorting

You can also sort the characteristics that are displayed in the evaluation, for example, descending or ascending by text or key. As you can see in Figure 2.23, these setting options can be accessed via an entry in the context menu.

		Order value	Order quantity	Billing value	Billing quantity	Not yet billed quantity
Material		EUR	PC	EUR	PC	PC
100-100	Back One Navigation Step		389	27,286	146	243
100-200	Back to Start		159			159
P-100	Convert to Formula		2,505	1,347,372	522	1,983
P-101			143	396,017	143	0
P-102	Select Filter Value...		75	225,726	74	1
P-103	Swap Material With ▶		30	99,702	30	0
P-104	Add Drilldown According To ▶		104	184,432	54	50
P-109	Remove Drilldown		596	1,728,295	596	0
P-402	Swap Axes		63	200,680	63	0
R-F100			4	7,800	3	1
R-F101	Sort Material ▶	Sort Ascending by Text				50
T-F110		Sort Descending by Text ☜				-250
Result	Properties...	Sort Ascending by Key			1	2,237
HD-1300	Query Properties...	Sort Descending by Key			1	12
Result	Goto ▶				1	12
E-1000			1			1

Figure 2.23   Sorting with the BEx Analyzer

In our example, the SORT MATERIAL DESCENDING BY TEXT option was selected to create the result shown in Figure 2.24.

Material	
P-402	Pump standard IDESNORM 100-402
P-104	Pump PRECISION 104
P-103	Pump PRECISION 103
P-102	Pump PRECISION 102
P-101	Pump PRECISION 101
T-F110	Pump PRECISION 100
P-100	Pump PRECISION 100
P-109	Pump cast steel IDESNORM 170-230
R-F100	Pump
R-F101	Pump
100-200	Fly wheel
100-100	Casing

Figure 2.24 Result of the Sort BEx Analyzer Option

Properties of the Characteristics

When defining the query, you can already predefine the properties of the characteristics, such as Display as Key, or Text or Suppress Results Rows. As the user, you have the option to customize these settings in the executed report according to your needs and requirements.

For example, if you want to map the MATERIAL characteristic with text instead of key and text, you must select the PROPERTIES option in the context menu of the corresponding material. In the window that opens, you can modify the display of the characteristic. Figure 2.25 shows the different display options.

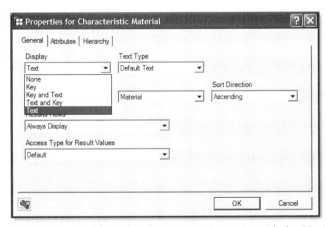

Figure 2.25 Modifying the Characteristic Properties with the BEx Analyzer

When the material display is changed to TEXT, you get a result as shown in Figure 2.26.

Table		
		Order value
Division	Material	EUR
High Tech	TFT Monitor, 17"	25,972
	Sunny Sunny 01	2,534
	Standard Keyboard - EURO Model	8,026
	Professional keyboard - NATURAL Model	10,414
	Motherboard M-3100	355
	Motherboard M-3100	1,129
	Maxitec-R 3100 Personal computer	523
	Maxitec-R 3100 Personal computer	1,995
	Maxitec-R 3100 Personal computer	3,721
	Harddisk, 20 GB	5,760
	Harddisk, 20 GB	2,494
	Harddisk, 20 GB	58,454
	Harddisk 21.13 GB / ATA-2	33,955
	Flatscreen MS 1775P	12,037
	Flatscreen MS 1585	11,425

Figure 2.26 Result of the Change Characteristic Properties BEx Analyzer Option

The control of the results rows can also be found at the corresponding display level in the characteristic properties. To illustrate this, the SALES UNIT characteristic was included in the drilldown. The characteristic is set in such a way that the system always displays the results rows. Figure 2.27 illustrates how this setting affects the display.

Table							
				Order value	Order quantity	Billing value	Billing quantity	Not yet billed quantity
Division	Material	Sales unit		EUR	PC	EUR	PC	PC
Pumps	Pump standard IDESN	piece(s)		200,680	63	200,680	63	0
		Result		200,680	63	200,680	63	0
	Pump PRECISION 104	piece(s)		344,955	104	184,432	54	50
		Result		344,955	104	184,432	54	50
	Pump PRECISION 103	piece(s)		99,702	30	99,702	30	0
		Result		99,702	30	99,702	30	0
	Pump PRECISION 102	piece(s)		228,611	75	225,726	74	1
		Result		228,611	75	225,726	74	1
	Pump PRECISION 101	piece(s)		396,017	143	396,017	143	0
		Result		396,017	143	396,017	143	0

Figure 2.27 Change Results Rows in the BEx Analyzer

Because our evaluation maps the values only in the PIECE(S) sales unit, you shouldn't map an additional results row for each row. To change this, select the ALWAYS SUPPRESS option in the properties of the SALES UNIT characteristic. Figure 2.28 shows the corresponding result.

Table				Order value	Order quantity	Billing value	Billing quantity	Not yet billed quantity
Division	Material	Sales unit		EUR	PC	EUR	PC	PC
Pumps	Pump standard IDESN(	piece(s)		200,680	63	200,680	63	0
	Pump PRECISION 104	piece(s)		344,955	104	184,432	54	50
	Pump PRECISION 103	piece(s)		99,702	30	99,702	30	0
	Pump PRECISION 102	piece(s)		228,611	75	225,726	74	1
	Pump PRECISION 101	piece(s)		396,017	143	396,017	143	0

Figure 2.28   Result of the Change Results Rows BEx Analyzer Option

In addition to the ALWAYS DISPLAY and ALWAYS SUPPRESS options, you can also use the DISPLAY IF MORE THAN ONE VALUE option to display the results rows. Then, the results rows are only displayed when there is more than one attribute for the characteristic.

Query Properties

Irrespective of the characteristic properties, you can also change specific properties for the entire query. This includes particularly the following options:

▶ Navigational State

▶ Presentation and Display Options

▶ Currency Conversion

▶ Zero Suppression

You can generate a specific local view of the data via the navigational state. This enables you to change the display of the characteristics and key figures. In general, this corresponds to the already described navigation options that the context menu provides, for example, swapping characteristics or adding and removing drilldowns.

The QUERY PROPERTIES option in the context menu navigates you to the local query properties (see Figure 2.29).

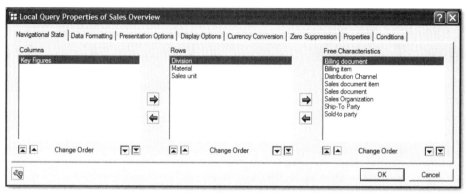

Figure 2.29 Navigational State BEx Analyzer Query Property

Here, you can swap any characteristics from columns, rows, and free characteristics by selecting the respective characteristic and clicking on the arrow keys. You can also change the order of the individual drilldown characteristics in the different areas. For this purpose, use the CHANGE ORDER option with the small icons below the corresponding area. It's also possible to modify the properties of the characteristics and key figures by clicking the right mouse button.

The PRESENTATION OPTIONS tab in Figure 2.29 enables you to change the position of the results rows in the report (right or left, top or bottom), as well as the presentation of mathematical signs and zeros. Additionally, you can select specific DISPLAY OPTIONS (see Figure 2.30).

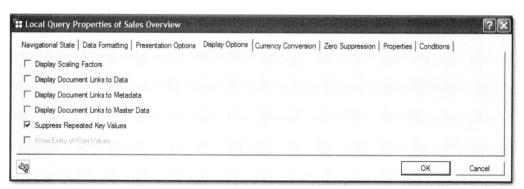

Figure 2.30 Display Options BEx Analyzer Query Property

Here you can display the scaling factors or links to documents. Furthermore, you can retroactively trigger the display of repeated key values, which are suppressed by default. For our sample query, the result from the deactivation of the suppression is shown in Figure 2.31.

Table							
			Order value	Order quantity	Billing value	Billing quantity	Not yet billed quantity
Division	Material	Sales unit	EUR	PC	EUR	PC	PC
Pumps	Pump standard IDESN(	piece(s)	200,680	63	200,680	63	0
Pumps	Pump PRECISION 104	piece(s)	344,955	104	184,432	54	50
Pumps	Pump PRECISION 103	piece(s)	99,702	30	99,702	30	0
Pumps	Pump PRECISION 102	piece(s)	228,611	75	225,726	74	1
Pumps	Pump PRECISION 101	piece(s)	396,017	143	396,017	143	0

Figure 2.31   Result of the Display Key Values BEx Analyzer Query Property

The query properties also provide a currency conversion option. Figure 2.32 shows its various settings.

Figure 2.32   Currency Conversion BEx Analyzer Query Property

The setting in Figure 2.32 converts our sales order and billing document values, which are currently mapped in EUR, to USD. The result is shown in Figure 2.33.

Table

Division	Material	Sales unit	Order value	Order quantity	Billing value	Billing quantity	Not yet billed quantity
			$	PC	$	PC	PC
Pumps	Pump standard IDESN	piece(s)	239,913	63	239,913	63	0
	Pump PRECISION 104	piece(s)	412,394	104	220,488	54	50
	Pump PRECISION 103	piece(s)	119,194	30	119,194	30	0
	Pump PRECISION 102	piece(s)	273,305	75	269,855	74	1
	Pump PRECISION 101	piece(s)	473,439	143	473,439	143	0
	Pump PRECISION 100	piece(s)	-709,544	-250			-250
	Pump PRECISION 100	piece(s)	7,466,820	2,505	1,610,783	522	1,983
	Pump cast steel IDESN	piece(s)	2,066,176	596	2,066,176	596	0
	Pump	piece(s)	12,433	4	9,325	3	1
	Pump	piece(s)	147,644	50			50
	Fly wheel	piece(s)	14,846	159			159
	Casing	piece(s)	88,897	389	32,621	146	243
	Result		10,605,518	3,868	5,041,794	1,631	2,237
Motorcycles	IDES Glad Boy configu	piece(s)	184,039	13	17,332	1	12
	Result		184,039	13	17,332	1	12
Elevators	Elevator model 1003 (	piece(s)	458,053	9			9
	Elevator model 1003 (	piece(s)	117,609	1			1
	Elevator Model 1001	piece(s)	358,650	1	0	0	1
	Elevator Model 1000	piece(s)	189,487	1			1
	Result		1,123,799	12	0	0	12

Figure 2.33 Result of the Currency Conversion BEx Analyzer Query Property

The query properties also enable you to control the suppression of zero values. Consequently, you can hide zero values under certain conditions. For example, you can have the system hide complete rows or columns if all of the values they contain are zero. In our query, this setting was already implemented in the query definition. If you want to change this in the executed report, you must navigate to the ZERO SUPPRESSION tab in the query properties. If you set the ZERO SUPPRESSION to NONE, all rows and columns of the query are displayed, even if the values are zero. As you can see in Figure 2.34, the result now also displays rows in which all key figures have the value zero.

Table			Order value	Order quantity	Billing value	Billing quantity	Not yet billed quantity
Division	Material	Sales unit	$	PC	$	PC	PC
Pumps	Pump standard IDESNC	piece(s)	239,913	63	239,913	63	0
	Pump PRECISION 104	piece(s)	412,394	104	220,488	54	50
	Pump PRECISION 103	piece(s)	119,194	30	119,194	30	0
	Pump PRECISION 102	piece(s)	273,305	75	269,855	74	1
	Pump PRECISION 101	piece(s)	473,439	143	473,439	143	0
	Pump PRECISION 100	piece(s)	-709,544	-250			-250
	Pump PRECISION 100	piece(s)	7,466,820	2,505	1,610,783	522	1,983
	Pump cast steel IDESN	piece(s)	2,066,176	596	2,066,176	596	0
	Pump	piece(s)	12,433	4	9,325	3	1
	Pump	piece(s)	147,644	50			50
	Fly wheel	piece(s)	14,846	159			159
	Casing	piece(s)	88,897	389	32,621	146	243
	Result		10,605,518	3,868	5,041,794	1,631	2,237
Motorcycles	IDES Glad Boy configu	piece(s)	184,039	13	17,332	1	12
	Result		184,039	13	17,332	1	12
Elevators	Elevator model 1003 (1	piece(s)	458,053	9			9
	Elevator model 1003 (1	piece(s)	117,609	1			1
	Elevator model 1003	piece(s)	0	0			0
	Elevator Model 1001	piece(s)	358,650	1	0	0	1
	Elevator Model 1000	piece(s)	189,487	1			1
	Result		1,123,799	12	0	0	12

Figure 2.34 Effect of the Zero Suppression BEx Analyzer Query Property

Adding Local Formulas

You can add your own local formulas to the executed report. This enables you to carry out specific calculations that the query definition doesn't include. Such calculations are generally also possible with the options provided by Excel. The advantage of the local formula option with BEx Analyzer is that calculations are integrated into the layout of the query and displayed as a predefined key figure in the query's result area.

To define local formulas, a formula editor is available that provides the existing key figures of the report as well as the basic arithmetic operations. Select the ADD LOCAL FORMULA option in the context menu (see Figure 2.35) to specify a local formula. This entry is only displayed if the cursor is positioned on the key figure header.

Order value	Order quantity	Billing value	Billing quantity	Not yet billed quantity
EUR				PC
200,680	Back One Navigation Step			0
344,955	Back to Start			50
99,702	Convert to Formula			0
228,611	Add Local Formula			1
396,017	Keep Filter Value			0
-593,513	Select Filter Value...			-250
6,245,772	Filter and Drill Down By ▶			1,983
1,728,295	Add Drilldown According To ▶			0
10,400				1
123,500	Swap Axes			50
12,418				159
74,360	Query Properties...			243
8,871,199	Goto ▶			2,237

Figure 2.35 Add Local Formula in the BEx Analyzer

As shown in Figure 2.36, a window with the formula editor now opens in which you must specify the desired arithmetic operation.

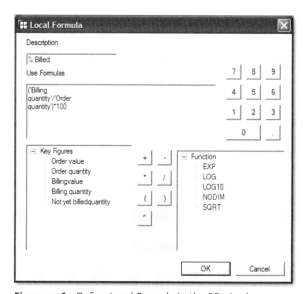

Figure 2.36 Define Local Formula in the BEx Analyzer

The formula defined in Figure 2.36 calculates the billed share of the sales order value as a percentage. After you have confirmed the definition by clicking OK, the system outputs the result (see Figure 2.37).

Table					Order value	Order quantity	Billing value	Billing quantity	Not yet billed quantity	% Billed
Division	Material		Sales unit		EUR	PC	EUR	PC	PC	
Pumps	P-402	Pump standard IDESN	piece(s)		200,680	63	200,680	63	0	100.0000
	P-104	Pump PRECISION 104	piece(s)		344,955	104	184,432	54	50	51.9231
	P-103	Pump PRECISION 103	piece(s)		99,702	30	99,702	30	0	100.0000
	P-102	Pump PRECISION 102	piece(s)		228,611	75	225,726	74	1	98.6667
	P-101	Pump PRECISION 101	piece(s)		396,017	143	396,017	143	0	100.0000
	T-F110	Pump PRECISION 100	piece(s)		-593,513	-250			-250	
	P-100	Pump PRECISION 100	piece(s)		6,245,772	2,505	1,347,372	522	1,983	20.8383
	P-109	Pump cast steel IDESI	piece(s)		1,728,295	596	1,728,295	596	0	100.0000
	R-F100	Pump	piece(s)		10,400	4	7,800	3	1	75.0000
	R-F101	Pump	piece(s)		123,500	50			50	
	100-200	Fly wheel	piece(s)		12,418	159			159	
	100-100	Casing	piece(s)		74,360	389	27,286	146	243	37.5321
	Result				8,871,199	3,868	4,217,310	1,631	2,237	42.1665
Motorcycles	HD-1300	IDES Glad Boy config	piece(s)		153,943	13	14,497	1	12	7.6923
	Result				153,943	13	14,497	1	12	7.6923

Figure 2.37 Result of the Define Local Formula BEx Analyzer Option

The system integrates the local formula into the result area. Consequently, the formula is mapped like all other key figures of the report.

In this context, note that this formula has only been locally integrated with the evaluation. When the evaluation is started the next time, the formula is no longer integrated. If you want to keep a specific local formula, you must save the evaluation as a workbook. You'll learn how to store your own workbooks later in this chapter.

Refreshing the Query

To change the selections made or request up-to-date data from the server, you can refresh the query by using the REFRESH button from the BEx Analysis Toolbox (see Figure 2.38).

Figure 2.38 Refresh Button in the BEx Analysis Toolbox

Then, the system displays the selection screen. After you confirm the selections, the system requests the data again from the SAP BW server.

Conditions and Exceptions

You can define *conditions* and *exceptions* in the query definition.

▶ **Conditions**

Conditions limit the displayed data according to specific requirements. For example, in our query, you can have the system only display records where the not yet billed quantity exceeds the value X or to analyze the top 10 customers.

▶ **Exceptions**

Exceptions enable you to highlight query results according to specific criteria. For example, you can highlight the not yet billed quantity in red if it exceeds a specific critical value, in order to identify such sales orders or customers more easily.

You can predefine several *conditions* and *exceptions* within the query definition. In the executed evaluation, you can activate and deactivate them as required. This enables you to select the appropriate settings for your requirements. Figure 2.39 shows a sample condition in the query definition.

Figure 2.39 Defining a Condition with the BEx Analyzer

If the condition illustrated in Figure 2.39 is active in the executed query, the system displays only the data records that have a not yet billed quantity greater than or equal to 1,000. You can also specify variable condition values, which enables you to define restrictive values for conditions yourself at runtime.

If the condition isn't active, the query displays all data records, irrespective of the value of the not yet billed quantity. In this case, you can activate a condition via the context menu in the executed report as shown in Figure 2.40.

Table			Order value	Order quantity	Billing value	Billing quantity	Not yet billed quantity
Division	Material		EUR	PC	EUR	PC	PC
Pumps	1389	Pump PRECISION 100	950	1,000			1,000
	1392	Pump PRECISION 100	124		*Back One Navigation Step*		130
	100-100	Casing	1,589,639	2,9	*Back to Start*		2,793
	100-101	CI Spiral casing (with	598		*Convert to Formula*		3
	100-200	Fly wheel	12,418				159
	C-1036	Steering Unit G54MB3	0		*Properties...*		24
	DA120	Casing	4,300		*Query Properties...*		0
	P-100	Pump PRECISION 100	8,561,219	3,3	*Key Figure Definition*		2,070
	P-101	Pump PRECISION 101	15 852 257	5 8			846
	P-102	Not yet billed quantity > X (Inactive)			*Toggle Condition State* ▶		753
	P-103	Not yet billed quantity > 1000 (Inactive)			*Create Condition* ▶		660
	P-104	Pump PRECISION 104	34,517,861	10,9	*Goto* ▶		887
	P-100	Pump cast steel IDEON	5 376 400	1 81 4			20

Figure 2.40 Activating a Condition with the BEx Analyzer

Activating the condition causes the system to display only records that have a not yet billed quantity greater than or equal to 1,000. Figure 2.41 illustrates the result of this navigation step.

Table			Order value	Order quantity	Billing value	Billing quantity	Not yet billed quantity
Division	Material		EUR	PC	EUR	PC	PC
Pumps	1389	Pump PRECISION 100	950	1,000			1,000
	100-100	Casing	1,589,639	2,954	197,834	161	2,793
	P-100	Pump PRECISION 100	8,561,219	3,394	3,438,013	1,324	2,070
	T-F101	Pump PRECISION 100	476,145	102,050	238,593	110	101,940
	Result		10,627,953	109,398	3,874,439	1,595	107,803
Motorcycles	1400-100	Deluxe Headlight	5,333,693	127,650	4,348,809	107,547	20,103
	1400-200	Deluxe Taillight	1,997,376	77,449	1,614,457	66,862	10,587
	1400-300	SunFun / 1200 cm3	67,812,905	9,352	63,114,805	8,297	1,055
	1400-400	Motorcycle Helmet - S	10,456,533	58,272	9,137,194	51,356	6,916
	1400-750	Deluxe Gas Tank Strip	1,887,159	122,039	1,448,671	90,572	31,467
	Result		87,487,665	394,762	79,663,935	324,634	70,128
High Tech	DPC1002	Harddisk 10.80 GB / S	9,371,341	44,776	8,653,497	41,007	3,769

Figure 2.41 Result of the Activate Condition BEx Analyzer Option

In contrast, if you activate a condition that you defined with a variable, the system uses the value that was entered in the selection screen. Figure 2.42 shows the selection screen in which this specification is configured.

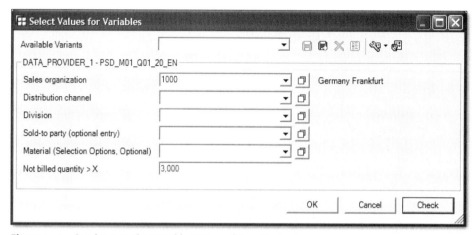

Figure 2.42   Condition in the Variable Screen of the BEx Analyzer

The result of this modification finally displays only records in which the not yet billed quantity is greater than 3,000 (see Figure 2.43).

Table			Order value	Order quantity	Billing value	Billing quantity	Not yet billed quantity
Division	Material		EUR	PC	EUR	PC	PC
Pumps	T-F101	Pump PRECISION 100	476,145	102,050	238,593	110	101,940
	Result		476,145	102,050	238,593	110	101,940
Motorcycles	1400-100	Deluxe Headlight	3,605,437	90,084	3,273,008	84,163	5,921
	1400-200	Deluxe Taillight	1,114,900	56,349	1,031,019	52,912	3,437
	1400-750	Deluxe Gas Tank Strip	1,457,598	87,803	1,343,677	82,204	5,599
	Result		6,177,935	234,236	5,647,704	219,279	14,957
High Tech	T-AU301	Diskette Drive, 3.5", HD	417,118	11,783	35	1	11,782
	Result		417,118	11,783	35	1	11,782
Overall Result			7,071,198	348,069	5,886,332	219,390	128,679

Figure 2.43   Result of the Variable Condition BEx Analyzer Option

You can activate and deactivate the conditions defined in the executed query as required. Multiple conditions can also be active simultaneously.

Exceptions for highlighting data are defined in a similar way. You configure the respective settings in the query definition. In our example, they could appear as shown in Figure 2.44.

Figure 2.44 Defining an Exception with the BEx Analyzer

Here, an ALERT LEVEL Bad 2 (dark red color) was selected for all values that are greater than 1,000. There are nine colors (variations of green, yellow, and red) to highlight the exceptions, and you can specify different colors for different value ranges. For each exception, you also have to define which key figures the exception is supposed to refer using the tabs from Figure 2.44. In our example, the exception affects the not yet billed quantity key figure; that is, the system highlights critical values.

The exception defined in our sample query has a result as shown in Figure 2.45.

Table		Order value	Order quantity	Billing value	Billing quantity	Not yet billed quantity
Material		EUR	PC	EUR	PC	PC
1389	Pump PRECISION 100	950	1,000			1,000
1392	Pump PRECISION 100	124	130			130
100-100	Casing	449,156	446	197,834	161	285
100-101	CI Spiral casing (with	598	3			3
100-200	Fly wheel	12,418	159			159
1300-1000	HD GLAD BOY powei	3,108	13	1,295	5	8
1400-100	Deluxe Headlight	3,605,437	90,084	3,273,008	84,163	5,921
1400-200	Deluxe Taillight	1,114,900	56,349	1,031,019	52,912	3,437
1400-300	SunFun / 1200 cm3	66,598,822	6,540	62,225,691	6,225	315
1400-310	CrossFun / 350 cm3	25,615,029	5,569	24,386,395	5,371	198
1400-315	CrossFun / 350 cm3	4,248,177	646	3,863,177	591	55
1400-400	Motorcycle Helmet - S	8,225,332	41,073	7,465,750	38,367	2,706
1400-750	Deluxe Gas Tank Strip	1,457,598	87,803	1,343,677	82,204	5,599
AM2-GT	SAPSOTA FUN DRIVE	79,577	3	79,577	3	0
B-7000	Brochure: New high t	0	19			19

Figure 2.45 Result of the Exception BEx Analyzer Option

The cells that are affected by the exception defined are highlighted with the respective color.

Workbooks

You can store an executed query with the current navigational state as a *workbook*. A workbook can be stored locally on your PC, like a common Excel file. As long as you're not logged on to the SAP BW system, this is a static file in which you can't navigate or refresh (i.e., request the most up-to-date data from the server) the data. As soon as you're logged on to the system, however, all navigation options are available again.

You can also store a workbook on the SAP BW server. In this case, you can make the workbook available for other users by storing a role that you then assign to the respective users. A workbook stored in favorites can only be called by the user that created the workbook.

The advantage of a workbook is that it can also store navigational states, that is, all navigation steps that you've performed (e.g., setting filters, adding further drill-down characteristics, changing the properties of characteristics or the query itself) are retained in a workbook. It's also possible to permanently integrate further design elements, such as your own company logo or additional charts. Figure 2.46 shows an example of such a workbook.

In general, the data content of the evaluation is stored with the workbook. However, you can define in the properties of the workbook that a selection screen is displayed when you call the corresponding workbook, which enables you to always request the most up-to-date data. This avoids the risk of evaluating obsolete data.

You can configure specific settings for the individual elements of the workbook and integrate additional elements, such as dropdown boxes or text elements, in a particular *design mode*.

To store a workbook locally on your PC, you use the standard Excel commands. If you want to store the workbook on a SAP BW server, you must select the SAVE button on the BEx Analysis Toolbox toolbar (refer to Figure 2.38). When clicking this button, you can store the workbook either in your favorites using the SAVE WORKBOOK AS option or in a predefined role on the SAP BW server.

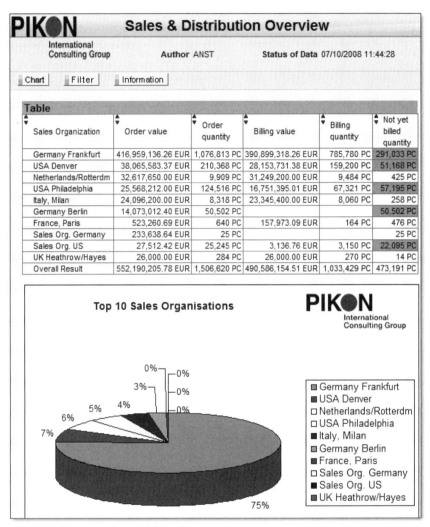

Figure 2.46 BEx Analyzer Workbook

2.4 Web Reporting

Now that you understand Excel reporting via BEx, let's move on to how to prepare and display analyses for the web. The following web reporting tools are available:

▶ Web Application Designer
▶ Web Analyzer

- ▸ Report Designer

- ▸ SAP NetWeaver Visual Composer

A comprehensive description of these tools is presented in the following sections.

2.4.1 Web Application Designer

The *Web Application Designer* is one of the most important tools for web reporting. It enables you to generate Internet pages by means of *web templates*. The content is dynamic and displays the result of one or more evaluations respectively. This enables you to carry out your analyses in the web. You start the Web Application Designer by choosing START • PROGRAMS • BUSINESS EXPLORER • WEB APPLICATION DESIGNER. Here, you can use an existing web template as the basis for a new template, or you can start with a blank web template and create it from scratch (see Figure 2.47).

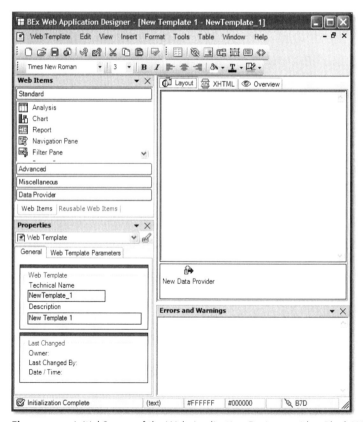

Figure 2.47 Initial Screen of the Web Application Designer with a Blank Web Template

The description of all details and options of the BEx Web Application Designer exceed the scope of this book, so, we'll only discuss the most critical elements to introduce you to the comprehensive options. For this purpose, you must first create a new web template.

In addition to providing storage options and many more program options, the menu bar and toolbar also enable you to carry out the layout operations necessary to create that new web template (see Figure 2.48). You can customize the toolbar to make frequently used functions available as symbols.

Figure 2.48 Web Application Designer Menu Bar and Toolbar

As you can see in Figure 2.47, the design area of the Web Application Designer has three tabs:

▶ LAYOUT

▶ XHTML

▶ OVERVIEW

You design the later layout of the template in the LAYOUT tab. However, first you must position the respective objects via drag and drop appropriately. While the developer is busy designing the layout, the system automatically generates the corresponding XHTML code in the background. You can view this code in the second tab, XHTML, anytime and edit it, if required.

Examples of Modifications of the XHTML Code

Practical examples where it makes sense to modify the XHTML code are merging cells of an inserted table or adding specific formats of the web template.

The OVERVIEW tab lists all objects in a table that are used for the current web template. You can view an example of this at the end of this section (see Figure 2.60 later in this chapter).

Below these three tabs, you find the area where the *DataProviders* are defined. You should first select the required DataProviders because they constitute the data to be displayed in your web template. In this context, DataProvider refers to one of the following objects:

- Query view
- Query
- InfoProvider

Double-clicking on NEW DATA PROVIDER adds a new DataProvider, and it's mandatory to configure at least one otherwise no data reference can be established. In our example, the query that is used in Section 2.3, Reporting Options in Microsoft Excel, is entered, and the default name DP1 is replaced by "SALES_DISTRIBUTION" for readability purposes. Figure 2.49 shows the settings for creating a new DataProvider.

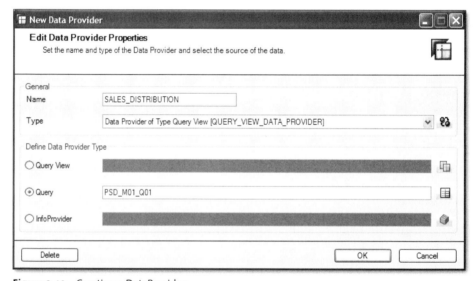

Figure 2.49 Creating a DataProvider

Of course, you can also use multiple DataProviders within a single web template and format their data in different ways.

The *web items* are the principal elements that you use to design the web analysis. They control how the data from the DataProviders is displayed within the web template. Figure 2.50 shows some of the web items that are available in the standard version:

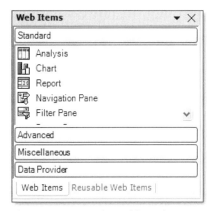

Figure 2.50   List of Possible Web Items

The STANDARD tab lists the ANALYSIS and CHART items, for example, which are used to display the data as tables or charts. You can easily place them in the LAYOUT window via drag and drop. As you can see in Figure 2.51, every web item has its own specific properties.

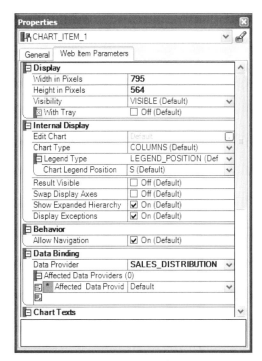

Figure 2.51   Property Settings of a Web Item

The GENERAL tab provides its technical name and description. Next to this tab there is the WEB ITEM PARAMETERS tab. In this tab, a DataProvider is assigned to the web item. Depending on the web item, the display of the parameters may vary. For graphical objects, you can, for example, define the size and type of the chart displayed (column, line, portfolio, heatmap, etc.).

In addition to the aforementioned web items, there are several other elements, which are also important when designing a web analysis, and these include:

- Navigation pane
- Filter pane
- Hierarchical filter selection
- Dropdown box
- Button group
- Info field
- Tab

Depending on the target group of a specific web report, you can modify the look and feel of the web page using these elements. In this context, you should ensure that the most critical information can be recognized at a glance when the report is displayed. Then, the use of additional web items can support and simplify the detailed analysis.

Designing the Layout

You can design different layouts using the objects described previously as shown in the following example.

The goal of this sample scenario is to enable web reporting whereby you can switch between a table of the displayed results and a corresponding chart by means of tabs.

To achieve this analysis we will use three web templates. The first template, Sales and Distribution Analysis, contains an XHTML table with individual web items. First, the structure of the table is defined and then added via the TABLE • INSERT TABLE menu. For the web items we will select an analysis, navigation pane and a filter pane. The analysis item already provides all navigation options via the context menu as described in Section 2.3, Reporting Options in Microsoft Excel. The additional web items supplement these options and increase usability.

The second template, Sales and Distribution Chart, contains the Chart web item. These two templates are then combined into a third template, Sales and Distribution Overview, using the extended Tab web item. Of course, you can also use all templates separately.

In our example, the two web templates, Sales and Distribution Analysis and Sales and Distribution Chart, are used as tabs. Alternatively, you could directly map the individual elements of the web templates using a container item on the tabs. Figure 2.52 once again illustrates the design view and shows how this layout is rendered in a browser.

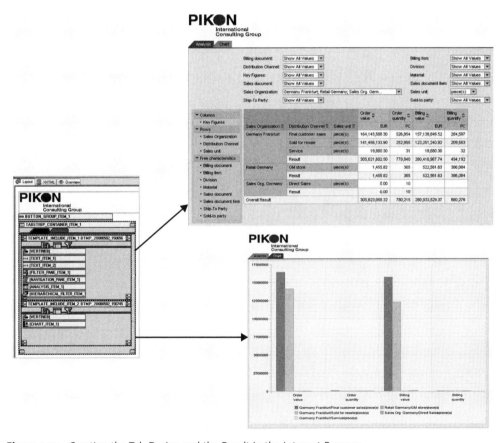

Figure 2.52 Creating the Tab Design and the Result in the Internet Browser

Functional Extension

The given template now ensures reporting for the defined query via the web. The display of the data is actually the date on which the DataProvider was last loaded with data is an interesting function frequently requested by users. For this purpose, two text elements are added to the Sales and Distribution web template (see Figure 2.53).

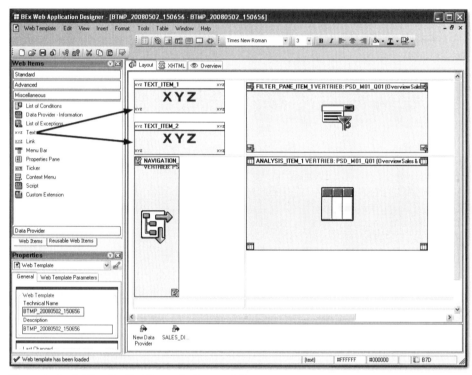

Figure 2.53 Adding the Text Items via Drag and Drop

We use the first item to display only text, which is defined as language-dependent text. For a German logon, the text will print *Letzte Änderungen*, whereas an English logon prints the text *Last changes*.

The second text element will display the date of the provider's last change. It's available in SAP standard and can be selected in the WEB ITEM PARAMETERS area.

Via the Sales and Distribution Overview template, we added a BUTTON GROUP, which can be used to define several buttons. A corresponding wizard enables you to link some inbuilt system functions with these buttons. In our example, we defined two buttons that allow users to save the displayed analyses in PDF or XLS file format. Then, the created web template can be checked for errors via the VALIDATE icon (see Figure 2.54).

Figure 2.54 Checking the Consistency of the Template

If no errors are found, you can run the template via the EXECUTE icon (see Figure 2.55) in the web browser.

Figure 2.55 Execution in the Web Browser

As a result, you obtain the web report shown in Figure 2.56. The newly added button objects are displayed in the top-left area of the screen.

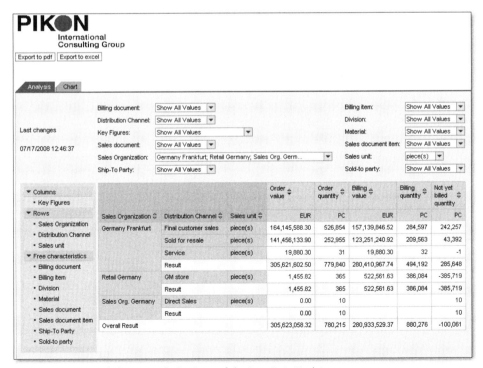

Figure 2.56 Extended View with the Date of the Last Data Update

In the next step, the Hierarchical Filter Selection web item is added to the template. We link it to the Material InfoObject so that the system displays the product hierarchy. The hierarchy must be explicitly activated in the query definition first. This object enables you to limit the analysis result to the area that you selected in the hierarchical filter selection (see Figure 2.57).

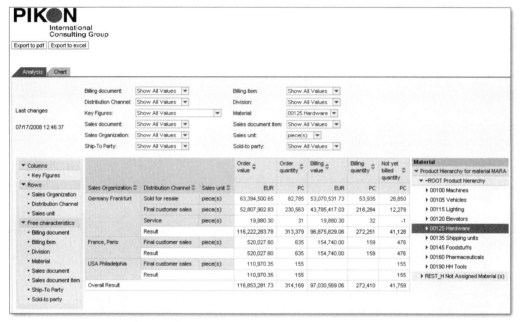

Figure 2.57 Analysis Result Due to the Hierarchical Filter Selection, Limited to the Hardware Material Group

At the beginning of this chapter, the main editing window with the three tabs, Layout, XHTML, and Overview, was introduced. However, except for a rudimentary script in the XHTML area, the tabs were initially empty. After the web templates have been created, it makes sense to display the result in detail with this format. For this purpose, we use the Sales and Distribution Overview template because it contains all web items of our example. The Layout tab is shown in Figure 2.58.

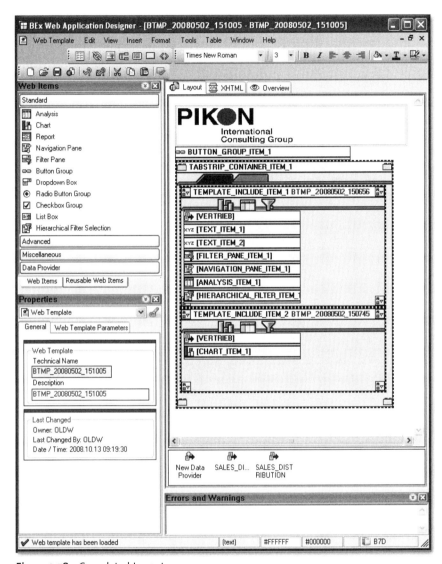

Figure 2.58 Completed Layout

Here, you can see the company logo, the previously added button group, and a tab item below containing the two templates, Sales and Distribution Analysis and Sales and Distribution Chart, as objects. The two DataProviders that were defined for the respective template are positioned in the bottom area. The XHTML tab (see Figure 2.59) now displays the design and parameter settings of all objects in the XHTML format.

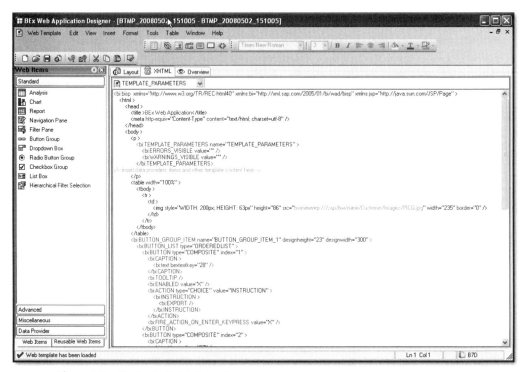

Figure 2.59 Design in Script Format

The third and last tab, OVERVIEW, contains the web items of all three templates (see Figure 2.60).

2.4.2 Web Analyzer

The *BEx Web Analyzer* enables you to perform and store ad-hoc analyses in the web. On the basis of a query, a query view, or an InfoProvider, you can customize the analyses according to your needs, store them in your favorites (on the portal), or make them available to other users via portal functions. Technically, this tool is based on the 0ANALYSIS_PATTERN web template from the Business Content provided by SAP. In addition to displaying the data in table or chart format, this web template provides the known navigation functions through filter and navigation items and the context menu. You can start the BEx Web Analyzer from the portal or by executing a query in the web.

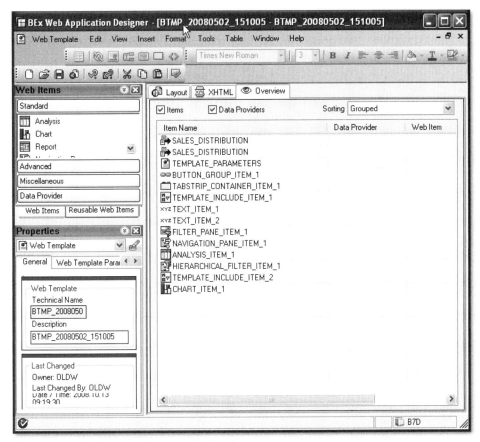

Figure 2.60 All Objects within the Web Template

2.4.3 Report Designer

The *BEx Report Designer* enables you to create formatted and optimized reports for printing data on the basis of queries or query views. However, this tool isn't described in detail here, because it's rarely used and will be removed from the SAP NetWeaver portfolio according to SAP. It will be replaced by an appropriate SAP NetWeaver version of the established *Crystal Reports* tool from Business Objects, an SAP company.

2.4.4   SAP NetWeaver Visual Composer

In contrast to the previously mentioned design tools of the BEx Suite, the *SAP NetWeaver Visual Composer* isn't an original SAP NetWeaver BI tool. Instead, this modeling tool has its roots in the SAP NetWeaver Portal environment where the integration of information and functions (e.g., SAP ERP, SAP CRM, SAP NetWeaver BI, and Web Services) from different systems assumes a critical role. You can use SAP NetWeaver Visual Composer to create flexible web applications, called *composite applications*, which provide information from different sources in a context that is logical for the user and enables cross-system interactions.

For example, you could display the sales orders from an SAP NetWeaver BI system together with other customer details from an SAP CRM system and the currently open items of the selected customer from the operational SAP ERP system on one Internet page. Additionally, you could enable the user to implement delivery blocks for the customer from the operational system, depending on the amount of the open items.

For the integration of BI data, the SAP NetWeaver Visual Composer contains a specific BI kit that you can use to integrate SAP NetWeaver BI queries (via the SAP NetWeaver BI Connector) and non-SAP data sources (via the BI Java Connector). Chapter 6, Cross-Sectional Evaluations, provides sample applications and modeling details regarding this aspect.

Technically, the SAP NetWeaver Visual Composer is based on a *model-driven architecture.* This approach enables the generation of web content without requiring in-depth programming knowledge. For example, you can model the user interface and the data flow via drag and drop and then use the compiler to convert it into the code that the application requires. The modeling itself is done in the web browser.

While a web application that was created with the Web Application Designer provides the functions that you already know from the BEx Analyzer for the query navigation (e.g., context menu), you must model the selection screens and navigation steps in the SAP NetWeaver Visual Composer manually. However, compared with the Web Application Designer, it has the advantage that you can directly integrate data sources and functions outside of SAP NetWeaver BI.

2.5   Summary

This chapter described the basic principles of SAP NetWeaver BI to lay the foundation for the sample scenario that Chapter 3 introduces and for the implementation options of the key figures that are discussed in Chapter 5.

The first sections dealt with modeling in SAP BW. Then the chapter explained the basic objects, such as InfoObjects, DSOs, and InfoCubes. It also introduced the data flow from the source system to the InfoProviders that are the basis for reporting with SAP NetWeaver BI. In this context, the data loading and transformation processes and the background of the data extraction in the source system were also described in detail.

This chapter also discussed the essential reporting options in BEx and the web environments to show you how to work with these tools following our sample scenario and use them efficiently for meaningful analyses.

This knowledge lays the foundation for the next chapter, which introduces you to a sample scenario in SAP BW where you'll find a lot of the concepts explained in this chapter put into action.

3   SD Sample Scenario

Chapter 2, SAP NetWeaver BI, described the basic principles of the modeling tools and objects in the SAP NetWeaver BI system, as well as the extraction options in the source system. The interrelations between the individual components and objects in the system finally constitute a *data model*. A proper data model is the basis for all evaluations in SAP NetWeaver BI. This chapter uses examples to introduce a possible data model as the basis for sales and distribution reporting.

3.1   The Basic Principles of Data Models

The goal of a data model should be to provide all required evaluations and meet the reporting requirements. However, when creating the data model, you should already consider possible future requirements to ensure a certain degree of *flexibility* and minimize the possible future customization effort as much as possible (cost minimization).

Another critical aspect of an optimized data model is the *performance*. In this context, you must distinguish between loading and reporting performance. The reporting performance is the most critical aspect here since it's perceivable for the users. For this purpose, the system provides the appropriate tools and configuration options that you can consider during the design phase of the data model to optimize the performance. Because you usually work with daily updated data or documents in sales and distribution controlling, you should also consider the loading performance when modeling and developing transformations. To ensure that the data is always up to date, you must supply the data targets with data at regular intervals, for example, each night.

This section introduces a possible data model that lays the foundation for sales evaluations using several examples. All of the evaluations later described as examples in Chapter 6, Cross-Sectional Evaluations, are based on this data model. It maps the entire data flow from the source system, to DSOs and InfoCubes, to the MultiProvider, as well as all of the key figures mentioned in this book.

The data model was largely developed using objects from the Business Content provided as standard. Because the Business Content can only partly meet some requirements, such as the mapping of orders on hand, we created bespoke objects to extend the data model. The update of the data between the individual objects was exclusively implemented via transformations.

3.2   DataSources

As already mentioned in Section 2.2, The Basic Principles of Data Retrieval, data extraction from the source system is controlled by DataSources. The Business Content already provides numerous DataSources for the extraction of sales and distribution data. These can roughly be divided into sales documents, deliveries, and billing documents. The following list includes the DataSources used in our sample scenario:

- ▶ **Sales documents**
  Quotations, orders, contracts, scheduling agreements:
  - ▶ 2LIS_11_VAHDR (Sales Document Header Data)
  - ▶ 2LIS_11_VASTH (Sales Document Header Status)
  - ▶ 2LIS_11_VAITM (Sales Document Item Data)
  - ▶ 2LIS_11_V_ITM (Sales-Shipping Allocation Item Data)
  - ▶ 2LIS_11_VASTI (Sales Document Item Status)
  - ▶ 2LIS_11_VAKON (Sales Document Condition)
  - ▶ 2LIS_11_VASCL (Schedule Line)
  - ▶ 2LIS_11_V_SCL (Sales-Shipping Allocation Schedule Line)
- ▶ **Order delivery**
  - ▶ 2LIS_11_V_SSL (Sales Document Order Delivery)
- ▶ **Deliveries**
  - ▶ 2LIS_12_VCHDR (Delivery Header Data)
  - ▶ 2LIS_12_VCITM (Delivery Item Data)
- ▶ **Billing documents**
  - ▶ 2LIS_13_VDHDR (Billing Doc. Header Data)

▶ 2LIS_13_VDITM (Billing Document: Item Data)

▶ 2LIS_13_VDKON (Billing Document Condition)

▶ **Other**

▶ 2LIS_02_ITM (Purchasing Data [Item Level])

All of these DataSources support delta updates. After an initialization, this enables you to transfer only the newly entered documents or the respective changes that were made to existing documents since the last loading process. This leads to a considerable performance increase for the data extraction but also makes the data update process in the SAP BW system more complex. You must consider this specific update method particularly for the implementation of routines within transformations.

3.3 Data Staging

In the *staging area*, the system initially stores the data that was extracted from the source system without any changes. The data isn't merged and standardized until the transformation into superordinate DataStores takes place. This procedure offers sufficient scope for your own logic but also provides the option to perform reporting on raw data, if necessary.

For the staging area in our data model, we use DSOs because they enable us to store data at the document level first and support the delta update of the corresponding DataSources. The used DSOs can be roughly divided into objects for order, delivery, and billing data. Furthermore, the header data, the item data, and also the schedule line data for orders are separated respectively. For additional sales data, such as order conditions, DSOs are also used.

3.3.1 DSOs for the Sales Document Area

This section introduces the DSOs for the sales document area, providing an overview of their purpose, structure, and the information they contain.

DSO "Order: Header Data"

This DSO contains general header and header status information on sales documents. The key of this DSO consists only of the *sales document* characteristic.

Besides numerous characteristics, it contains exactly one key figure, *number of sales documents*, which can be used as the basis for analyzing the number of orders per customer, for example.

The 2LIS_11_VAHDR DataSource provides general information on the sales document and the *number of orders* key figure. This DSO also includes the header status fields of the sales document, such as billing status and delivery status, which are delivered by the 2LIS_11_VASTH DataSource.

All fields are updated in the two transformations on a 1:1 basis. For this process, no start and end routines are required.

DSO "Order: Item Data"

This DSO is required to store data of sales document items in the staging area. This data includes information on the item and on the delivery of the sales documents as well as item-dependent status information. The DSO also stores condition data on the corresponding items. Its key consists of the *sales document* and *sales document item* characteristics.

General information on the sales document item is updated into the DSO using the 2LIS_11_VAITM DataSource. This information is supplemented by status information via the 2LIS_11_VASTI DataSource, and delivery information via the 2LIS_11_V_ITM DataSource.

A special feature of this DSO is the update of the item's condition data. Because only specific condition types are interesting for reporting in most cases, the selected condition data records are also stored directly at item level. For each required condition type, for example, conditions for freight, cash discount, rebate, and customer discount, you define a specific key figure here and extend the DSO by these key figures. Of course, depending on the requirements for later reporting processes, other condition types are also possible. The individual condition data records are mapped to the corresponding items within the transformation. The example in Figure 3.1 illustrates this.

Condition Record

Sales Document	Item	Condition Type	Counter Condition	Condition Value
100000001	10	**BO01**	0001	10.00
100000001	10	**HD00**	0001	15.00
100000001	10	**SKTO**	0001	20.00

Target Record

Sales Document	Item	...	Rebate	Freight	Cash Discount
100000001	10	...	**10.00**	0.00	0.00
100000001	10	...	0.00	**15.00**	0.00
100000001	10	...	0.00	0.00	**20.00**

Figure 3.1 Transformation of the Condition Records to Target Records

This procedure is supposed to simplify the query definition because the necessary key figures are directly available at item level.

DSO "Order: Schedule Lines"

An additional DSO is required to store order schedule lines. In addition to the sales document number and sales document item, its key also includes the schedule line number. This DSO is filled by the 2LIS_11_VASCL and 2LIS_11_V_SCL Data-Sources. Here, the 2LIS_11_VASCL DataSource delivers the schedule line information, and the 2LIS_11_V_SCL DataSource provides open delivery quantities and values at schedule line level for delivery-relevant sales orders.

DSO "Order"

After updating all data of a sales document into separate DSOs, you can basically directly update them into an InfoCube. However, we use an additional DSO as a clipboard before the data is updated into the InfoCube. This DSO first combines the header, item, and schedule line information of the sales documents. To ensure correct delta management, the implementation of additional logic in the form of your own source code within a transformation to an InfoCube can become quite time-consuming and complex. Our data model provides the option to map this logic into the second-level DSO via transformations during the data update. Consequently, you can completely avoid specific implementations during the update into the InfoCube. Figure 3.2 illustrates this process.

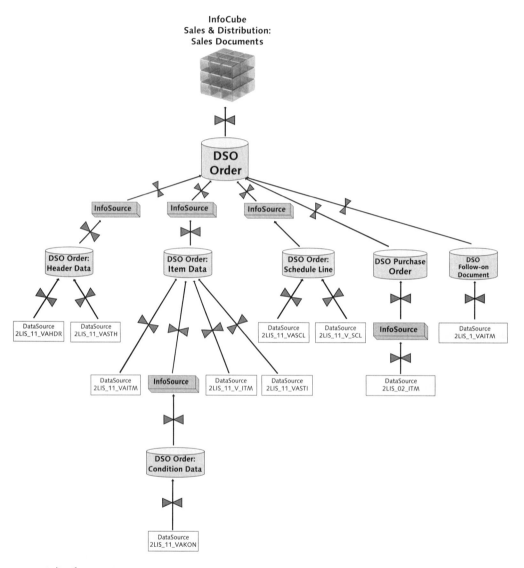

Legend: ▶◀ = Transformation + DTP

Figure 3.2 Data Flow in the Orders Area

3.3.2   DSOs for the Delivery Area

Now that we've covered all of the DSOs in the sales documents area, let's move on to the objects in the delivery area.

DSO "Delivery: Header Data"

This DSO stores delivery header data and is supplied with data from the source system by the 2LIS_12_VCHDR DataSource. The *delivery* characteristic is its only key. The DataSource contains general information on the delivery, such as the customer, shipping details, goods issued and associated key figures, including the number of deliveries, total volume of the delivery, total weight, and so on. The data is updated on a 1:1 basis into the DSO.

DSO "Delivery: Items"

Similar to the sales document items, we also use a specific DSO to store the delivery items. This DSO is supplied with data by the 2LIS_12_VCITM DataSource. In addition to the *delivery* and *delivery item* key information, this data also includes item-related information on the goods issue (e.g., the date of the actual goods issue), on the customer (e.g., ship-to party, payer), on the material (e.g., material, material group, storage location), and on the distribution channel. Besides the characteristics, it also provides important key figures for the delivery item, such as information on the weight, volume, and shipping processing time. All characteristics and key figures are transferred from the source system, that is, the DataSource, and stored in the DSO without any changes.

DSO "Delivery"

Just as we did for the sales documents, we use an additional DSO in the delivery data flow that merges the header and item data and provides that data for further updates into the InfoCube (see Figure 3.3).

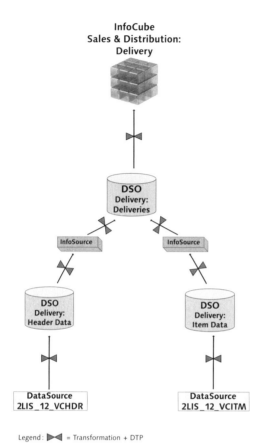

InfoCube
Sales & Distribution:
Delivery

DSO
Delivery:
Deliveries

InfoSource   InfoSource

DSO
Delivery:
Header Data

DSO
Delivery:
Item Data

DataSource
2LIS_12_VCHDR

DataSource
2LIS_12_VCITM

Legend: ▶◀ = Transformation + DTP

Figure 3.3 Data Flow in the Delivery Area

3.3.3 DSOs for the Order Delivery Area

Now that we've considered the basic information on sales documents and deliveries in our data model, we'll now discuss the update process for detailed information on order deliveries.

In the Business Content, the 2LIS_11_V_SSL DataSource is provided for the extraction of the data. The delta creation is triggered when changes are made to an order or to the corresponding deliveries. The DataSource thus provides the respective delivery details for all order schedule lines. This includes status information on the delivery, on dates (e.g., the actual delivery or the actual goods issue date), and general information on scheduling lines. The DataSource also delivers the *confirmed order schedule line quantity* or *delivered quantity* key figures.

DSO "Order Delivery"

Because this DataSource provides combined information on orders and the corresponding delivery, the key of our DSO must be structured accordingly. It consists of the order number, order item, and order schedule line, as well as the delivery and delivery item. All other characteristics and key figures are initially updated directly and without any adaptations into the DSO.

To improve the analysis options in reporting, we extended the DSO by the two key figures, *deviation on delivery date – requested delivery date* and *deviation on delivery date – confirmed delivery date*. You can also determine such key figures in the query definitions. However, to do this within the transformation has the following advantages:

▶ **Reduced workload**
The key figures are already available for the creation of the query and don't have to be defined for each query again.

▶ **Higher transparency**
The determination of the key figures is globally specified once, which allows for comparing individual queries.

▶ **Less complexity**
The determination in transformations is less complex than a determination in the query definition.

The basic principles of determination for the key figures implemented in key figure routines of the transformation are described in Section 5.3.3, Delivery Performance (On-Time Delivery Performance, Delivery Time).

Unfortunately, the DataSource doesn't provide all information on the order schedule lines to link them efficiently with data of other sources. Consequently, you need to enrich the data. Sometimes it's useful to have additional information on delivery dates (e.g., a score on the delivery reliability using the *deviation on delivery date – requested delivery date* and *deviation on delivery date – confirmed delivery date* key figures, see Section 5.3.3). The DataSource doesn't provide this information, so to enrich the information on the order schedule line and delivery date you must update the data into the *order: delivery details* DSO.

DSO "Order: Delivery Details"

This DSO consists of all characteristics and key figures of the *order delivery* DSO. In addition, further characteristics for schedule lines as well as key figures for measuring the on-time delivery performance are included. Filling and determining these additional characteristics and key figures takes place within the transformation. To locate the relevant characteristics for schedule lines, we use our own logic in the start routine; to determine the key figures, individual key figure routines are used.

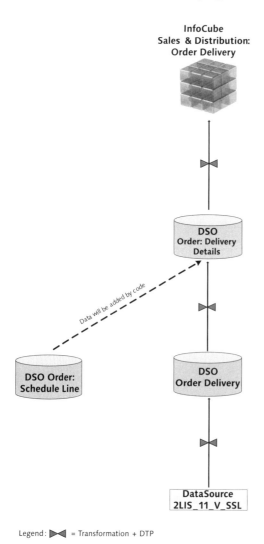

Legend: ▶◀ = Transformation + DTP

Figure 3.4 Data Flow in the Order Delivery Area

The following characteristics are enriched in the example of the *order: schedule lines* DSO:

- Material
- Company code
- Sales office
- Sales group
- Sales organization
- Division
- Plant

Figure 3.4 illustrates the data flow of the order delivery information of the Data-Source from the storage of the data in different DSOs to the InfoCube on which the respective analyses are based.

3.3.4 DSO Objects for the Billing Document Area

To complement the scenario from the point of view of sales and distribution reporting, the final section deals with billing documents. The Business Content also already provides DataSources for header and item data of billing documents. The following section explains the DSOs that are used in this context in detail.

To show and evaluate key figures, such as *revenue* or *sales quantity*, in reporting, the SAP BW system must also provide billing data. For this purpose, SAP delivers the 2LIS_13_VDHDR, 2LIS_13_VDITM and 2LIS_13_VDKON DataSources. Just as with sales documents, this data is updated first into separate DataStore objects.

DSO "Billing Document: Header Data"

The header data of a billing document is updated into a particular DSO. The billing document number is the key of the DSO. The DSO contains characteristics, such as *company code*, *billing document type*, *customer*, and information on sales areas, in addition to the *number of billing documents* key figure. The data is updated from the 2LIS_13_VDHDR DataSource on a 1:1 basis.

DSO "Billing Document: Item Data"

As you can see in Figure 3.5, two DataSources supply the *billing document: item data* DSO with data. We use the 2LIS_13_VDITM DataSource to update the actual item data and also update condition data into this DSO, similarly to the *order: item data* DSO. The key consists of the billing document number and the billing item.

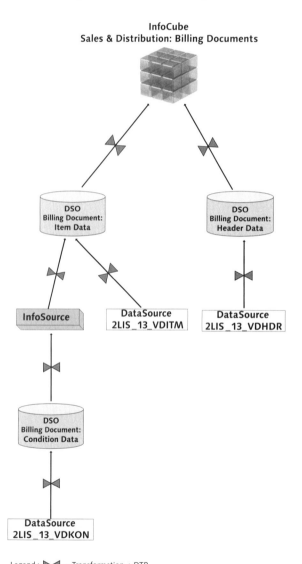

Figure 3.5 Data Flow in the Billing Documents Area

The 2LIS_13_VDITM DataSource can deliver, for example, information on the customer, on the material, and on organization units that you can directly update into the DSO.

For billing documents, we also update different condition types, initially into specific *billing document: condition data* DSOs. We use this DSO as the DataSource for the direct update of predefined condition types (overhead rate, rebate, freight, cash discount, etc.) into our *billing items* DSO. Here, the same logic (own source code) was used as was used for the order items (see Figure 3.2).

3.4   InfoProviders

InfoCubes are used to create report, analyses and can be a component of MultiProviders. In our model, we use separate InfoCubes for sales documents, deliveries, order delivery, and billing documents. The data is updated from a specific DSO; however, as already mentioned, we didn't include own implementations (source code) in the transformation for the InfoCube. The InfoCubes contain many characteristics and key figures of the underlying DSOs. Furthermore, in our model, the data is updated into the InfoCubes at document level because the analyses described in Chapter 5, Implementing the Key Figures in SAP NetWeaver BI, are partly based on this level of detail. However, this isn't always necessary and depends on the respective requirements. Of course, an aggregated storage of the data in the InfoCubes is possible.

Note on Performance

Document numbers, such as order number, should be included in the InfoCube in a *line-item dimension*, if possible. The system then doesn't have to create a dimension table. In this case, the master data ID (SID) table of the characteristic replaces the dimension table. This results in the following benefits:

▶ **Improvement of the loading performance**
The system doesn't have to generate master data IDs when transaction data is loaded.

▶ **Improvement of the reporting performance**
The execution of SQL (Structured Query Language) statements can be facilitated when calling queries.

However, a line-item dimension can only contain one characteristic, so retroactively adding characteristics isn't possible.

3.5 MultiProviders

In general, you should map your analyses—also known as queries in the SAP NetWeaver BI environment—to MultiProviders to ensure the highest possible degree of flexibility. This procedure has the advantage that you can easily integrate later added InfoCubes into the MultiProvider, which makes this data also available for evaluations.

The entire reporting in our data model is based on a MultiProvider (see Figure 3.6). It merges the data from all aforementioned InfoCubes and enables cross-InfoCube analysis. However, you can also carry out evaluations based on data of individual InfoCubes. In addition to all characteristics and key figures of the assigned Info-Cubes, the MultiProvider also provides their navigation attributes.

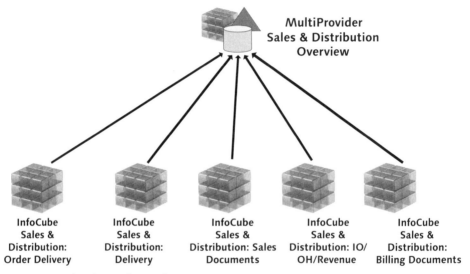

Figure 3.6 InfoCubes/MultiProvider

3.6 Extended Data Model

The previous examples mainly discussed the objects of the Business Content and consequently laid the foundation for sales and distribution reporting. These objects enable you to map numerous sales key figures in reports and analyses. However, this is often not sufficient to map all reporting requirements of sales and distribution. The following sections describe approaches to solve the following issues:

▸ Incoming orders/orders on hand

▸ Consideration of cross-company stock transfers/purchase orders

▸ Follow-on documents

In this context, the parts of the already described data model (that aren't discussed in detail again) are linked with further requirement-specific objects.

3.6.1 Incoming Orders/Orders on Hand

Mapping the incoming orders, orders on hand, and the revenue is an additional requirement for sales and distribution controlling and a challenge for the developers of the data model, too. Because this requires — particularly for incoming orders — an evaluation of the changes of the sales order value, our previously introduced data model can't meet this requirement.

The difficulty here is that, for item data of sales documents, the 2LIS_11_VAITM DataSource provides only the current status of the documents from the source system but no history or changes of the current item value and of the current quantity. In short, the Business Content doesn't provide an appropriate solution for this problem.

However, to still meet this requirement, we update the item data of the sales document into an additional DSO, *incoming orders*. To determine the revenue that is also necessary for mapping the orders on hand, you can use the already described DSO, *billing items*. The data of these two DSOs is updated into a separate InfoCube and is then available for reporting the required key figures.

The following sections explain this solution in detail. First, the DSO for the incoming orders is discussed. Because the changes of the sales order value are mapped historically, a time characteristic must be added to the actual item data key that consists of sales document number and sales document item. Which time characteristic you use depends on the requirement for analyzing the incoming orders. For example, if you only want to see monthly changes of the incoming orders per sales order item, the *calendar year/month* characteristic would be sufficient. To map the complete history (if you want to trace all changes of an order item), you must extend the key by the *calendar day* characteristic and by the *time* characteristic. In our example, we use the *calendar year/month* characteristic to evaluate the incoming orders on a monthly basis.

Record Mode

The technical characteristic, 0RECORDMODE, which is delivered by all DataSources, indicates the type of data record. The most common attributes are as follows:

▶ X   = Before image

▶ blank = After image or new record

▶ R   = Reverse image (deletion record)

Within the transformation from the 2LIS_11_VAITM DataSource into the *incoming orders* DSO, we map the actual logic for the determination of the incoming orders. For this quite complex determination of the key figures, we use the start routine. In this context, we distinguish between the following cases for each sales order item:

1. **New creation**
   If a new record (0RECORDMODE = blank) is delivered, that is, a document item was entered in the source system, the key figures are updated on a 1:1 basis for the current month. In this simple case, the incoming orders value corresponds to the net value of the order item:
   Incoming Orders Value = Net Value of the Order Item

2. **Change of an existing order item**
   In this case, the source system provides two data records for the order item. A before image (0RECORDMODE = X) with the original characteristic and key figure values and an after image (0RECORDMODE = blank) with the current characteristic and key figure values. To determine the incoming orders (positive or negative), you must create a delta between the old and the new net sales order value. However, because you merge the incoming orders on a monthly basis, it isn't sufficient to consider the before and after image. You must check whether the sales order value has already changed in the current month. This value must also be taken into account for the determination. This results in the following formula for the determination of the incoming orders value:
   Incoming Orders Value = Incoming Orders Value (Current Month)
   + Δ(After Image Net Value/Before Image Net Value)

3. **Deletion record or rejection of the sales order item**

If the source system provides a deletion record or a reverse image (0RECORD-MODE = R), you must cancel the incoming order that has been updated up until that time.

Incoming Orders Value = - Σ (All Already Updated Net Values of the Order Item)

The calendar month, which is a part of the key, is determined using the statistics date. You can use the same logic to determine the incoming orders per day. To do this, you only need to replace the calendar month by the statistics date in the key.

Example of the Development of the Dataset in the DSO

On 02/01/2008 a sales order item with a net value of 1,000 USD is created (see Tables 3.1 and 3.2).

Record Mode	Sales Order	Item	Statistics Date	Net Value	Document Currency
	4711	10	02/01/2008	1,000.00	USD

Table 3.1 Data Record in the Data Package

Sales Order	Item	Calendar Month	Net Value	Document Currency
4711	10	02/2008	1,000.00	USD

Table 3.2 Data Records in the DSO

On 3/5/2008, the net value of the sales order item is increased to 1,200.00 USD (see Tables 3.3 and 3.4).

Record Mode	Sales Order	Item	Statistics Date	Net Value	Document Currency
X	4711	10	02/01/2008	1,000.00	USD
	4711	10	03/05/2008	1,200.00	USD

Table 3.3 Data Records in the Data Package After the Sales Order Item Was Increased

Sales Order	Item	Calendar Month	Net Value	Document Currency
4711	10	02/2008	1,000.00	USD
4711	10	03/2008	200.00	USD

Table 3.4 Data Records in the DSO After the Sales Order Item Was Increased

In the same month (03/20/2008), the net value is increased again (see Tables 3.5 and 3.6).

Record Mode	Sales Order	Item	Statistics Date	Net Value	Document Currency
X	4711	10	03/05/2008	1,200.00	USD
	4711	10	03/20/2008	1,500.00	USD

Table 3.5 Data Records in the Data Package After Repeated Increase

Sales Order	Item	Calendar Month	Net Value	Document Currency
4711	10	02/2008	1,000.00	USD
4711	10	03/2008	500.00	USD

Table 3.6 Data Records in the DSO After Repeated Increase

On 4/10/2008 the sales order item is deleted (see Tables 3.7 and 3.8).

Record Mode	Sales Order	Item	Statistics Date	Net Value	Document Currency
R	4711	10	04/10/2008	–1,500.00	USD

Table 3.7 Data Records in the Data Package After the Sales Order Item Was Deleted

Sales Order	Item	Calendar Month	Net Value	Document Currency
4711	10	02/2008	1,000.00	USD
4711	10	03/2008	500.00	USD
4711	10	04/2008	–1,500.00	USD

Table 3.8 Data Records in the DSO After the Sales Order Item Was Deleted

As you can see in Table 3.8, the history for the incoming orders was completely stored in the DSO and considered the different cases (new creation, change, and cancellation).

The prerequisites for storing the data at the DSO level are fulfilled. This data is now updated into a separate InfoCube.

Let's get back to our original requirement — mapping the incoming orders and orders on hand. To get the orders on hand, you require the incoming orders key figure and the revenue key figure. For this purpose, we can use our *billing item* DSO as a DataSource to receive the corresponding billing document values additionally. The incoming orders (positive sign) and the revenue (negative sign) are then updated into the *orders on hand* key figure.

In this context, the manual billing documents without sales order reference represent a special case. Here, a revenue is generated that reduces the orders on hand according to our logic. However, there is no corresponding incoming orders value because there is no corresponding sales order. This may have the result that a negative value for the orders on hand is output in the respective reports, which doesn't correspond to the definition. To avoid this situation, artificial incoming orders with the amount of the corresponding billing value are generated for billing documents without reference to a sales order. The logic for this was implemented within the transformation of the *billing items* DSO into the *Sales & Distribution: IO/OH/Revenue* InfoCube. Figure 3.7 illustrates the complete data flow for this.

In summary, mapping the *incoming orders*, *orders on hand* and *revenue* key figures in SAP NetWeaver BI is a great challenge for the designers and developers of the data model. Due to the different requirements of enterprises, no all-in-one solution can be given here. You could also imagine that the logic for determining the incoming orders in the source system is implemented to reduce the complexity of the data update in the SAP BW system. Nevertheless, you can use the data model described here as a guide for your own developments.

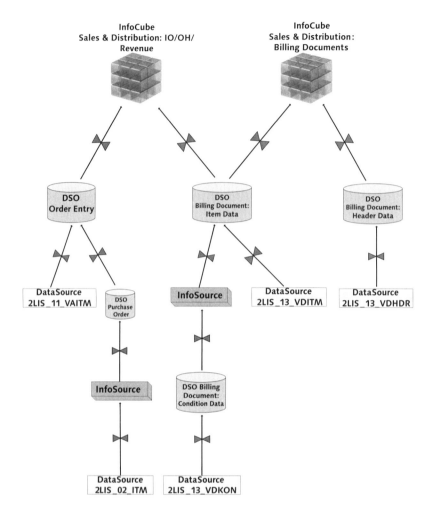

Figure 3.7 Data Flow in the Billing Documents and Incoming Orders/Orders on Hand/Revenue Area

3.6.2 Cross-Company Stock Transfers/Purchase Orders

The following section deals with two further issues that cannot be mapped without an extension of the current data model — cross-company sales or cross-company stock transfers. In both cases, the respective process in SAP ERP doesn't generate all required documents. Consequently, these must be provided artificially for evaluations.

Cross-Company Sales

Similar to the case of the manual billing documents without sales order reference described earlier, the order information isn't completely available for cross-company sales. In this case, a sales order is first created in the sales area of the selling company code. However, the delivery is made by a plant of an associate company. For this purpose, the system generates two billing documents: one for the end customer and an internal billing document for the selling company code (Sections 4.5, Delivery Key Figures, and 4.6, Billing Key Figures, provide more detailed information on this issue).

Our data model maps the documents in the selling company code correctly. However, in the delivering company code, there is only a billing document but no order. This order needs to be generated again. For this purpose, a check is carried out during the update of the orders in the start routine to determine whether the process is a cross-company sales process. In this case, the data record is initially copied on a 1:1 basis to generate a new additional data record for the delivering company code. For this data record then additional derivations are necessary, for example, to find the correct sales area. Furthermore, the internal transfer price is determined and calculated as a net value from the DSO for order conditions (see Section 5.5.2, Cross-Company Stock Transfer).

Cross-Company Stock Transfers

A typical scenario of a data model for sales and distribution data usually doesn't consider the purchase orders for sales reporting. However, this data is also interesting for some particular aspects of sales and distribution controlling, for example, for cross-company stock transfers where a company code purchases goods at another company code. An order is generated in the system of the purchasing company code. The delivering company code delivers the goods to the purchasing company code and bills them. In this process, however, no sales order is generated in the system of the delivering company code, and consequently no incoming orders and orders on hand are updated (see Section 4.5, Delivery Key Figures). But you as the sales employee of the delivering company code want to know the total order volume, irrespective of whether this is a sales order of an external customer or a sales order of an affiliated company. This illustrates that it isn't sufficient to only consider sales orders that are loaded from the source system into the SAP BW system by the Business Content DataSources.

The source system cannot provide sales orders for cross-company stock transfers for extraction because no sales document was generated for this process. However, we require the respective information for reporting in some way.

You can extract the generated purchase order or its items using the 2LIS_02_ITM DataSource. This enables you to determine at least the information that is relevant for our requirements. The final concept is to generate artificial sales order items from the document items of this purchase order in the SAP BW system.

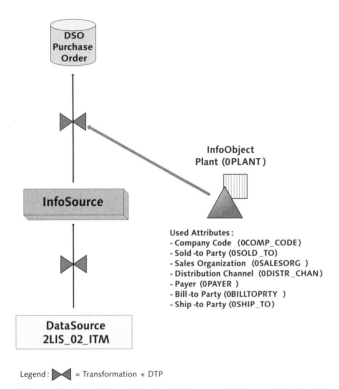

Legend: ▶◀ = Transformation + DTP

Figure 3.8 Data Flow of the Stock Transport Orders and Derivations in Transformation

For this purpose, the document items are first stored in a separate *purchase orders* DSO on a 1:1 basis. However, a check whether this is a relevant stock transfer order is already carried out in the start routine. The system discards all other data records and doesn't update them into the *purchase orders* DSO. It then implements derivations for the remaining relevant data records. The DataSource cannot deliver sales-relevant characteristics, such as the sales organization and distribution channel. Because these characteristics are relevant for reporting, you must always determine them accordingly (see Section 5.5.2, Cross-Company Stock Transfer). Figure 3.8 illustrates the data flow of these stock transport orders and the required derivations.

After implementing all checks and derivations, you must now turn your attention to the key that consists of the purchasing document and sales document number. Number ranges for purchasing documents and for sales documents may overlap. As a result, a purchasing document may overwrite an existing sales document during further updates. If separate number ranges cannot be ensured, you must assign a specific number for the artificial sales document through source code in a characteristic routine.

As you can see in Figure 3.9, these order items that were converted to sales order items are now updated into our *order* DSO. The same holds true for the *incoming orders* DSO (see Figure 3.7).

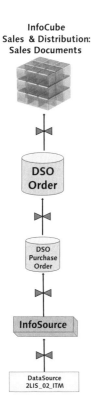

Legend: ▶◀ = Transformation + DTP

Figure 3.9 Data Flow in the Cross-Company Stock Transport Orders Area

We have now achieved our goal — considering the incoming orders and orders on hand resulting from cross-company stock transfers. You can now evaluate the artificially generated sales order items in reporting.

3.6.3 Follow-on Documents

In the last part of the data model, further questions arise in sales and distribution controlling that we can't answer at the moment with regard to the model's current status. These questions may be, for example:

▸ How long is the period between the submission of the quotation and the award?

▸ Which quotations have been completely accepted (quotation value = sales order value)?

To answer these questions, you must add some additional information to the sales documents. In this context, you must provide the following information that can be later used for reporting:

▸ Sales order value of the follow-on document

▸ Sales order quantity of the follow-on document

▸ Creation date of the follow-on document

▸ Number of follow-on order items

This requires several steps; first, you must extend the data model once again. We mainly set up the update of sales documents items into a new DSO, *follow-on documents*.

When the data is updated, the data records that don't have a preceding document or that have a reason for rejection must be filtered first. You can recognize them by the VGBEL and ABGRU fields of the DataSource. The filter was changed using a snippet of ABAP source code within the start routine of the transformation.

As you can see in Figure 3.10, the system then updates the relevant data records into the new DSO, *follow-on documents*. However, in this process, only the following characteristics and key figures are considered:

▸ Sales document (part of the key)

▸ Sales document item (part of the key)

▸ Document number of the reference document

- ▸ Item number of the reference document

- ▸ Net value of the order item in document currency

- ▸ Document currency

- ▸ Cumulative order quantity in sales units

- ▸ Sales unit

- ▸ Sales order items

- ▸ Calendar day

**InfoCube
Sales & Distribution:
Sales Documents**

**DSO
Order**

**DSO
Follow-on
Document**

**DataSource
2LIS_11_VAITM**

Legend: ▶◀ = Transformation + DTP

Figure 3.10 Data Flow in the Follow-on Documents Area

The data records are then updated into the already described *orders* DSO. First, the necessary key figures, *sales order value of the follow-on document*, *sales order quantity of the follow-on document*, and *number of follow-on order items*, and the *creation date of the first follow-on document* characteristic must be included in the DSO.

The goal is now to add all information of the follow-on document to the data record of the actual document. This is done via simple mapping where the *document number of the reference document* is mapped to the DSO document number (part of the key), and the *item number of the reference document* is mapped to the item number (part of the key). Figure 3.11 illustrates this procedure, including the update of the key figures.

Source Fields	DSO Follow-on Document		Target Fields	DSO Orders
0REFER_DOC	Document number of the reference document	→	*0DOC_NUMBER*	*Sales document*
0REFER_ITM	Item number of the reference item	→	*0S_ORD_ITEM*	*Sales document item*
0DOC_CURRCY	Document currency	→	0DOC_CURRCY	Document currency
0SALES_UNIT	Sales unit	→	0SALES_UNIT	Sales unit
0CML_OR_QTY	Cumulative order quantity in sales units	→	PSD_FOLME	Follow-up quantity
0ORD_ITEMS	Sales order item	→	PSD_ORD_I	Number follow-up ordered items
0REFER_DOC	Document number of the reference document	→	PSD_SACY*	First follow-up date
0REFER_ITM	Item number of the reference item	→	PSD_FOLWT	Follow-up value
0NET_VALUE	Net value of the order item in document currency	→		*Determined by own code

Figure 3.11 Transformation of the Follow-on Documents

This procedure doesn't generate new data records but enriches existing sales documents with additional information. Chapter 4, Key Figures in the Sales and Distribution Process, and Chapter 5, Implementing the Key Figures in SAP NetWeaver BI, contain further information on how these characteristics and key figures can be used to answer the question mentioned previously in reporting.

3.7   Summary

This chapter used multiple examples to introduce a data model based on objects from the Business Content, which didn't require additional enhancements to a large extent. This chapter also illustrated by means of an extended model that you can map very specific requirements. However, experience has shown that requirements can largely vary in different enterprises; therefore this model isn't a standard solution. Nevertheless, you can use it as a basis for designing your own data model.

4 Key Figures in the Sales and Distribution Process

The previous chapters introduced you to SAP NetWeaver Business Intelligence (SAP NetWeaver BI) and provided a sample scenario. To set up a key figure system in SAP NetWeaver BI, you must know the development process of data in the source system. This chapter deals with the key figures relevant for the sales and distribution (S&D) process. Initially, we address the general fundamentals of how basic information in SAP ERP is developed and look at which data is required for creating key figures in SAP NetWeaver BI. This is followed by a description of quotation key figures, order key figures, delivery key figures, billing key figures, and key figures for the cross-company business.

4.1 Sales and Distribution Key Figures — General Basics

In general, a *key figure* is an indicator for evaluating a subject. Business key figures are aggregated data, which is usually evaluated with reference to a period at characteristic level in order to measure the success or attainment of goals in specific areas. For the various enterprise areas (production, material management, sales, accounting and balancing, controlling, etc.), key figure systems have been developed that correlate the individual key figures to achieve transparency of the success contribution of the respective subareas.

For the subarea of S&D, numerous key figures and key figure systems have been developed. Every enterprise must decide individually which key figures are supposed to be considered for the evaluation of S&D. The following criteria can be decisive:

- Related industry
- Business model
- Size of the enterprise

▸ Market situation

▸ Sales strategy and concept

From this, it follows that for each enterprise, a suitable set of key figures needs to be configured, or rather that the relevant indicators must be selected from the existing key figure definitions. At this point, we don't want to discuss a complete key figure system and map it in the system. We'd rather show you, using some sample key figures, how raw data is created in the S&D process of the SAP ERP application, which then is processed into key figures in SAP NetWeaver BI.

For this purpose, the S&D process is subdivided into the following steps: quotation, order, delivery, and billing. After we describe the corresponding key figures for each step, we outline the specifics in the cross-company business.

4.2   Quotation Key Figures

The following key figures form the basis for evaluations in the quotation area:

▸ Quotation value

▸ Quotation quantity (total of all items)

▸ Number of quotation documents

These key figures form the basis for the success analysis of the sales activity in this phase of the S&D process. The aim is to determine an enterprise's success in the market, find the reasons for this success, and define the problem areas.

> **Building on that, the following questions must be considered for the success analysis:**
>
> ▸ What's the total amount of quotation value, quotation quantity, and number of documents (or number of document items) within a certain period?
>
> ▸ What are the absolute numbers of the open quotation value (or quotation quantity, number of documents, number of document items)?
>
> ▸ What's the quota of open quotations?
>
> ▸ What's the absolute value of accepted quotations?
>
> ▸ What's the quota of accepted quotations (success quota of quotations)?

- What's the absolute value of rejected quotations?
- What's the quota of rejected quotations?
- What's the value of all quotations that have already expired?
- What's the quota of expired quotations?

For the description of key figures, the following pattern is used. First, you receive a brief description of the business background of key figures. Then, we outline where you can find the required raw data in the SAP ERP source documents for calculating the key figures. Following that, you learn which characteristics are interesting in addition to the "classic" characteristics (*customer, country, material, sales area,* etc.). The entire discussion is rounded off with a system example.

4.2.1 Quotation Value, Quotation Quantity, Number of Quotations

Quotation value, quotation quantity, number of quotation documents, and number of quotation items are counted among to the basic key figures in S&D. Here, no distinction is made with regard to the status ("open," "accepted," "rejected"). Rather, all quotations are considered that have been recorded within the analysis period specified as the selection period by the user. These values are also suitable to make period comparisons as well as target/actual comparisons.

Period comparisons and target/actual comparisons provide early indicators for the demand for products and services offered by the enterprise. The *quotation value* is the net value of all chargeable items of the quotation. The *quotation quantity* is the cumulative quantity of all items of a document. Here, you must make sure to not only evaluate the cumulative value of all items. Usually, the users want to know how the quotation value is distributed to the materials (or material groups and product hierarchies). This necessitates a quotation value for each quotation item.

We now gradually examine a source document in SAP ERP based on a system example. Figure 4.1 shows the item overview of a quotation.

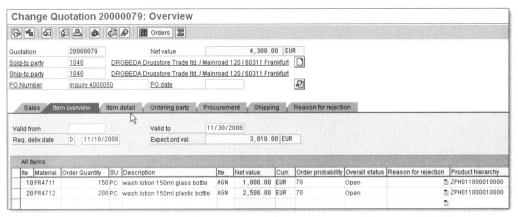

Figure 4.1 Item Overview in the Quotation in the SD Component (Transaction VA22)

The quotation for the customer (DROBEDA Drugstore Trade Ltd. with Sold-to-party-number 1040) contains two items: one for material PR4711 and one for material PR4712. The NET VALUE field in the item row indicates the quotation value for the individual items. This value is stored in Table VBAP (Sales Documents: Item Data) in the NETWR field. The order quantity is stored in the KWMENG field of the same table. This information represents the source information for the key figures, *quotation value* and *quotation quantity*.

Figure 4.2 shows the same quotation as illustrated in Figure 4.1; now, however, the SALES tab is activated. The ORDER REASON dropdown list provides the input options available, which are defined in the Customizing area of SAP ERP (Field AUGRU in Table VBAK Sales Document Header Data). This field enables you to analyze the key figures *quotation value, quotation quantity,* and *number of documents according to order reasons* in addition to the classic key figures (*sales area, country, customer, customer group, material, material group,* etc.). This allows you to also evaluate the efficiency of the different sales instruments (advertisement, field sales, and campaigns). The fact that the field is called ORDER REASON and not quotation reason is confusing in this context because you need to specify here which sales activity the *quotation* is based on. In SAP ERP, however, all S&D documents (quotations, orders, returns orders, credit memo and debit memo requests) are mapped in the same tables so that the fields are identical.

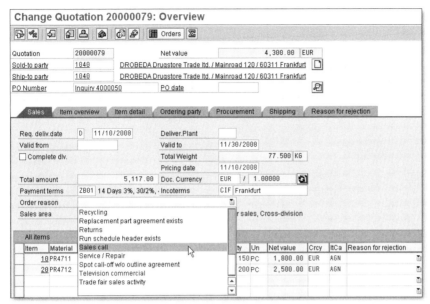

Figure 4.2 Selecting the Quotation Reason, Order Reason in the SD Component (Transaction VA22)

The order reasons are maintained in the sales and distribution (SD) component via the Customizing path SPRO • SALES AND DISTRIBUTION • SALES • SALES DOCUMENTS • SALES DOCUMENT HEADER • DEFINE ORDER REASONS. You must select the order reason during the quotation entry.

4.2.2 Order Probability and Expected Order Value

You can specify the order probability for each item as an additional value in the quotation document. Via the order probability and based on the quotation value, the system calculates the expected order value.

Calculating the Expected Order Value	
Net value:	4,300 EUR
Order probability:	70 %
Expected order value:	3,010 EUR

In the following sections, we continue with this example. Figure 4.1 shows that an order probability of 70% is specified for each item respectively (VBAP-AWAHR field). This is the basis for calculating the expected order value. The system calculates a default value for the order probability, which you can vary when entering or changing the quotation.

The default value is based on Customizing settings and the master data maintenance, which can be changed during the creation of a document — as it's frequently the case in SAP ERP. In Customizing of the SD component, an order probability is defined for the order type (in our case, QT for the quotation). Figure 4.3 shows the Customizing for the "QT" sales document type.

Figure 4.3 Customizing of the QT Order Type in the SD Component (Transaction VOV8)

An order probability of 70% was specified for the "QT" sales document type. Moreover, an order probability is stored for the customer in the customer master (ORDER PROBAB. field; see Figure 4.4).

The default value is calculated based on these two values, which is then displayed in the quotation entry. In our case, the system calculates as shown in the following box.

Calculating the Default Value

70% in the document

= customer master "1040":   100%

"QT" order type: 70%

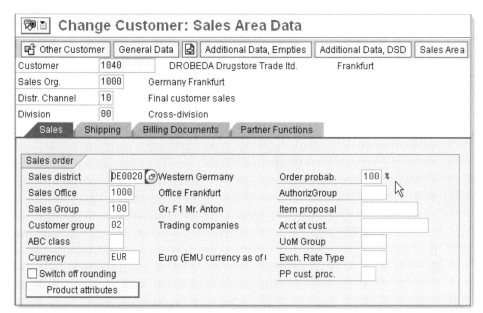

Figure 4.4 Changing the Sales Area Data of the Customer Master Record in the SD Component (Transaction VD02)

You can change the default value. From the order probability, you can calculate the key figure, *expected order value*, for reporting. In the corresponding evaluations, you can compare the *quotation value* and *expected order value* key figures. This enables you to evaluate the existing quotations in a differentiated manner.

Note for the Dynamic Calculation of the Expected Order Value

The expected order value isn't stored in Tables VBAK and VBAP but is always calculated dynamically during the transaction. Similar to the key figure, *expected order value*, you can also establish the key figure, *expected order quantity*. In contrast to the expected order value, this value isn't displayed in the SD quotation.

4.2.3 Open Quotations

Open quotations are considered for further analysis; these are all quotations for which no order has been placed or quotations that haven't been rejected. For displaying them in SAP NetWeaver BI, you must decide whether quotations whose validity period has been exceeded should be considered as open quotations. With regard to open quotations, you must differentiate the following key figures:

- Open quotation value
- Open quotation quantity
- Number of open documents
- Number of open document items

Note that quotations can be partly open, partly accepted, and partly rejected.

The key figures for open quotations must also be differentiated via the characteristic *order reason* (or *quotation reason*, see Section 4.2.1, Quotation Value, Quotation Quantity, Number of Quotations). With regard to the system example, let's consider Figure 4.1 once again. For each item, the net value and order probability is displayed. The overall status of both items is OPEN because neither follow-on documents nor reasons for rejection have been entered. Figure 4.5 shows the document flow for this quotation.

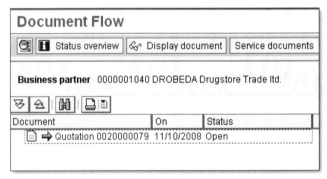

Figure 4.5 Document Flow for the Quotation in the SD Component (Transaction VA22)

The document flow contains only the quotation with no additional documents. The overall status of the quotation is OPEN. The following list shows the values of the key figures:

- Open quotation value: 4,300 EUR
- Number of open quotations: 1
- Number of open quotation items: 2
- Open quotation quantity material PR4711:   150 pieces
- Open quotation quantity material PR4712:   200 pieces

4.2.4   Success Quota and Accepted Quotation

A quotation is accepted if the customer places an order with reference to a quotation. As a result, the following key figures are decreased:

▶ Open quotation value

▶ Open quotation quantity

▶ Number of open documents

▶ Number of open document items

At the same time, the following key figures increase:

▶ Quotation value of successful quotations

▶ Quotation quantity of successful quotations

▶ Number of accepted documents

▶ Number of accepted document items

One of the essential criteria for measuring the S&D success is the success quota of quotations. For this purpose, the key figures for the successful quotations are put into relation to the key figures for the quotations in total. This way, you can calculate a success quota for each customer, which, in turn, can be used as a comparison value for maintaining the order probability in the customer master.

Here, the reasons for successful quotations are also interesting to focus future S&D activities accordingly. To analyze these reasons, you need to take into account the order reasons in the sales order.

Now let's examine how the quotation shown in Figure 4.1 and the corresponding key figures change if a sales order is entered that references the quotation. For Item 10 from the quotation, a sales order was entered for the complete item quantity. Figure 4.6 shows the item selection when entering the sales order. The user has only set the checkmark for Item 10, so only this item is accepted in the order.

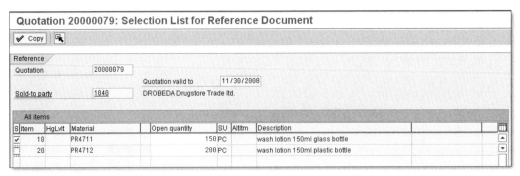

Figure 4.6 Item Selection During the Sales Order Creation with Reference to the Quotation in the SD Component (Transaction VA01)

Figure 4.7 shows the sales order with the order item accepted from the quotation. The user selected EXCELLENT PRICE as the ORDER REASON, which was the reason why the customer decided in favor of the quotation.

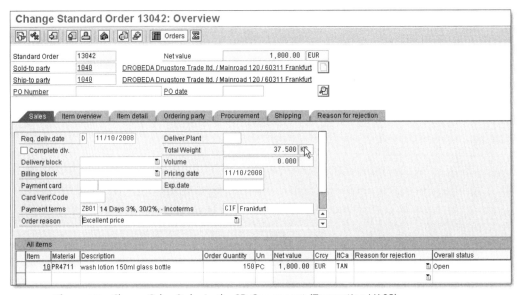

Figure 4.7 Change Sales Order in the SD Component (Transaction VA02)

In our quotation, both the document flow and the document status have changed. Figure 4.8 shows the document flow in the quotation.

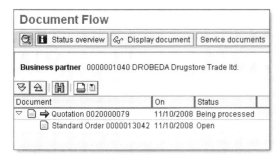

Figure 4.8 Document Flow in the Quotation in the SD Component (Transaction VA22)

Unlike previously, the document flow now includes the first follow-on document (Sales Order 13042). The overall status of the quotation is "Being processed" because one part of the quotation items is still open. In this regard, we take a look at the item overview of the quotation once again.

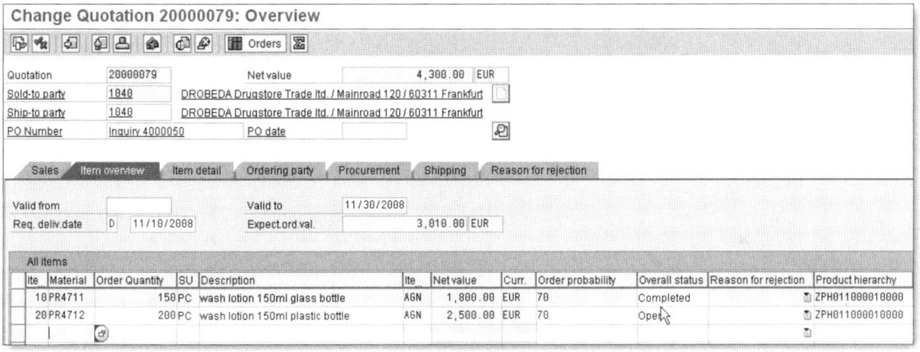

Figure 4.9 Change Quotation, Item Overview in the SD Component (Transaction VA22)

Figure 4.9 shows a change in the overall status of Item 10, which is now set to "Completed." Based on the shown document flow, the key figures defined earlier have developed as follows:

- ▶ Open quotation value: 2,500 EUR
- ▶ Number of open quotations: 1
- ▶ Number of open quotation items: 1
- ▶ Open quotation quantity material PR4711: 0 pieces
- ▶ Open quotation quantity material PR4712: 200 pieces
- ▶ Quotation value of successful quotations: 1,800 EUR

- Number of successful quotations: 1
- Number of successful quotation items: 1
- Quotation quantity of successful quotations
  - Material PR4711:   150 pieces
  - Material PR4712:   0 pieces

From the key figures for the successful quotations, you can derive the following quotas:

- Success quota value: 42%
- Success quota number of documents: 100%
- Success quota number of items: 50%
- Success quota quotation quantity material PR4711:   100%
- Success quota quotation quantity material PR4712:   0%

This overview shows that the quota for the number of successful documents has a restricted value because, in this case, both the quota of successful and unsuccessful quotations is 100%. It makes more sense to analyze the success quota for the quotation value.

4.2.5   Rejected Quotations

The key figure for rejected documents is also of special interest just like the key figure for values, quantities, and documents of accepted quotations. If a customer rejects a quotation, a reason for rejection is maintained for each item. Reasons for rejection can be set up in Customizing and defined depending on the requirements of the respective enterprise. The evaluations in SAP NetWeaver BI should additionally enable a drilldown according to reason of rejection.

By entering the reason for rejection in the quotation item, the following key figures are decreased:

- Open quotation value
- Open quotation quantity
- Number of open documents
- Number of open document items

At the same time, the following key figures increase:

► Quotation value of rejected quotations

► Quotation quantity of rejected quotations

► Number of rejected documents

► Number of rejected document items

Just like for the success quota, you should identify both the absolute values and the relative values for the rejected quotations (value, quantity, number of documents). For this purpose, the key figure, *rejected quotations*, is put into relation to the overall value of the quotations.

Now let's continue with the system example of this chapter. Our quotation 20000079 still includes the open ITEM 20 with a quantity of 200 pieces. Initially, the customer places an order of 80 pieces. Figure 4.10 shows the sales order.

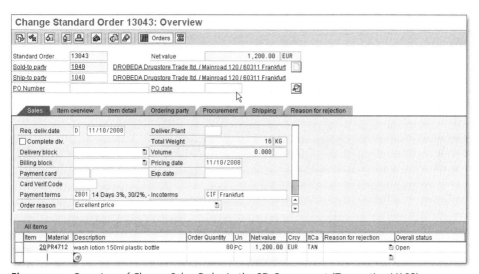

Figure 4.10 Overview of Change Sales Order in the SD Component (Transaction VA02)

Again, "Excellent price" was selected as the order reason. However, only a quantity of 80 pieces was ordered. In the quotation, a quantity of 200 pieces had been entered.

Figure 4.11 shows the document flow after the entry of the sales order. Compared to Figure 4.8, you can now see two sales orders (13042 and 13043). The status of the quotation is still "Being processed" because a specific part of ITEM 20 is still open.

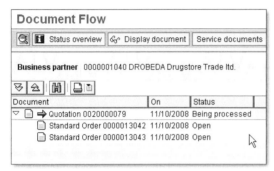

Figure 4.11 Display of the Document Flow for the Quotation in the SD Component (Transaction VA22)

Now let's analyze the document status of the quotation; for this purpose, the item overview for QUOTATION 20000079 is displayed again (see Figure 4.12).

Change Quotation 20000079: Overview

Quotation	20000079	Net value		4,300.00	EUR
Sold-to party	1040	DROBEDA Drugstore Trade ltd. / Mainroad 120 / 60311 Frankfurt			
Ship-to party	1040	DROBEDA Drugstore Trade ltd. / Mainroad 120 / 60311 Frankfurt			
PO Number	Inquiry 4000050	PO date			

Sales | Item overview | Item detail | Ordering party | Procurement | Shipping | Reason for rejection

Valid from		Valid to	11/30/2008	
Req. deliv.date	D 11/10/2008	Expect.ord.val.	3,010.00	EUR

All items

Ite	Material	Order Quantity	SU	Description	Ite	Net value	Curr.	Order probability	Overall status	Reason for rejection
10	PR4711	150 PC		wash lotion 150ml glass bottle	AGN	1,800.00	EUR	70	Completed	
20	PR4712	200 PC		wash lotion 150ml plastic bottle	AGN	2,500.00	EUR	70	Being processed	

Figure 4.12 Change Quotation, Item Overview in the SD Component (Transaction VA22)

While ITEM 10 in QUOTATION 20000079 is marked as "Completed," ITEM 20 still has the status "Being processed" because it contains an open (not referenced) quantity of 120 pieces. After the second sales order, the key figures can't be taken directly from the S&D documents but must be calculated. They have the following values:

- Open quotation value: 1,300 EUR
- Number of open quotations: 1
- Number of open quotation items: 1
- Open quotation quantity material PR4711: 0 pieces
- Open quotation quantity material PR4712: 120 pieces

- Quotation value of successful quotations: 3,000 EUR
- Number of successful quotations: 1
- Number of successful quotation items: 2
- Quotation quantity of successful quotations
  - Material PR4711: 150 pieces
  - Material PR4712: 80 pieces

From the key figures for the successful quotations, you can derive the following quotas after the second sales order:

- Success quota value: 70%
- Success quota number of documents: 100%
- Success quota number of items: 100%
- Success quota quotation quantity material PR4711: 100%
- Success quota quotation quantity material PR4712: 40%

In this case, the success quota provides unusable values with regard to the number of quotation items if a partial order exists for an item because the key figure, *success quota number of items*, has a value of 100% although only a partial quantity was ordered for an item.

To conclude this system example, the customer rejects the remaining quantity of ITEM 20. For this purpose, a REASON FOR REJECTION is entered for the item. Figure 4.13 shows the item overview of the quotation.

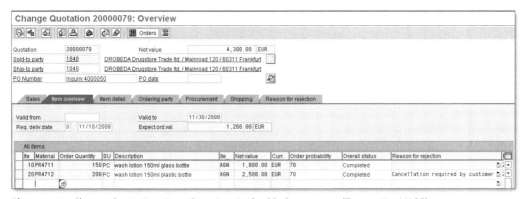

Figure 4.13 Change Quotation, Item Overview in the SD Component (Transaction VA22)

For ITEM 20, "Cancellation required by customer" was entered as the REASON FOR REJECTION. Consequently, the status of the quotation's second item is now "Completed." Finally, you must consider how the key figures developed after the rejection.

- Open quotation value: 0 EUR
- Number of open quotations: 0
- Number of open quotation items: 0
- Open quotation quantity material PR4711: 0 pieces
- Open quotation quantity material PR4712: 0 pieces
- Quotation value of successful quotations: 3,000 EUR
- Number of successful quotations: 1
- Number of successful quotation items: 2
- Quotation quantity of successful quotations
  - Material PR4711: 150 pieces
  - Material PR4712: 80 pieces
- Quotation value of rejected quotations: 1,300 EUR
- Number of rejected quotations: 1
- Number of rejected quotation items: 1
- Rejected quotation quantity material PR4711: 0 pieces
- Rejected quotation quantity material PR4712: 120 pieces

From the key figures for the successful quotations, you can derive the following quotas after the rejection for ITEM 20:

- Rejection quota value: 30%
- Rejection quota number of documents: 100%
- Rejection quota number of items: 100%
- Rejection quota quotation quantity material PR4711: 0%
- Rejection quota quotation quantity material PR4712: 60%

The restricted information value of quotas for the key figures, *rejection quota number of documents,* and *rejection quota number of document items*, has already been pointed out. This problem can be solved by distinguishing partially rejected items. However, the resulting information value isn't proportional to the required effort and detracts from the clarity.

4.2.6 Expired Quotations

For each quotation, you define the validity period in the document header. For evaluations in SAP NetWeaver BI, you must decide whether quotations whose validity period has been exceeded should still be indicated as open quotations. The validity period of a quotation is defined in the document header (VALID FROM, VALID TO fields; refer to Figure 4.1). In any case, it makes sense to provide an evaluation of the quotations whose validity period has already expired. As already outlined in Section 4.2.4, Success Quota and Accepted Quotations, for example, you should also indicate the quota of expired quotations (value, quantity, number of documents) here, that is, the ratio of the expired quotations to the overall value of quotations. These relative key figures enable a better evaluation of information that is provided to the user.

4.2.7 Sales Cycle

The sales cycle is a key figure indicating how much time elapses between the quotation and the customers purchase decision. Here, it's assumed that only successful orders are taken into account. Accordingly, the sales cycle is determined from the period between the quotation creation and the first sales order, which is entered with reference to the quotation.

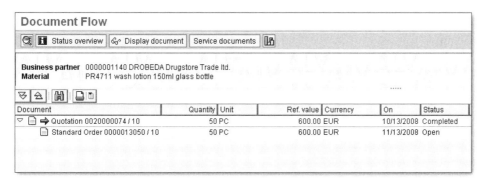

Figure 4.14 Document Flow for the Quotation in the SD Component (Transaction VA22)

Figure 4.14 shows the document flow for Quotation 20000074. The document was created on 10/13/2008. The corresponding sales order 13050 was created on 11/13/2008 in the system. As a result, the sales cycle for this document is 23 workdays. In SAP NetWeaver BI, it makes sense to calculate and evaluate the average sales cycle per document.

4.3   Order Key Figures

In this book, the presentation of the process-oriented S&D key figures is based on the S&D process, which is subdivided into the following steps: quotation processing, order processing, delivery, and billing. In the previous sections, you learned about the key figures resulting from quotation processing. So, let's continue our discussion with the order processing. In SAP ERP, you can create orders with reference to the quotation. For this purpose, data from the preceding document is copied to the order so that duplicate entries are eliminated. You can also enter orders without any reference to the preceding document. Another option is to transfer orders in electronic form and create the order automatically in the system. Generally, this has no influence on the development of key figures.

4.3.1   Incoming Orders and Orders on Hand

Among the most important S&D key figures are incoming orders and orders on hand. We use these terms synonymously for order entry (incoming orders) and order backlog (orders on hand). Practical experience shows that in some regions these terms are in use too. These are early indicators that anticipate the future turnover development. The longer the lead times of sales orders within an enterprise, the more important the orders on hand key figure is.

Whereas the incoming orders key figure is always considered per period (day, week, month, quarter), the orders on hand key figure constitutes a cumulated figure on a specific key date. The orders on hand include all open orders that haven't generated any revenues yet. With regard to a period, the calculation shown in the following box applies.

Determining the Orders on Hand	
Orders on hand at the end of the period:	*850*
= Orders on hand at the beginning of the period:	*1,000*
+ Incoming orders of the period:	*250*
− Revenues of the period:	*400*

The following sections describe the development of the *incoming orders* and *orders on hand* key figures based on the same systematics used for the previous quotations. For this purpose, the system example initiated in Section 4.2, Quotation Key Figures, is continued.

At this point, however, you can also use the Sales Information System (SIS) of SAP ERP. This approach is discussed additionally in Section 4.4, Excursus: Orders on Hand and Incoming Orders via the SIS. Within SIS, data is stored in separate statistics tables, including key figures, characteristics, and periods in the SAP ERP system at an aggregated level. Updates are controlled in Customizing of SIS. The statistics data of SIS can be loaded into the SAP NetWeaver BI system and used as the basis for evaluations. For the approach described in this book, documents and their follow-on documents in SAP BW are loaded in the SAP NetWeaver BI system. The connection of information between documents and the data aggregation to characteristics and periods is carried out in SAP NetWeaver BI.

This way, all raw data is available in SAP NetWeaver BI. All settings and rules for the aggregation, connection, and preparation of data are mapped centrally in SAP NetWeaver BI. This enables employees in both business and its departments to concentrate their know-how on this system and its tools and then map specific requirements therein. You don't need any detailed knowledge of SIS update.

On the other hand the advantage of the SIS solution is primarily that suitable SIS structures, including update rules, are already defined in many enterprises. Consequently, you don't have to establish a completely new solution for the implementation of SAP NetWeaver BI. SIS tables can be extracted easily into the SAP NetWeaver BI system.

Let's go back to the system example that we started in Section 4.2, Quotation Key Figures. The quantity-based and value-based development of the *incoming orders* and *orders on hand* key figures is described in a process-oriented way. That is, you learn how key figures develop within the different processes of the SD component. The following processes are described as examples:

- Standard order processing
- Credit memo and debit memo processing
- Returns processing
- Third-party order processing
- Consignment

Standard Order Processing

For the quotation shown earlier in Figure 4.1, two sales orders exist. The first Sales Order 13042 (refer to Figure 4.7) contains ITEM 10 with MATERIAL PR4711 and a NET VALUE of 1,800 EUR. The second Sales Order 13043 (refer to Figure 4.10) comprises ITEM 20 with MATERIAL PR4712 and a NET VALUE of 1,200 EUR. Figure 4.15 shows the document flow for Sales Order 13043.

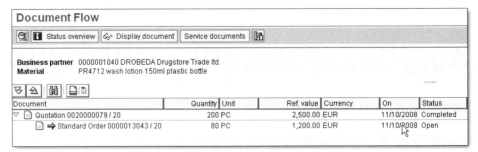

Figure 4.15 Document Flow for Sales Order 13043 in the SD Component (Transaction VA02)

Once again, Figure 4.15 indicates that the sales order was created with reference to Quotation 20000079. Moreover, it's clear that no follow-on documents exist for the sales order. The following list shows the values of the key figures resulting from the two Sales Orders 13042 and 13043:

▶ Incoming orders (value):   3,000 EUR

▶ Orders on hand (value):   3,000 EUR

▶ Incoming orders (quantity)

  ▷ Material PR4711:   150 pieces

  ▷ Material PR4712:   80 pieces

▶ Orders on hand (quantity)

  ▷ Material PR4711:   150 pieces

  ▷ Material PR4712:   80 pieces

Similar to the quotation key figures, it's also possible to create the following key figures:

▶ Number of order documents

▶ Number of document items

▸ Rejected sales orders (value, number of documents, number of items)

▸ Rejection quota (ratio of rejected orders to incoming orders)

Because the systematics have already been described in detail in Section 4.2, Quotation Key Figures, this isn't outlined again in the following. Instead, the system example is continued, and a delivery document is created for the orders.

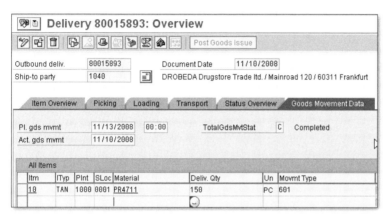

Figure 4.16 Delivery Document in the SD Component (Transaction VL02N)

Figure 4.16 shows the delivery document 80015893 with reference to Sales Order 13042. The TotalGdsMvtStat ("C", Completed) field indicates that the goods issue posting has already been implemented. This document is now also included in the document flow for the sales order, which is shown in Figure 4.17.

```
Document Flow
  Status overview  |  Display document  |  Service documents

Business partner  0000001040 DROBEDA Drugstore Trade ltd.
Material          PR4711 wash lotion 150ml glass bottle
```

Document	Quantity	Unit	Ref. value	Currency	On	Status
▽ ☐ Quotation 0020000079 / 10	150	PC	1,800.00	EUR	11/10/2008	Completed
▽ ☐ ➡ Standard Order 0000013042 / 10	150	PC	1,800.00	EUR	11/10/2008	Completed
▽ ☐ Delivery 0080015893 / 10	150	PC			11/10/2008	Being processed
☐ WMS transfer order 0000002943 / 1	150	PC			11/10/2008	Completed
☐ GD goods issue:delvy 4900037303 / 1	150	PC	825.00	EUR	11/10/2008	complete

Figure 4.17 Document Flow for the Sales Order in the SD Component (Transaction VA02)

Creating the delivery and the goods issue posting hasn't yet changed the *incoming orders* and *orders on hand* key figures. This is done in the next step during the sales order billing. The billing document is shown in Figure 4.18.

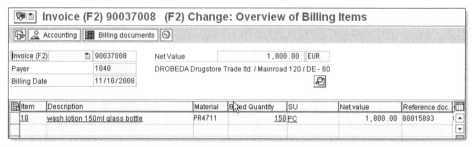

Figure 4.18 Billing Document for the Delivery in the SD Component (Transaction VF02)

Similar to the delivery document, the document flow of the sales order is now updated by the billing document. This example involves a delivery-related billing document, which means that the invoice is created based on the delivery data. The essential information (ship-to party, delivery quantity, delivery date) is copied from the delivery document to the billing document. This also includes information about which sales order forms the basis for the delivery and consequently for the billing document. Figure 4.19 shows the document flow of Sales Order 13042 after the billing document 90037008 has been created.

Document Flow

Status overview | Display document | Service documents

Business partner 0000001040 DROBEDA Drugstore Trade ltd.
Material PR4711 wash lotion 150ml glass bottle

Document	Quantity	Unit	Ref. value	Currency	On	Status
▽ Quotation 0020000079 / 10	150	PC	1,800.00	EUR	11/10/2008	Completed
▽ ➡ Standard Order 0000013042 / 10	150	PC	1,800.00	EUR	11/10/2008	Completed
▽ Delivery 0080015893 / 10	150	PC			11/10/2008	Completed
WMS transfer order 0000002943 / 1	150	PC			11/10/2008	Completed
GD goods issue:delvy 4900037303 / 1	150	PC	825.00	EUR	11/10/2008	complete
▽ Invoice (F2) 0090037008 / 10	150	PC	1,800.00	EUR	11/10/2008	FI Document Created
Accounting document 0100000710	150	PC			11/10/2008	Not cleared

Figure 4.19 Document Flow for the Sales Order in the SD Component (Transaction VA02)

In the process, the documents, quotation, sales order, and delivery are completed. The billing document is OPEN because the payment still needs to be done by the customer. The billing document reduces the orders on hand and simultaneously increases the sales. The incoming orders as a cumulated figure remain unchanged. The following list shows the value of the respective key figures after processing the entire process:

- Incoming orders (value): 3,000 EUR
- Orders on hand (value): 1,200 EUR
- Incoming orders (quantity)
  - Material PR4711: 150 pieces
  - Material PR4712: 80 pieces
- Orders on hand (quantity)
  - Material PR4711: 0 pieces
  - Material PR4712: 80 pieces
- Sales: 1,800 EUR

Credit Memo and Debit Memo Processing

Credit memos and debit memos are standard business processes. However, this isn't just about posting a credit memo or debit memo in the FI component (SAP ERP Financials) but also about documenting the agreement that was stipulated with the customer. This is done in the SD component using the credit memo and debit memo requests. These are billed on an order-related basis by means of credit memos and debit memos. The following sections resume the system example from Standard Order Processing in Section 4.3.1 and describe how the key figures change in these processes. Figure 4.20 shows a credit memo request that was created for the customer 1040.

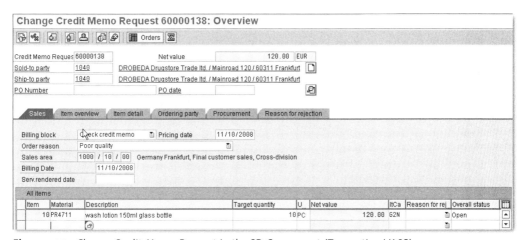

Figure 4.20 Change Credit Memo Request in the SD Component (Transaction VA02)

The ORDER REASON ("Poor quality") indicates that quality defects occurred for some parts of the delivered products. For this reason, the customer receives a credit memo for 10 pieces with a net value of 120 EUR. The status of the credit memo request is "open" because the corresponding billing document, which posts the credit memo in the FI component, has not been created yet. Due to this document, the key figures change as follows:

- Incoming orders (value):   2,880 EUR
- Orders on hand (value):   1,080 EUR
- Incoming orders (quantity)
  - Material PR4711:   140 pieces
  - Material PR4712:   80 pieces
- Orders on hand (quantity)
  - Material PR4711:   –10 pieces
  - Material PR4712:   80 pieces
- Sales: 1,800 EUR

You can see that the key figure incoming orders is reduced by 120 EUR due to the credit memo request. The orders on hand are reduced with regard to the quantity (10 pieces) and value (120 Euro) because a credit memo request exists. In this example, the *orders on hand* (quantity) key figure even becomes negative for material PR4711 because no additional open sales orders are available for this material.

Initially, the sales remain unchanged. This is changed in the next step during the creation of the billing document for the credit memo request. For this purpose, you need to remove the BILLING BLOCK ("Check credit memo") in the document (see Figure 4.20). You can then bill the document.

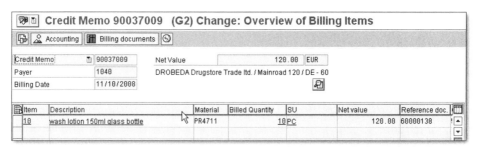

Figure 4.21   Change Credit Memo in the SD Component (Transaction VF02)

Figure 4.21 shows the billing document for Credit Memo Request 90037009. The credit memo request is now completed and the sales for the credit memo are posted in the FI component. Now, the key figures have the following status:

- Incoming orders (value): 2,880 EUR
- Orders on hand (value): 1,200 EUR
- Incoming orders (quantity)
  - Material PR4711: 140 pieces
  - Material PR4712: 80 pieces
- Orders on hand (quantity)
  - Material PR4711: 0 pieces
  - Material PR4712: 80 pieces
- Sales: 1,680 EUR

Incoming orders remain unchanged because the credit memo requests have already been subtracted. The orders on hand in terms of quantity (10 pieces) and value (120 EUR) are reset to their original value because the credit memo request has been billed and completed. The sales are reduced by the posted credit memo amounting to 120 EUR.

In this example, the key figures, *incoming orders* (quantity and value), *orders on hand* (quantity and value), and *sales,* have each been reduced by the credit memo request (*incoming orders, orders on hand*) or the billing document (*sales*), respectively. In the real business world, however, this can't be implemented quite as easily. We still opted for this approach in order to keep the example clear and comprehensible. Let's now consider some aspects that are important in this context.

It doesn't always make sense to directly reduce the *incoming orders, orders on hand,* and *sales* key figures by credit memo requests and credit memos. Another option is to define a separate key figure (e.g., *credit memos on hand*) for credit memo requests, which provides information about how many credit memos have been issued within a specific period and the total credit memo value. This can then be evaluated based on order reasons (credit memo request reasons) in a differentiated manner. This key figure can be compared to the "positive" orders on hand to enable a differentiated evaluation (e.g., *orders on hand – credit memos on hand = cleansed orders on hand*).

Particularly for the quantity, you must make a distinction between value credit memos and quantity credit memos. This example actually includes a classic value credit memo because the customer doesn't return the material. Especially in this case, it often makes sense to not reduce the quantity in the evaluations. The management of quantity and value may be different (the value is reduced; the quantity isn't reduced).

In SAP NetWeaver BI, whether these quantity or value updates are implemented is defined. For example, you can exclude documents of a specific document type (credit memo with document type "G2," refer to Figure 4.21) or items of a specific item category (in this example, the credit memo item has the item category "G2N," refer to Figure 4.20) in specific reports in SAP NetWeaver BI without considering their values. We'll come back to this aspect later on for the implementation of key figures. At this point, two things can be identified: The layout of the information system is done centrally in SAP NetWeaver BI. However, knowledge of the development and temporal-logical sequence of source documents in SAP ERP is indispensable if you want to master this task successfully.

Basic Rules for Debit Memos

For debit memos, the same rules apply as for credit memos — just with the opposite mathematical signs. For example, credit memos are required to calculate additional services (e.g., transport, assembly, commissioning, training) or to compensate orders that have been invoiced too low with a subsequent debit.

Returns Processing

With regard to the effects on the *incoming orders*, *orders on hand*, and *sales* key figures, the procedure for returns processing is very similar to the procedure for credit memo processing. This process comprises three basic steps that are mapped through separate documents:

1. **Returns order**
   In the returns order, it specifies which materials are returned in which quantity and by whom. By means of the pricing function, you can determine the item and order value. The returns document forms the basis for returns credit memos — just like the credit memo requests, which have been described in Credit Memo and Debit Memo Processing in Section 4.3.1. For this reason, the *incoming orders* and *orders on hand* key figures are reduced initially.

2. **Returns delivery**
   The returns delivery is entered with reference to the returns order and results in a goods receipt posting in the returns stock. The delivery doesn't change the key figures considered here.

3. **Returns credit memo**

The returns credit memo is created with reference to the returns order and is, in contrast to standard order processing (see Standard Order Processing in Section 4.3.1), order-related. The returns credit memo reduces the *sales* key figure. Similar to the process of credit memo and debit memo request, this sales posting increases the *orders on hand* key figure.

The same quantity and value handling information applies as was discussed in Credit Memo and Debit Memo Processing in Section 4.3.1. Here, it can also make sense to create user-defined key figures for the returns incoming orders or the returns orders on hand. In this case, the detail control is also implemented based on the document type and the item category in SAP NetWeaver BI.

Third-Party Order Processing

In third-party order processing, the end customer places an order at his vendor. However, the vendor doesn't deliver the goods himself but, in turn, places a purchase order at his vendor who sends the goods directly to the end customer using *third-party order processing*. Figure 4.22 shows the flow of goods and documents in third-party order processing.

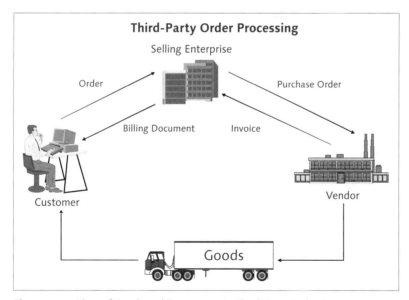

Figure 4.22 Flow of Goods and Documents in Third-Party Order Processing

In the selling enterprise, a sales order is created in SAP ERP that includes a third-party item (item category "TAS"). With reference to this item, a purchase requisition is created in the material management component (MM) of SAP ERP, which is then converted into a purchase order. The purchase order is sent to the vendor. The vendor sends the goods directly to the end customer and then issues a billing document to the selling enterprise, which, in turn, sends a billing document to the end customer. To describe this process, we'll use a new system example; in contrast to the previous example, we only focus on the order values and won't consider any quantities. The first step involves the third-party order (see Figure 4.23).

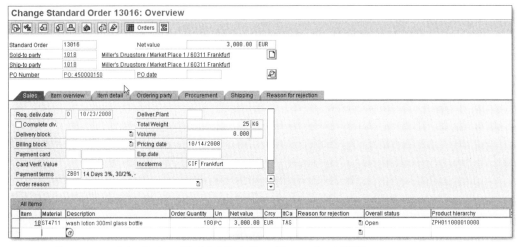

Figure 4.23   Sales Order with Third-Party Item (Transaction VA02)

You can recognize the third-party item by the item category "TAS." The ORDER QUANTITY is 100 pieces and the order NET VALUE is 3,000 EUR. First, the key figures develop just as they do in standard order processing:

▸ Incoming orders (value):   3,000 EUR

▸ Orders on hand (value):   3,000 EUR

▸ Sales: 0 EUR

In the MM component, the purchase requisition has already been converted to the purchase order 4500053490 as you can see in the document flow for Sales Order 13016 in Figure 4.24.

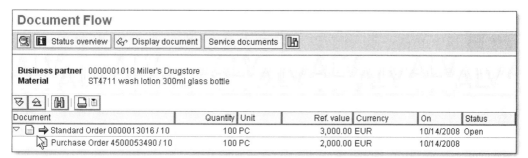

Figure 4.24 Document Flow for Third-Party Item in the Sales Order (Transaction VA02)

The Purchase Order was created in the MM component with reference to the third-party item in Sales Order 13016/10 of the SD component. The purchase order has a deviating document value that results from the quantity and purchase price of the vendor. So, we can now extend the key figure concept with the on-order stock:

- Incoming orders (value):   3,000 EUR
- Orders on hand (value):   3,000 EUR
- Open purchase order value (value): 2,000 EUR
- Business volume: 0 EUR
- Sales: 0 EUR

Because you can filter third-party items in SD and in MM via the order type or the item category "TAS" in SAP NetWeaver BI reports, this enables you to compare the third-party orders on hand with the third-party open purchase order value. In the next step, Vendor 1085 directly delivers to the end customer from the sales order and sends a corresponding vendor invoice that is posted in the invoice verification of the MM component.

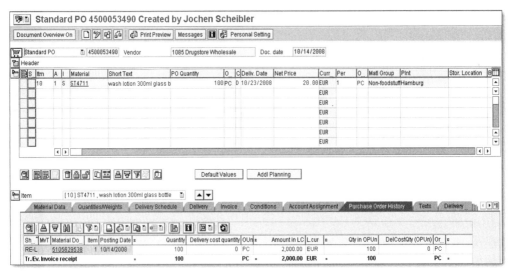

Figure 4.25 Purchase Order History of Purchase Order 4500053490 (Transaction ME22N)

Figure 4.25 shows the purchase order history for the third-party purchase order. The vendor invoice was entered with the document bearing the number 5105629538. This reduces the open purchase order value while increasing the purchase value or business volume at the same time. The key figures indicate the following:

▶ Incoming orders (value):   3,000 EUR

▶ Orders on hand (value):   3,000 EUR

▶ Open purchase order value: 0 EUR

▶ Business volume: 2,000 EUR

▶ Sales: 0 EUR

The next step is to create an invoice for the end customer. Because the goods were not delivered to the end customer by the selling enterprise, no delivery document is required. The billing document is order-related with reference to the third-party order item.

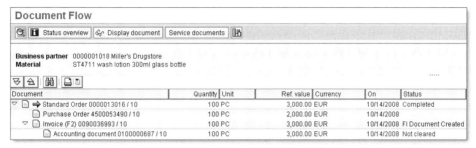

Figure 4.26 Document Flow for Third-Party Item in the Sales Order (Transaction VA02)

After billing, the document flow (see Figure 4.26) shows the third-party order item (Sales Order 13016/10), the purchase order in the MM component (Purchase Order 4500053490/10), and the outgoing invoice (Invoice 90036993/10) to the end customer. Unfortunately, the vendor invoice for the purchase order isn't visible here but only in Figure 4.25. After billing to the end customer, the key figures show the following results:

- Incoming orders (value):   3,000 EUR
- Orders on hand (value):   0 EUR
- Open purchase order value: 0 EUR
- Business volume: 2,000 EUR
- Sales: 3,000 EUR

Consignment

A consignment business entails that consignment stores are set up at the customer's site. The vendor fills these stores but remains the owner of the stock. The customer withdraws goods from this stock as required and notifies the vendor accordingly. This consignment issue is billed by the vendor. With this process, customers decrease the capital tie-up in the stock. In detail, the process comprises the following steps:

1. Consignment fill-up
2. Consignment issue
3. Consignment pick-up
4. Consignment returns

For the *consignment fill-up*, a sales order is entered whose items have no value and are not relevant for billing. Consequently, the *orders on hand* key figure doesn't change due to this sales order. A delivery is created with reference to this order whose goods issue posting results in a transfer of the customers consignment stock. This stock is located at the customer's site in consignment stores. Regarding the value, the stock is still owned by the vendor. Figure 4.27 shows a stock overview for MATERIAL PR4711.

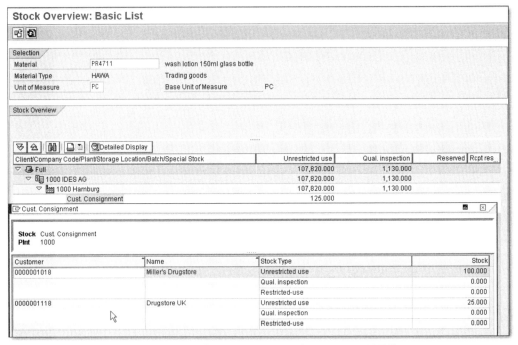

Figure 4.27 Stock Overview in the MM Component (Transaction MMBE)

In total, 125 pieces are located at the consignment stores of the customer, of which 100 pieces are at Customer 1018 (Miller's Drugstore). The corresponding transfer was performed through a consignment fill-up (sales order with order type "CF"), which had no effect on the key figures *incoming orders* and *orders on hand*. For this reason, the sales order isn't displayed here.

In the second step of *consignment issue,* the customer reports an issue of 50 pieces from the consignment stores. For this purpose, a sales order is entered with the order type "CI" (consignment issue). You can see this order in Figure 4.28.

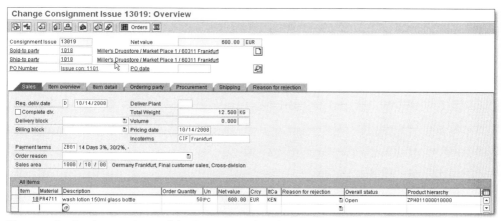

Figure 4.28 Consignment Issue of the Customer with Order Type "CI" (Transaction VA02)

The order item has the item category (ITCA) "KEN" (consignment issue). With regard to the *incoming order* and *orders on hand* key figures, this is a regular sales order that involves a delivery and billing document. Through the sales order, the key figures change as follows:

▶ Incoming orders (value):   600 EUR

▶ Orders on hand (value):   600 EUR

▶ Sales: 0 EUR

The goods issue posting of the corresponding delivery (Delivery 80015879/Item 10, see Figure 4.29) clears the stocks from the consignment stock, which has no impact on the key figures. With reference to this delivery document, a billing document (Invoice 90036994/10) is created for the settlement of the customer issue. The document flow for the issue order looks as shown in Figure 4.29 after billing the consignment issue.

Document	Quantity	Unit	Ref. value	Currency	On	Status
▽ ⇒ Consignment Issue 0000013019 / 10	50	PC	600.00	EUR	10/14/2008	Completed
▽ Delivery 0080015879 / 10	50	PC			10/14/2008	Completed
GI iss: cust.consgmt 4900037262 / 1	50	PC	275.00	EUR	10/14/2008	complete
▽ Invoice (F2) 0090036994 / 10	50	PC	600.00	EUR	10/14/2008	FI Document Created
Accounting document 0100000688 / 10	50	PC	600.00	EUR	10/14/2008	Not cleared

Figure 4.29 Document Flow for Consignment Issue (Transaction VA02)

After billing of the consignment issue, the key figures change as follows:

▶ Incoming orders (value):   600 EUR

▶ Orders on hand (value):   0 EUR

▶ Sales: 600 EUR

In contrast to the consignment fill-up, the issues of the customer from the consignment stock constitute a regular sales order that increases the *incoming orders* and *order on stock*.

In the consignment business, the customer may not require all stock from the consignment stores. This stock is then returned to the vendor, or the vendor picks the stock up at the customer's site. This is an optional third step in the consignment process, which is referred to as *consignment pick-up*. It's the reverse process of fill-up. For this purpose, the consignment pick-up order type ("CP") is provided. Just like the fill-up, the pick-up has no impact on the *incoming orders* and *orders on hand* key figures.

Consignment returns includes the returns to the consignment stock of the vendor. For this purpose, the consignment returns order type ("CONR") is provided. It corresponds to the returns process and has the same impact on the key figures.

Free of Charge Delivery

There are different reasons why customers receive free deliveries (e.g., samples, subsequent delivery). For this purpose, SAP ERP provides the "FD" order type that is delivered using a standard delivery. The value-based key figures are not affected here because no values are determined and stored within the orders. However, by means of the order type and the item categories in SAP NetWeaver BI, you can determine whether the quantity-based key figures are to be updated accordingly or not.

Outline Agreement

Outline agreements map long-term agreements with customers. In SAP ERP, a distinction is made between contracts and scheduling agreements. Quantity and value contracts define purchase quantities and prices for a specific period. With reference to contracts, release orders are created to map the release order behavior of the customer. By contrast, a scheduling agreement is a sales order whose release orders are implemented by entering the schedule lines in the scheduling agreement to control the various delivery dates. A separate release order (as in the contract) isn't required.

The following paragraphs detail the development of the key figures for contracts and scheduling agreements with examples. You'll also see additional key figures that are important in this context.

Figure 4.30 shows a contract for a specific chocolate selection. Selections combine multiple concrete material masters. The customer decides on a specific material only during the release order. This example includes a contract with Customer 95000, William's Food Trade.

A value contract (document number 40000216) with a volume of 100,000 EUR was stipulated with the customer; until now, the customer hasn't placed a release order (VALUE RELEASED: 0 EUR). For this reason, the key figures for the *incoming orders* and *orders on hand* have not changed. For contract management, the following additional key figures may be interesting:

▶ Contract stock

▶ Contract quantity (in case of quantity contract)

▶ Release order quantity

▶ Release order values

▶ Expired contracts

▶ Completed contracts

Figure 4.30 Change Contract in the SD Component (Transaction VA42)

Let's take a look at the document flow of the first release order for the contract shown in Figure 4.30.

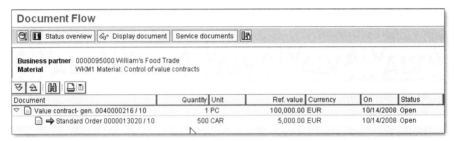

Figure 4.31 Document Flow in the Release Order for the Contract in the SD Component (Transaction VA02)

Figure 4.31 indicates that the release order (document number 13020) is a regular sales order that was entered with reference to the contract. Due to the release order, the key figures for orders on hand change as follows:

▸ Incoming orders (value):   5,000 EUR

▸ Orders on hand (value):   5,000 EUR

▸ Sales: 0 EUR

To conclude this example, let's take a look at the contract and the release order statistics. In Figure 4.32, you can see the release value that is based on the release orders. The VALUE RELEASED field now contains the value "5,000.00" EUR. The user can determine the level of the contract consumption and see the outstanding value to adjust the business activities accordingly. This way, negotiations for a follow-up contract can be scheduled, for example.

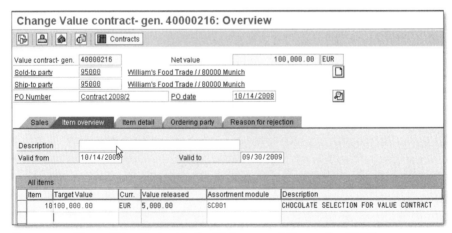

Figure 4.32 Change Value Contract in the SD Component (Transaction VA02)

In the previous example, you saw how the *incoming orders*, *orders on hand*, and *sales* key figures are changed by value contracts and the related release orders. The next example shows you how the *incoming orders* and *orders on hand* key figures develop by entering scheduling agreements and schedule lines. As mentioned previously, a scheduling agreement doesn't require a release order. The delivery dates are entered as schedule lines for the individual items.

Figure 4.33 shows an item overview for the scheduling agreement bearing the document number 30000061. For MATERIAL SC11000, a TARGET QUANTITY of "10,000" units was entered in Item 10 of the contract. For outline agreements, the validity period is always important. The scheduling agreement in this example is valid from 11/01/2008 to 04/30/2009. During this period, the customer can procure the specified materials in accordance with the stipulated conditions.

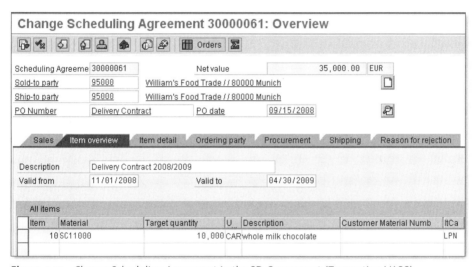

Figure 4.33 Change Scheduling Agreement in the SD Component (Transaction VA32)

A schedule line for the scheduling agreement item is entered for each delivery date. Figure 4.34 shows that schedule lines with corresponding delivery dates have already been entered for this item.

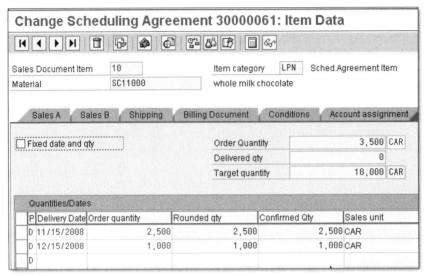

Figure 4.34 Schedule Lines for the Scheduling Agreement Item (Transaction VA32)

Two delivery dates have already been defined for Contract 30000061 with a target quantity of 10,000 cardboard boxes (car) of whole milk chocolate. One delivery is on 11/15/2008 and the other one on 12/15/2008. Via the two schedule lines, 3,500 cardboard boxes are released cumulatively. Because the price per box is 10 EUR (this item isn't displayed in the figures), the net value amounts to 35,000 EUR. The *incoming orders* and *orders on hand* key figures only change when an item schedule line is entered. Previously, these values were zero. The following list shows the values of the key figures after entering the item schedule lines in the scheduling agreement:

▶ Incoming orders (value):   35,000 EUR

▶ Orders on hand (value):   35,000 EUR

▶ Sales: 0 EUR

The process of scheduling agreement processing is continued by entering a delivery for each schedule line. This is followed by the billing document. The billing document reduces the orders on hand and increases the sales accordingly. In this regard, this process doesn't differ from the regular standard order processing any longer. Additional key figures for the scheduling agreement processing might include the following:

▶ Scheduling agreement quantity

▶ Delivery release orders (according to schedule lines)

Unlike in SAP ERP, in SAP NetWeaver BI, you can evaluate scheduling agreement quantities, including the prices, without having to specify schedule lines. Then you can compare the target value and the release order value for scheduling agreements.

4.3.2   Orders with Delivery or Billing Blocks

Users can set delivery or billing blocks for order documents, which prevent the creation of follow-on documents. They enable you to clarify technical or business details before the order is actually processed. Incoming orders and orders on hand are updated despite the delivery block. However, in SAP NetWeaver BI, it's useful and also possible to also evaluate the corresponding key figures for the incoming orders and orders on hand according to these criteria. This way, the S&D management can determine how many orders must be clarified and which order values are associated with this process.

4.3.3   Analysis of Business Processes

In SAP ERP, different business processes are mapped via order types and item categories. Section 4.3.1, Incoming Orders and Orders on Hand, described how these processes impact the value development of the corresponding key figures for incoming orders, orders on hand, and sales.

An analysis of the order types and item categories additionally provide information about how the incoming orders distribute over the individual processes. Besides the order value, the order quantities and the number of respective documents are also interesting. For example, the evaluation provides the information listed in Table 4.1.

Business Processes	Values	Number of Documents
Standard orders	250,000 EUR	100
Third-party orders	75,000 EUR	25
Direct purchase orders	60,000 EUR	20
Consignment fill-up	0 EUR	30
Consignment issue	35,000 EUR	15
Returns orders	10,000 EUR	14
Credit memo requests	2,500 EUR	1
Debit memo requests	5,000 EUR	3
Outline agreements	500,000 EUR	3
Outline agreement releases	125,000 EUR	10

Table 4.1 Partial Evaluation for Order Types and Item Categories

Here, you must consider that, for example, the consignment fill-up always involves free-of-charge orders because the transfer to the consignment stores isn't billed. The customer only has to pay for issues from the consignment stores.

This evaluation also provides information about the significance of individual business processes, which can be increased by presenting the relative significance (percentage of the total value). Analyzing the order reasons provides information about the business transactions. This enables you to answer the following questions:

▶ **Why are goods returned?**
For example, due to incorrect delivery, quality defects, repair, or order cancellation.

▶ **What was the reason for a third-party order processing or a direct purchase order?**
Probably the goods were not available, were not listed in the selection, or the delivery included spare parts or samples.

▶ **Why was a credit memo granted?**
For example, due to wrong pricing, damage, or delivery delay.

▶ **Why was a debit memo granted?**
For instance, due to wrong pricing or additional services.

A prerequisite is, however, that the corresponding order reasons have been set in Customizing of the SD component and that these are entered by the user during order processing.

4.4 Excursus: Orders on Hand and Incoming Orders via the SIS

The SIS of the SD component provides numerous key figures, characteristics, and information structures. In the information structures, aggregated information is updated at the characteristic level for a specific periodicity (day, week, and month). This section describes the specifics for updating the *incoming orders*, *orders on hand*, and *sales* key figures in the form of an excursus.

The orders on hand are mapped by the *open orders* key figure. This includes all orders that have not yet been delivered. Hence, in many enterprises, the problem arises that the *open orders* key figure is reduced with the creation of the SD delivery, but no sales have been generated yet. If the creation of the delivery and the billing document are within the same period, this doesn't affect the calculation for determining the orders on hand (see Section 4.3.1, Incoming Orders and Orders on Hand). If this isn't the case, however, the calculation is incomplete, which is considered problematic in many enterprises. Let's consider how the key figure develops in the course of the S&D process based on a system example. In the first step, you enter a sales order (see Figure 4.35).

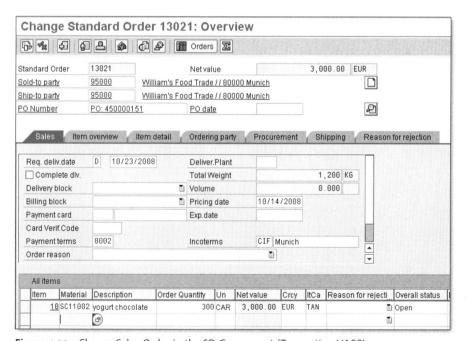

Figure 4.35 Change Sales Order in the SD Component (Transaction VA02)

Sales order 13021 (see Figure 4.35) contains an order item with a NET VALUE of 3,000 EUR. The evaluation of the *incoming orders, orders on hand (open orders)*, and *sales* key figures in SIS provides the values shown in Figure 4.36.

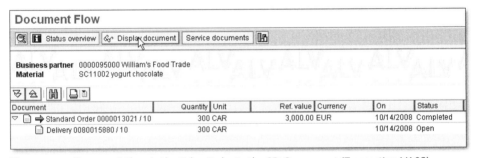

Figure 4.36   Evaluation in SIS in the SD Component (Transaction MC(A))

For the corresponding selection, the *incoming orders* have a total of 3,000 EUR. The *open orders* key figure has the same value. The *Sales* key figure hasn't been generated yet. In the next step, a delivery for the sales order is created. Figure 4.37 shows the document flow of the sales order after creating the delivery.

Document Flow

Document	Quantity	Unit	Ref. value	Currency	On	Status
▽ ⇨ Standard Order 0000013021 / 10	300	CAR	3,000.00	EUR	10/14/2008	Completed
Delivery 0080015880 / 10	300	CAR			10/14/2008	Open

Business partner   0000095000 William's Food Trade
Material   SC11002 yogurt chocolate

Figure 4.37   Document Flow in the Sales Order in the SD Component (Transaction VA02)

The delivery hasn't been picked yet and the goods issue has not been posted. Nevertheless, the orders on hand (or the key figure, *open orders*) have already been reduced as is shown in Figure 4.38.

Customer Analysis: Incoming Orders: Drilldown

Sold-to party   95000 William's Food

No. of Material: 1

Material		Incoming orders	Open orders	Sales
Total		3,000.00 EUR	0.00 EUR	0.00 EUR
SC11002	yogurt chocolate	3,000.00 EUR	0.00 EUR	0.00 EUR

Figure 4.38   Evaluation in SIS in the SD Component (Transaction MC(A)

As expected, the *open orders* key figure was reduced. Because no billing document has been posted, the *sales* key figure isn't updated yet. This is done in the next step for posting the billing document. Figure 4.39 shows the document flow in the sales order after billing.

Document Flow

Status overview | Display document | Service documents

Business partner   0000095000 William's Food Trade
Material   SC11002 yogurt chocolate

Document	Quantity	Unit	Ref. value	Currency	On	Status
Standard Order 0000013021 / 10	300	CAR	3,000.00	EUR	10/14/2008	Completed
Delivery 0080015880 / 10	300	CAR			10/14/2008	Completed
Picking request 20081014 / 10	300	CAR			10/14/2008	Completed
GD goods issue:delvy 4900037264 / 1	300	CAR	1,500.00	EUR	10/14/2008	complete
Invoice (F2) 0090036995 / 10	300	CAR	3,000.00	EUR	10/14/2008	FI Document Created
Accounting document 0100000689	300	CAR			10/14/2008	Not cleared

Figure 4.39   Document Flow in the Sales Order in the SD Component (Transaction VA02)

When you create the billing document in the SD component, this also involves the sales posting in the FI component and the update of the *sales* key figure in the SIS of the SD component. You can see this by opening the evaluation in the SIS again (see Figure 4.40).

Customer Analysis: Incoming Orders: Drilldown

Sold-to party   95000 William's Food

No. of Material: 1

Material		Incoming orders	Open orders	Sales
Total		3,000.00 EUR	0.00 EUR	3,000.00 EUR
SC11002	yogurt chocolate	3,000.00 EUR	0.00 EUR	3,000.00 EUR

Figure 4.40   Evaluation in SIS in the SD Component (Transaction MC(A)

Unlike previously, the *sales* key figure is now 3,000 EUR as well. As discussed earlier, it's desirable to reduce the orders on hand (key figure, *open orders*) when posting the billing document. However, this option isn't provided in the update of key figures in the SD component readily. Here, you have to define separate information structures with corresponding update rules in Customizing. Also the SIS has some weak points in the cross-company process, which will be discussed later (see Section 4.7, Key Figures in the Cross-Company Business). SIS structures are usually not extracted to SAP NetWeaver BI for these reasons. We usually recommend transforming information concerning the different documents (offers, orders, deliveries, invoices) to SAP NetWeaver BI in order to implement evaluations on this basis.

4.5 Delivery Key Figures

Let's now consider the process-oriented key figures for the delivery processing. In SAP ERP, these documents are used to map the picking and shipping. Delivery documents are created with reference to the orders. An order can include multiple deliveries, and a delivery can include multiple orders.

4.5.1 Delivery Quantity, Delivery Value, and Documents

Many delivery analyses are based on the following key figures:

▶ Delivery quantity

▶ Delivery volume

▶ Number of deliveries

▶ Number of delivery items

Frequently, the *delivery value* key figure is also requested, which isn't available in the SAP standard because at the time of delivery, the focus is on the quantity in the SAP ERP application. In SAP NetWeaver BI, you can determine the delivery value via the corresponding order item, for example. The formula is shown in the following box.

> **Determining the Delivery Value**
>
> *delivery value*
> *= order value / order quantity x delivery quantity*

Depending on the document status, the mentioned key figures can be differentiated as follows:

▶ **Open deliveries**
The delivery document is created; picking has not been executed yet.

▶ **Picked deliveries**
Picking has been carried out; goods issue is open.

▶ **Goods issues**
The goods issue of the deliveries is posted.

▶ **Completed deliveries**
The billing document is created for deliveries that are relevant for billing. Goods issue is posted for deliveries not relevant for billing.

Basically, you can evaluate the work list and create the following key figures:

▶ Deliveries to be picked

▶ Goods issue to be posted

▶ Deliveries to be billed

However, this information should be evaluated already in SAP ERP so that the corresponding transactions can be executed directly. For this reason, in this section we focus on the evaluation of key figures that depend on the document status (*open, picked, goods issue posted, billed*).

Again, we'll describe the development of key figures based on an example that starts with the sales order creation shown in Figure 4.41.

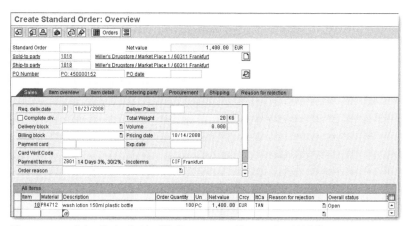

Figure 4.41 Sales Order in the SD Component (Transaction VA01)

The sales order contains an item for MATERIAL PR4712 with a quantity of 100 pieces, with a NET VALUE of 1,400 EUR. In the next step, the delivery document with number 80015881 is created with reference to this sales order. Its status is shown in Figure 4.42.

Figure 4.42 Change Delivery Document in the SD Component (Transaction VL02N)

In Figure 4.42, the OVRLLPICKSTATUS field indicates that the document is to be picked and that picking has not been carried out yet. Therefore, the PICKED QTY field has the value "0". Note at this point that it is possible to create delivery documents in SAP ERP that are not relevant for picking (e.g., returns deliveries).

The development of the key figures is as follows (we only refer to the *open delivery quantity* and *open delivery value* key figures):

▶ Open delivery quantity: 100

▶ Open delivery value: 1,400 EUR (value from the order)

▶ Picked delivery quantity: 0

▶ Picked delivery value: 0

▶ Goods issue quantity: 0

▶ Goods issue value: 0

▶ Delivery quantity (completed):   0

▶ Delivery value (completed):   0

The delivery value needs to be calculated based on the order because the delivery document itself doesn't contain any price or value information. After picking has been carried out, the delivery document looks like Figure 4.43.

Figure 4.43 Delivery Document After Picking in the SD Component (Transaction VL02N)

Picking is now complete as indicated in the picking status (OVRLLPICKSTATUS field) and the PICKED QTY fields. The OVRLLPICKSTATUS field now has the value "C" (FULLY PICKED). The PICKED QTY field now includes the quantity of "100" pieces.

At this point, you must consider that partial pickings are also possible. In this case, picking is implemented in several successive steps: in our example, the delivery document has been fully picked. The following list shows how the delivery key figures change in this example:

▶ Open delivery quantity: 0

▶ Open delivery value: 0

▶ Picked delivery quantity: 100

▶ Picked delivery value: 1,400 EUR (from the order)

▶ Goods issue quantity: 0

▶ Goods issue value: 0

▶ Delivery quantity (completed):   0

▶ Delivery value (completed):   0

In the next step of this example, we take a look at the delivery after the goods issue posting (see Figure 4.44).

In Figure 4.44, you can see the changes in Delivery 80015881 after the goods issue posting. The TOTALGDSMVTSTAT field now has the value "C" (COMPLETED), which indicates that the goods issue posting was carried out. With this goods issue posting, the stock quantities of the MM component were reduced as well. Moreover, the stock value in FI was updated by means of a corresponding accounting document. The following list shows how the key figures have changed due to the goods issue posting:

- ▶ Open delivery quantity: 0
- ▶ Open delivery value: 0
- ▶ Picked delivery quantity: 100
- ▶ Picked delivery value: 1,400 EUR (from the order)
- ▶ Goods issue quantity: 100
- ▶ Goods issue value: 1,400 EUR (from the order)
- ▶ Delivery value (completed):   0
- ▶ Delivery quantity (completed):   0

Figure 4.44   Delivery Document After the Goods Issue Posting (Transaction VL02N)

This delivery is relevant for billing. By means of billing, the customer is invoiced for the delivery and the document is considered complete. Figure 4.45 shows the status overview for the delivery document after the billing document has been created.

Delivery 80015881 now has the status FULLY INVOICED. This status is shown in the BILL.DOCS field. It indicates that the document is completed. As a result, the delivery key figures change as follows:

- Open delivery quantity: 0
- Open delivery value: 0
- Picked delivery quantity: 100 pieces
- Picked delivery value: 1,400 EUR (from the order)
- Goods issue quantity: 100 pieces
- Goods issue value: 1,400 EUR (from the order)
- Delivery quantity (completed):   100 pieces
- Delivery value (completed):   1,400 EUR (from the order or billing document)

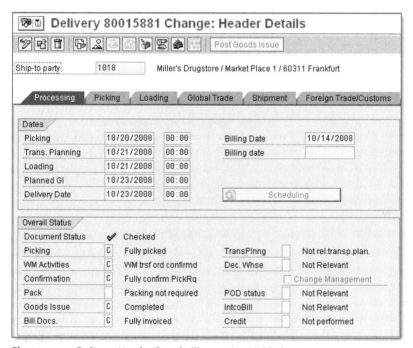

Figure 4.45   Delivery Header Details (Transaction VL02N)

The *open delivery quantity* and *open delivery value* key figures have already been set to "0" after picking. The remaining key figures have been increased to 100 pieces (quantity-related key figures) or 1,400 EUR (value-based key figures), respectively, by means of the picking, goods issue posting, and billing actions.

4.5.2   On-Time Delivery Performance

On-time deliveries are an important prerequisite for customer satisfaction. Therefore, the *on-time delivery performance* key figure is particularly crucial. To determine the on-time delivery performance you need the scheduled and the actual delivery date.

In this context, it's not an easy task to determine the *scheduled* delivery date in the underlying sales order. When the sales order is entered, the customer's requested delivery date is entered as well at the document header level. The availability check is used to determine whether the customer's requested delivery date can be adhered to. If not, the system specifies the earliest possible delivery date and creates a new schedule line for the order item. This schedule line contains the confirmed quantity and the corresponding delivery date. The customer is notified of this date in the order confirmation. You now have to consider whether you should use the originally requested delivery date of the customer or the date confirmed to the customer for calculating the on-time delivery performance. Within reporting, more questions arise:

▶ **How do you calculate the on-time delivery performance with an aggregated view?**
First, the on-time delivery performance is calculated per schedule line because the date information is stored at this level. For an order item of 10 pieces, it's possible that 7 pieces are delivered on time and 3 pieces are delivered with a delay of 5 days. But how do you evaluate the on-time delivery performance for this item as a whole? You could assume the maximum (5 days), the average (2.5 days), or a weighting based on the quantity (1.5 days). The same applies to other aggregation levels, for instance, per material.

▶ **Do you evaluate a delivery that is performed before the requested delivery date of the customer as positive or negative?**
If such a delivery with a negative value is included in the calculation of the on-time delivery performance, this improves the overall result. Consequently, delays of other deliveries are compensated. To avoid this, you can consider such deliveries as on-time and set the number of days to "is equal to 0." Frequently, it's requested to incorporate deliveries that arrive before the confirmed delivery date as a delivery that isn't on time.

These two problems can be solved if you evaluate the on-time delivery performance by means of scoring. In doing so, each goods receipt obtains a score that can then be aggregated accordingly (per material, customer, customer group). Table 4.2 shows a possible score structure.

Deviation from the Delivery Date in Days	Score
0-1 day too late	100
2-4 days too late	95
5-7 days too late	75
8-10 days too late	50
More than 10 days too late	25
More than 20 days too late	1
0-1 day too early	100
2-4 days too early	95
5-7 days too early	75
More than 7 days too early	50

Table 4.2 Scoring Scheme for the On-Time Delivery Performance

Moreover, there is a close connection between the on-time delivery performance and the quantity reliability. You must consider the question of how to evaluate an on-time delivery whose quantity is less than specified. For this purpose, the scoring can be additionally weighted with the quantity, for example. Then, the score is multiplied by the proportionate quantity (if the score = 100, and the quantity proportion = 50%, this results in a score of 50).

Let's now consider the scoring of the on-time delivery performance based on a system example. Figure 4.46 shows Sales Order 13045. The customer has specified 11/10/2008 as the requested delivery date.

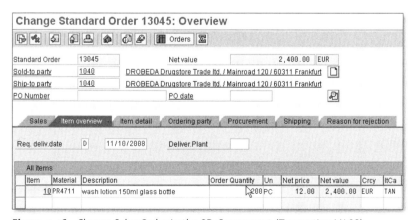

Figure 4.46 Change Sales Order in the SD Component (Transaction VA02)

By means of the availability check of the SD component, the system determined 11/13/2008 as the delivery date for the order item. Figure 4.47 shows the corresponding schedule lines for this item. The schedule lines are used to schedule the individual delivery dates for an order item. Therefore, 11/13/2008 is confirmed as the delivery date.

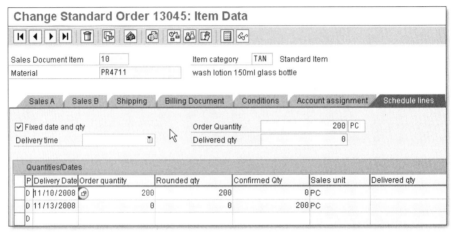

Figure 4.47 Schedule Lines for the Order Item in the SD Component (Transaction VA02)

However, the actual delivery was on 11/21/2008. The corresponding delivery document is shown in Figure 4.48. Here, the actual goods issue date (ACTUAL GI DATE) is on 11/21/2008.

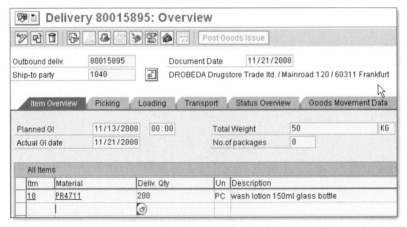

Figure 4.48 Item Overview in the Delivery in the SD Component (Transaction VL02N)

Depending on which date you want to use as the basis (requested delivery date, confirmed date) and based on Table 4.2, you can establish the following scores:

- Requested delivery date: 11/10/2008
- Confirmed date: 11/13/2008
- Actual delivery date: 11/21/2008
- Deviation (requested delivery date):   9 days (score: 50)
- Deviation (confirmed date):   6 days (score: 75)

Note that the date for the actual goods issue and the delivery date are identical in this example. Of course, the transport time isn't taken into account here. However, SAP ERP doesn't recalculate the delivery date automatically (the day on which the goods arrive at the customer's site). The delivery document still includes the originally planned delivery date that was scheduled based on the confirmed date. You can change this date manually, but you take the risk that you might forget to make this setting. Therefore, it's advisable in most cases to use the actual goods issue date.

4.5.3 Delivery Time

The delivery time is another criterion for the performance of an enterprise. In the following, delivery time is considered as the time between the incoming orders and the outbound delivery. For the incoming orders date, you must determine whether you want to use the requested delivery date of the customer or the entry date of the order item. An argument against the requested delivery date is that it's assigned once at the header level and then transferred to all items. As a result, the requested delivery date is also transferred to those items that are added at a later point. This is also the case if the requested delivery date is already in the past. With regard to the delivery time, for instance, the following information might be interesting:

- Average delivery time
- Maximum deviation from the average delivery time
- Average deviation from the average delivery time
- Median of the delivery time

The evaluation of the delivery time in SAP NetWeaver BI is particularly interesting because the standard SAP ERP application includes only a few evaluations. Consequently, you depend on additional programming within SAP ERP.

4.6   Billing Key Figures

After quotation processing, order processing, and delivery, the S&D process con-
cludes with billing. Billing can be order-related or delivery-related. An example
for order-related billing is third-party order processing. This section presents the
relevant key figures for billing documents.

4.6.1   Sales, Sales Volume

Among the most important billing-related key figures are the following:

▶ Sales

▶ Sales quantity

▶ Number of billing documents

▶ Number of billing items

Sales is the product of the item quantity (sales quantity) and the price. The key
figures for the number of billing documents and the associated document items
provide information about the document volume.

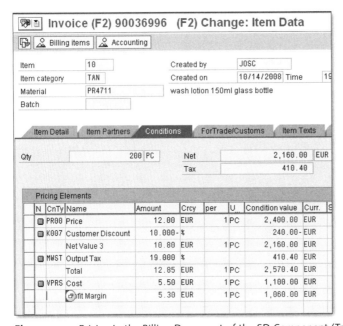

Figure 4.49   Pricing in the Billing Document of the SD Component (Transaction VF02)

In principle, quotations, orders, and billing documents allow for differentiated pricing. In a pricing procedure, values such as prices, discounts, surcharges, and output taxes are taken into account. The pricing procedures are defined in Customizing. Figure 4.49 shows the structure of pricing in sales documents based on a billing document.

The information provided in pricing can be used as the basis for deriving additional key figures. These are described in the following sections.

4.6.2 Pricing Analysis

From the individual condition values, which you can find in the rows of the pricing procedure (see Figure 4.49), you can derive the following key figures:

▶ Granted discounts, such as sorted by customer discount, material discount, promotion discount

▶ Surcharges, such as fees or services

▶ Total value for the output tax

In Customizing, you can set up additional condition types and pricing procedures depending on the respective requirements of the enterprise. This enables you to evaluate the respective price components in SAP NetWeaver BI at an aggregated level.

4.6.3 Margin

The margin analysis is a special form of the pricing analysis (see Section 4.6.2, Pricing Analysis). The VPRS condition type (refer to Figure 4.49) shows the (planned) production costs of the material. These are read from the evaluation screen of the material master, for example. This enables you to evaluate the profit margin via the net value of the item and the cost. In Figure 4.49, the value is indicated in the PROFIT MARGIN subtotal. If you put the profit margin in relation to the sales, you obtain the key figure for the *margin*.

4.7   Key Figures in the Cross-Company Business

Frequently, different delivery relationships exist between various groups or corporate units. To support these relationships, the SAP ERP application provides *cross-company processes*. You must distinguish the following scenarios:

▶ Cross-company sales

▶ Cross-company stock transfer

With regard to the evaluation of the *incoming orders* and *orders on hand* key figures, a problem arises for these processes where no solution is available in the SIS of the SD component. The following sections describe the scenarios briefly and address the information required for the *incoming orders* and *orders on hand* key figures. The implementation is detailed in Chapter 5, Mapping the Key Figures in SAP NetWeaver BI.

4.7.1   Scenarios of the Cross-Company Processes

In the first scenario, cross-company sales, a legally independent enterprise (selling company code) sells goods from the stock of an affiliated company (delivering company code). The prerequisite is that both companies work in the same SAP ERP client. For this purpose, a sales order is created in the sales area of the selling company code. In this order, a plant from the company code of the affiliated company (delivering company code) is determined as the delivering plant. The goods issue posting is carried out in the delivering company code and the goods are delivered directly to the customer. Two billing documents are created with reference to the delivery. The end customer is the payer of the external billing document. The internal billing document is used for the settlement of the delivering company code to the selling company code. Thus, the selling company code is the payer.

In the second scenario of cross-company stock transfer, one company code purchases goods from another company code. For this purpose, in the MM component, a stock transfer order is created in the purchasing company code. Similar to the scenario of the cross-company sales, a delivery is created in the delivering company code, but this time with reference to the stock transfer order. The goods are delivered to the purchasing company code and received there together with the goods receipt posting. An internal billing document is created with reference to the delivery. This way, the selling company code bills its delivery to the purchasing company code. The purchasing company code is the payer of the internal billing document.

In both scenarios, neither the incoming orders nor the orders on hand are updated in the SD SIS of the delivering company code. Because many enterprises consider the evaluation of this key figure as an important early indicator for the business development, it's often necessary to update the incoming orders in these organizational units as well. For the sake of completeness, please note that at this point in SAP SIS in the scenario of the cross-company sales, the corresponding key figures for the incoming orders and the orders on hand (respectively Open Orders see Section 4.4: Excursus: Orders on Hand and Incoming Orders via the SIS) are updated for the selling company code, but not for the delivering company code.

4.7.2 System Examples

Now let's consider two system examples to help describe the requirements of the update for the incoming orders and the orders on hand. First, we'll outline the process of cross-company sales and then the process of cross-company stock transfer.

In the first step, a sales order is entered. Figure 4.50 shows a section of the header data of a sales order. You can see that the order was created for the British subsidiary in the sales area 2000/10/00 (sales organization, distribution channel, division).

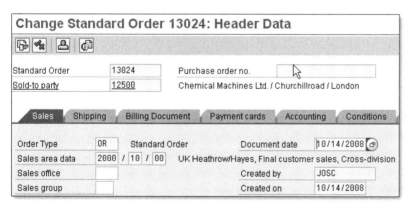

Figure 4.50 Document Header Data in the Cross-Company Sales Order in the SD Component Transaction VA02)

The sales order is assigned to the sales organization 2000 and the company code 2000. The item data of the sales order shown in Figure 4.51 indicates that the delivery is carried out by plant 1000 (see the field PLNT), which, in turn, is assigned to the company code 1000 within the customizing component.

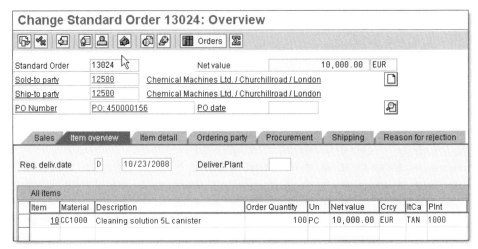

Figure 4.51 Item Data in the Cross-Company Sales Order in the SD Component (Transaction VA02)

In the SIS, the *incoming orders* and *orders on hand* key figures are only updated in the selling sales area 2000/10/00 as follows:

▶ Incoming orders: 10,000 EUR

▶ Orders on hand: 10,000 EUR

▶ Sales: 0 EUR

The key figures are not updated in the delivering company code. However, incoming orders can also be noted in the delivering company code. The amount of the incoming orders depends on the price that the delivering company code will bill to the selling company code in the internal billing document. This price can already be found in the cross-company sales order 13024 shown in Figure 4.51. For this purpose, you need to take a look at the conditions in pricing as shown in Figure 4.52.

Figure 4.52 Pricing in the Cross-Company Sales Order in the SD Component (Transaction VA02)

The condition type "PI01" (see Figure 4.52) includes the price of the inter-company billing between the two company codes (in this example: 75 EUR). Consequently, in the delivering company code, the key figures have to be updated as follows:

- Incoming orders: 7,500 EUR
- Orders on hand: 7,500 EUR
- Sales: 0 EUR

In the selling company code, the key figures develop due to the delivery and the billing document, as described in Section 4.3.1, Incoming Orders and Orders on Hand. In the delivering company code, the orders on hand are decreased due to the internal billing document. Figure 4.53 shows the internal billing document for the sales order.

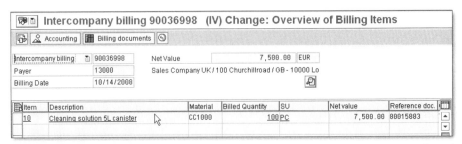

Figure 4.53 Inter-company Billing Between the Delivering and the Selling Company Code in the SD Component (Transaction VF02)

The internal billing document (see Figure 4.53) indicates a net value of 7,500 EUR. This document is the billing document of the delivering company code to the selling company code. The customer master record 13000 (Sales Company) represents the sales organization of company code 2000. The key figures of the delivering company code develop as follows:

- Incoming orders: 7,500 EUR
- Orders on hand: 0 EUR
- Sales: 7,500 EUR

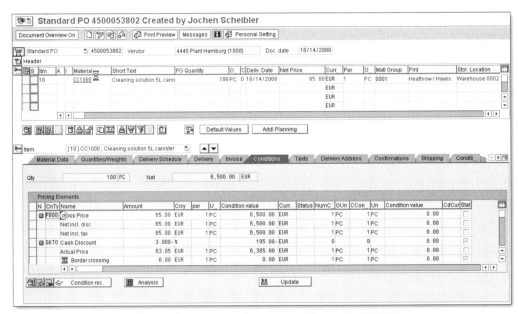

Figure 4.54 Purchase Order in the MM Component (Transaction ME22N)

In the second system example, we want to describe the process of cross-company stock transfer. In the purchasing company code 2000, a purchase order is entered for Vendor 4445 (see Figure 4.54). The vendor represents the delivering plant 1000 (Plant Hamburg). The system determines the price for procuring the material from another plant by means of the vendor material info record in the MM component. In this example, the price per piece is 65 EUR.

In the case of cross-company stock transfer, the *incoming orders* and *orders on hand* key figures aren't updated in the SIS in the delivering company code 1000 either. However, these key figures have to be updated as follows:

- Incoming orders: 6,500 EUR
- Orders on hand: 6,500 EUR
- Sales: 0 EUR

With reference to the stock transfer order shown in Figure 4.54, a replenishment delivery is created in the SD component. This doesn't affect the *incoming orders* and *orders on hand* key figures. Subsequently, an internal billing document is entered for billing the goods delivery with reference to the stock transfer order (see Figure 4.55).

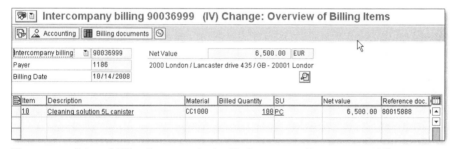

Figure 4.55 Internal Billing Document in the SD Component (Transaction VF02)

The customer master record 1186 represents the purchasing company code. The internal billing document reduces the orders on hand and updates the sales. As a result, the key figures have the following values:

- Incoming orders: 6,500 EUR
- Orders on hand: 0 EUR
- Sales: 6,500 EUR

For the pricing in the internal billing document, the price is transferred from the purchase order. This way, you can avoid deviations between the *orders on hand*

and the sales update. This setting also prevents price deviations occurring during the posting of the corresponding vendor invoice in the purchasing company code (2000). You can find the required Customizing settings in the copying control for billing documents (Transaction VTFL). For the copying control of the delivery document (NLCC: replenishment delivery cross company) to IV (inter-company billing document), you select option "A" (price source "purchase order") as the price source at the item level (item category "NLC"). This way it's ensured that the prices are transferred from the purchase order.

4.8 Summary

This chapter presented process-oriented key figures. This presentation focused toward the S&D process, which are divided into the phases of quotation processing, order processing, delivery, and billing. Moreover, we outlined the specifics of the cross-company process, which plays an important role in many companies. You learned how raw data is created in the SAP ERP application, which forms the basis for mapping the corresponding key figures in SAP NetWeaver BI.

The *quotation* key figures focus on the success analysis question. This information is supposed to determine the reasons for the results of sales activities to draw conclusions for the future.

The *order* key figures predominately include the key figures for *incoming orders*, *orders on hand*, and *sales*. You saw how the different process variants of the SAP ERP application influence these key figures.

The key figures help you analyze the performance of the delivery process. Questions such as how fast the delivery is and how good the on-time delivery performance is can be answered using the delivery key figures.

Billing key figures round off the process-oriented key figures. These primarily focus on the evaluations with regard to sales and sales volume.

The section on cross-company processes is also important. The standard version of SAP ERP doesn't provide any option to create the *incoming orders* and *orders on hand* key figures in the delivering units. The discussion of cross-company processes in this chapter provides many enterprises approaches to the solution.

The following chapters detail how you can map these key figures in SAP NetWeaver BI.

5 Implementing the Key Figures in SAP NetWeaver BI

A BI system subsists on changing content, information, various user groups, and new requirements. This section deals with aspects of analyzing basic key figures of S&D, which constitute the basis for many analyses.

The previous chapters introduced you to the objects and options in SAP NetWeaver BI and explained them using clear examples. They also illustrated the procedures for creating and changing key figures in the S&D process. This chapter shows you how SAP BW can support analyses of the S&D processes. In this context, it describes the various options for implementing the individual S&D key figures as well as their advantages and disadvantages.

As is often the case in IT, there's usually more than one solution for a concrete problem in the BI environment. Likewise, there are different modeling methods and the query definition provides several options to map the required key figures. The goal here is to provide and format the information for the report's recipient in the most efficient and most optimized way.

As described in Chapter 3, SD Sample Scenario, our data model is largely based on the DataSources for S&D documents provided as standard in SAP Business Content. However, within data modeling it was ensured that relationships between individual documents copied onto the SAP BW system independently of each other were explicitly restored (such as the reference of an order to a particular quotation). This allows for flexible reporting of the corresponding key figures. All evaluations detailed in this chapter are based on the *sales and distribution overview* MultiProvider, which means that we're not restricted to the data of a single DataProvider. If required, you can easily add more S&D key figures to the reports. For performance optimization, however, all queries in the filter are restricted to only the DataProviders required in the evaluation.

The following sections focus on the S&D process and describe the key figures mentioned in Chapter 4, Key Figures in the Sales and Distribution Process, with regard to quotation, delivery, billing document, and cross-company business in SAP NetWeaver BI.

5.1 Quotation Key Figures

Many quotation analyses use the following key figures: *quotation value, quotation quantity, number of quotations*, and *number of quotation items*. These key figures are subsequently restricted to certain characteristics in varying ways and put into relation with the evaluations requirements.

Because our data model includes all quotations (together with the orders and contracts) within a single InfoCube, the queries in the filter are restricted to the *sales and distribution: sales documents* InfoProvider. For quotations, a filter was additionally set to the sales document category "B" to ensure that only *quotation* key figures are used for these evaluations.

5.1.1 Quotation Value, Quotation Quantity, Number of Quotations

The *quotation value, quotation quantity, number of quotations*, and *number of quotation items* key figures — evaluated by different criteria — indicate the demand for the products or the potential of existing customers and new customers at an early stage of the S&D process. Initially, these key figures are usually analyzed for a specific period and sales area in SAP NetWeaver BI. Figure 5.1 provides a possible selection screen of such a report.

To show a useful selection of quotations during a specified period, you must ensure in the modeling phase that the relevant time characteristics are enabled and updated accordingly. For example, a monthly selection is possible on the basis of the following date information:

- ▶ Creation date of the quotation
- ▶ Creation date of the quotation item
- ▶ Requested delivery date
- ▶ Validity period of the quotation (*valid from* or *valid to*)

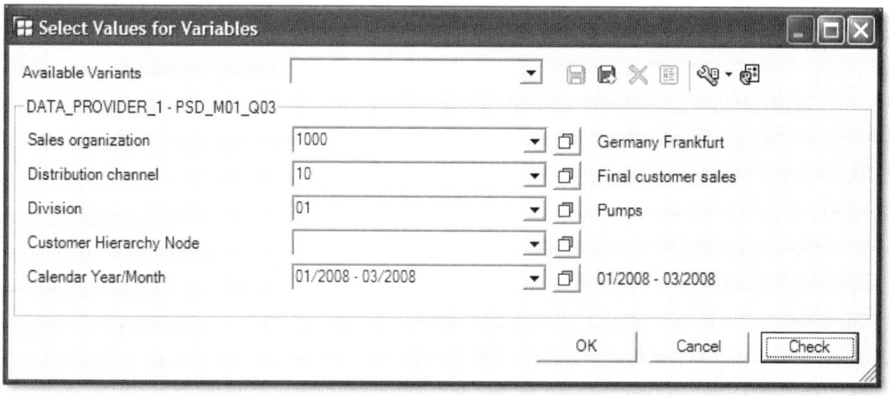

Figure 5.1 Selection of the Quotations

In this example, the creation date of the respective object is selected; that is, *number of quotations* refers to the creation date of the quotation, and *number of quotation items* refers to the creation date of the item. Figure 5.2 shows the result.

Sold-to party		Reason for quotation	Quotation value	Quotation quantity	Number of quotations	Number of quotation items
1000	Becker Berlin	Trade fair sales activ	727 EUR	60 PC	4	5
		Television commercia	85,385 EUR	25 PC	1	1
		Customer recommend	375 EUR	5 PC	1	1
		Excellent price	375 EUR	5 PC	1	1
		Result	86,862 EUR	95 PC	7	8
1018	Miller's Drugstore	Fast delivery	5,900 EUR	400 PC	2	4
		Limited pilot order	7,800 EUR	600 PC	3	6
		Result	13,700 EUR	1,000 PC	5	10
1040	DROBEDA Drugstore	Newspaper advertise	8,100 EUR	650 PC	2	4
		Excellent price	1,200 EUR	100 PC	1	1
		Free of charge samp	5,200 EUR	400 PC	1	3
		Limited pilot order	600 EUR	50 PC	1	1
		Result	15,100 EUR	1,200 PC	5	9
Overall Result			115,662 EUR	2,295 PC	17	27

Filter pane characteristics:
Calendar Year/Month
Customer
Distribution Channel — Final customer sal
Division
Key Figures — ,Quotation value,Q
Material
Reason for order
Reason for rejection
Sales document item
Sales document
Sales group
Sales Office
Sales Organization — Germany Frankfur
Sold-to party — 1000 Becker Berlin
Valid to

Figure 5.2 Quotation Key Figures per Customer

Our example analyzes the quotation data per customer and the reason for the quotation. The FILTER pane of the evaluation provides further characteristics as examples for additional drilldowns. For example, you can filter all quotations whose validity will shortly expire and create a drilldown by quotation number. Later we will show (in Figure 5.21) how you can integrate the validity of quotations into an evaluation. Of course, you can adapt the provided characteristics according to your requirements.

In practice, for example, it's often necessary to analyze the mentioned key figures per material (see Figure 5.3).

Table					
Material		Quotation value	Quotation quantity	Number of quotations	Number of quotation items
NT100	power supply NT-100	750 EUR	10 PC	0	2
P-104	Pump PRECISION 104	85,385 EUR	25 PC	0	1
PR4711	wash lotion 150ml glass bottle	15,613 EUR	1,245 PC	0	14
PR4712	wash lotion 150ml plastic bottle	13,914 EUR	1,015 PC	0	10
#	Not assigned	0 EUR	0	17	0
Overall Result		115,662 EUR	2,295 PC	17	27

Figure 5.3 Quotation Key Figures per Material

In this context, it shows clearly that the *number of quotations* key figure can't be easily mapped per material because it's based on information in the document header, which doesn't contain the material. In these cases, the system generates an additional row that displays the *material* characteristic as NOT ASSIGNED.

To output this information per material, you can create a specific formula in the query definition. This formula is based on a key figure of the quotation item, for example, *number of quotation items*.

Figure 5.4 Determination of Number of Quotations (Formula—Step 1)

The formula shown in Figure 5.4 first still outputs the number of quotation items. To determine the *number of quotations* key figure, you must add an exception aggregation that counts the number of sales document (see Figure 5.5).

Figure 5.5 Determination of Number of Quotations (Formula—Step 2)

Because the *number of quotation items* key figure is provided per material, you can also use this formula to evaluate the *number of quotations* key figure per material. Figure 5.6 shows the result for comparison.

Material		Quotation value	Quotation quantity	Number of quotations	Number of quotations calculated	Number of quotation items
NT100	power supply NT-100	750 EUR	10 PC	0	2	2
P-104	Pump PRECISION 104	85,385 EUR	25 PC	0	1	1
PR4711	wash lotion 150ml glass bottle	15,613 EUR	1,245 PC	0	14	14
PR4712	wash lotion 150ml plastic bottle	13,914 EUR	1,015 PC	0	9	10
#	Not assigned	0 EUR	0	17	0	0
Overall Result		115,662 EUR	2,295 PC	17	17	27

Figure 5.6 Number of Quotations per Material

Here, you must ensure that the total of the displayed single values in the NUMBER OF QUOTATIONS CALCULATED column (26 in our example) doesn't correspond to the OVERALL RESULT (17 in our example) because a quotation may include various materials.

You can determine the *number of customers* or *number of materials* key figures in the query and implement them, for example, per sales area in a similar way. At this point, we should also mention that using such exception aggregations may have a negative effect on the report, because these calculations must be done at the details level when the report is called. Consequently, you should only use these options in such queries for which the *number of customers* or *number of materials* key figures is explicitly required.

5.1.2 Order Probability and Expected Order Value

As described in Section 4.2, Quotation Key Figures, you can determine or maintain an order probability per quotation item, that is, the probability of a sales order being placed from a quotation. The document extractors of the Business Content first transfer this information as a characteristic to the SAP BW system. The following sections describe various options to implement the order probability and the resulting key figures, *expected order quantity* and *expected order value*.

Because the order probability is provided as a characteristic, you can use it for selection. A variable enables you to decide the value in the selection screen without hard coding it into the query definition, for example, you only want to analyze such documents that have an order probability of 70 to 100% in this evaluation, as illustrated in Figure 5.7.

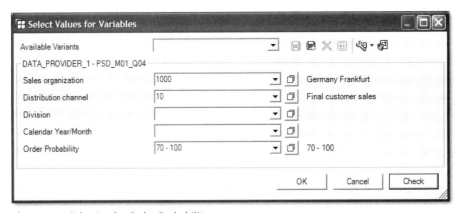

Figure 5.7 Selection by Order Probability

Regardless of this, you can also filter or drill down this evaluation using the *order probability* characteristic (see Figure 5.8).

However, this doesn't mean that the *expected order* key figures are calculated. If you want to determine these key figures, you can use a formula variable that determines the order probability from the characteristic using a replacement path. Figure 5.9 shows the definition of such a variable.

Table

Sold-to party		Sales document	Sales document item	Order probability	Quotation value	Quotation quantity
1000	Becker Berlin	20000051	10	70	114 EUR	10 PC
			20	70	214 EUR	15 PC
		20000050	10	70	114 EUR	10 PC
		20000047	10	70	171 EUR	15 PC
		20000046	10	70	114 EUR	10 PC
		20000032	10	70	375 EUR	5 PC
		20000031	10	70	375 EUR	5 PC
		20000017	10	70	85,385 EUR	25 PC
		Result			86,862 EUR	95 PC
1018	Miller's Drugstore	20000020	10	70	1,400 EUR	100 PC
		20000019	10	70	1,400 EUR	100 PC
			20	80	1,200 EUR	100 PC
		20000018	10	70	1,400 EUR	100 PC
			20	80	1,200 EUR	100 PC
		20000016	10	70	1,400 EUR	100 PC
		20000015	10	70	1,400 EUR	100 PC
		Result			9,400 EUR	700 PC
1040	DROBEDA Drugstore	20000064	10	70	1,200 EUR	100 PC
		20000063	10	70	2,400 EUR	200 PC
			20	70	1,400 EUR	100 PC
			30	70	1,400 EUR	100 PC
		20000062	10	70	1,800 EUR	150 PC
			20	70	2,500 EUR	200 PC
		Result			10,700 EUR	850 PC
Overa					106,962 EUR	1,645 PC

Figure 5.8 Evaluation per Order Probability

Now you can use this variable in formulas, which allows you to determine the expected values and quantities.

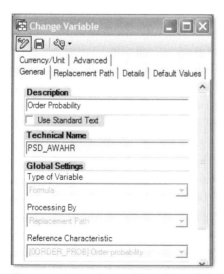

Figure 5.9 Formula Variable Order Probability

The result is shown in Figure 5.10. In this example, the order probability is displayed twice, that is, as a characteristic and as a key figure. This is for illustration purposes only.

Table		Order probability	Probability by formula variable	Quotation value	Expected order value calculated from variable	Quotation quantity	Expected order quantity calculated from variable
Sold-to party							
1000	Becker Berlin	70	70	86,862 EUR	60,803 EUR	95 PC	67 PC
	Result		70	86,862 EUR	60,803 EUR	95 PC	67 PC
1018	Miller's Drugstore	10	10	1,200 EUR	120 EUR	100 PC	10 PC
		55	55	1,550 EUR	853 EUR	100 PC	55 PC
		65	65	1,550 EUR	1,008 EUR	100 PC	65 PC
		70	70	7,000 EUR	4,900 EUR	500 PC	350 PC
		80	80	2,400 EUR	1,920 EUR	200 PC	160 PC
	Result		56	13,700 EUR	8,800 EUR	1,000 PC	640 PC
1040	DROBEDA Drugstore	35	35	600 EUR	210 EUR	50 PC	18 PC
		45	45	2,400 EUR	1,080 EUR	200 PC	90 PC
		55	55	1,400 EUR	770 EUR	100 PC	55 PC
		70	70	10,700 EUR	7,490 EUR	850 PC	595 PC
	Result		51	15,100 EUR	9,550 EUR	1,200 PC	758 PC
Overall Result			56	115,662 EUR	79,153 EUR	2,295 PC	1,464 PC

Figure 5.10 Expected Order Quantities and Order Values with Formula Variable

A disadvantage of this solution is that these calculations are only correct at order probability level; that is, the drilldown of the report must contain the characteristic. You can slightly adapt the presentation of the totals rows (e.g., for the probability per formula variable it was set to average); however, it's generally not useful to calculate percentages at the aggregated level. Figure 5.11 shows the result of removing the drilldown of the *order probability* characteristic.

Table		Probability by formula variable	Quotation value	Expected order value calculated from variable	Quotation quantity	Expected order quantity calculated from variable
Sold-to party						
1000	Becker Berlin	X	86,862 EUR	X	95 PC	X
1018	Miller's Drugstore	X	13,700 EUR	X	1,000 PC	X
1040	DROBEDA Drugstore	X	15,100 EUR	X	1,200 PC	X
Overall Result		X	115,662 EUR		2,295 PC	

Figure 5.11 Formula Variable Without Drilldown by Order Probabilities

As described for the *number of quotations* (see Section 5.1.1, Quotation Value, Quotation Quantity, Number of Quotations), you can use exception aggregations again to determine the expected values and quantities. If you set the *order probability* reference characteristic for the *totals* exception aggregation for both formulas, you also obtain correct values at the aggregated level (see Figure 5.12). In this case, the system multiplies the individual quotation items by the order probability and aggregates the resulting single values at the customer level.

Sold-to party		Quotation value	Expected order value calculated with exception aggr.	Quotation quantity	Expected order quantity calculated with exception aggr.
1000	Becker Berlin	86,862 EUR	60,803 EUR	95 PC	67 PC
1018	Miller's Drugstore	13,700 EUR	8,800 EUR	1,000 PC	640 PC
1040	DROBEDA Drugstore Trade ltd.	15,100 EUR	9,550 EUR	1,200 PC	758 PC
Overall Result		115,662 EUR	79,153 EUR	2,295 PC	1,464 PC

Figure 5.12 Expected Quantities and Values with an Exception Aggregation

To avoid using a formula variable, you can also create an additional key figure, *order probability*, already in the modeling process and have the system supply each data record directly with the characteristic value. Then, the required calculations can directly refer to this key figure and are also correct at the document level. However, the problem of the aggregation of the order probability isn't resolved. Then, the calculation is first implemented as specified in the key figure definition, for example, using the probability total or average. So, you must use exception aggregations once again.

A solution to facilitate the creation of the query and avoid problems with aggregation is to determine the separate key figures, *expected order quantity* and *expected order value*, within data modeling. Here, the determination is implemented for each document item, that is, at the detailed level when the data is loaded. A presentation as shown earlier in Figure 5.10 is still possible. Also, you can aggregate those pre-calculated key figures as required because they are no longer percentages but real quantities or values (see Figure 5.13).

Table						
Sold-to party		Reason for order	Quotation value	Expected order value	Quotation quantity	Expected order quantity
1000	Becker Berlin	Trade fair sales activity	727 EUR	509 EUR	60 PC	42 PC
		Television commercial	85,385 EUR	59,770 EUR	25 PC	18 PC
		Customer recommendation	375 EUR	263 EUR	5 PC	4 PC
		Excellent price	375 EUR	263 EUR	5 PC	4 PC
		Result	86,862 EUR	60,803 EUR	95 PC	67 PC
1018	Miller's Drugstore	Fast delivery	5,900 EUR	3,820 EUR	400 PC	260 PC
		Limited pilot order	7,800 EUR	4,980 EUR	600 PC	380 PC
		Result	13,700 EUR	8,800 EUR	1,000 PC	640 PC
1040	DROBEDA Drugstore	Newspaper advertisement	8,100 EUR	4,860 EUR	650 PC	390 PC
		Excellent price	1,200 EUR	840 EUR	100 PC	70 PC
		Free of charge sample	5,200 EUR	3,640 EUR	400 PC	280 PC
		Limited pilot order	600 EUR	210 EUR	50 PC	18 PC
		Result	15,100 EUR	9,550 EUR	1,200 PC	758 PC
Overall Result			115,662 EUR	79,153 EUR	2,295 PC	1,464 PC

Figure 5.13 Expected Quantities and Values Without a Drilldown by Order Probabilities

From the point of view of reporting, this is the best and fastest solution. The query definition is simple, and the query runtimes aren't affected. Nevertheless, this solution is often not used for the following reasons:

▶ **Manipulation of the data model**
If the DataProvider supplies the quotation quantity in different units of measure (such as base unit of measure, sales unit) and the value in different currency units (e.g., document currency, company code currency), it also provides the corresponding number of key figures because a key figure always refers to exactly one unit. To store all of the corresponding "expected quantities" and "expected values," the same number of key figures are additionally required, which means that the data model must be considerably extended.

▶ **Restructuring of the data**
If this requirement did not exist when the DataProvider was created, the extension requires that the data must be reloaded to fill the new key figures for already existing documents retroactively. If there are numerous documents, this may lead to long loading times and high reconciliation work with other users.

Particularly if such determined information is required quite often and in different contexts, it's useful to extend the data model by additional key figures. If the data model doesn't provide this option, you can proceed as described earlier.

5.1.3 Open, Rejected, and Accepted Quotations

As described in Sections 4.2.3 to 4.2.5, the status of the quotation changes as soon as an order is created for this quotation. However, because the quotation document has only indirectly changed (i.e., the document data of the quotation in the sales and distribution [SD] component isn't changed), it's rather difficult to transfer the individual status changes to the SAP BW system. This functionality isn't provided in SAP's standard version. To analyze which quotations are open, accepted, partly open or partly accepted, this information is provided in the relevant orders and, within our data model, was already added to the quotation when the data was updated (see Section 3.6.3, Follow-on Documents). This enables you to access the additional key figures, *accepted quotation value*, *accepted quotation quantity*, and *number of accepted items*, for each quotation item. Again, the best way to determine the cross-sectional key figure, *number of quotations* (regardless of open, accepted, or rejected), is to use exception aggregations in the query because the reference to the reason for rejection or follow-on documents is provided only for the items but not for the document header (see Section 5.1.1, Quotation Value, Quotation Quantity, Number of Quotations).

By extending the data model, the key figures on accepted quotations are consequently delivered to the DataProvider. These are shown in Figure 5.14.

Table

Sold-to party		Total number of quotation items	Number of accepted quotation items	Total quotation value	Accepted quotation value	Total quotation quantity	Accepted quotation quantity
1000	Becker Berlin	8	5	86,862 EUR	86,306 EUR	95 PC	50 PC
1018	Miller's Drugstore	10	2	13,700 EUR	2,800 EUR	1,000 PC	200 PC
1040	DROBEDA Drugstore	9	4	15,100 EUR	6,000 EUR	1,200 PC	480 PC
Overall Result		27	11	115,662 EUR	95,106 EUR	2,295 PC	730 PC

Figure 5.14 Accepted Quotations

The rejected quotation items, however, can be recognized by the reason for rejection. To illustrate this, the reasons for rejection of the quotations were added to Figure 5.14 (see Figure 5.15 for the result).

Table

Sold-to party		Reason for rejection	Total number of quotation items	Number of accepted quotation items	Total quotation value	Accepted quotation value	Total quotation quantity	Accepted quotation quantity
1000	Becker Berlin	Delivery date too late	2	0	328 EUR	0 EUR	25 PC	0 PC
		Poor quality	1	1	114 EUR	57 EUR	10 PC	5 PC
		Not assigned	5	4	86,420 EUR	86,249 EUR	60 PC	45 PC
		Result	8	5	86,862 EUR	86,306 EUR	95 PC	50 PC
1018	Miller's Drugstore	Not assigned	10	2	13,700 EUR	2,800 EUR	1,000 PC	200 PC
		Result	10	2	13,700 EUR	2,800 EUR	1,000 PC	200 PC
1040	DROBEDA Drugstore	Guarantee	2	0	2,800 EUR	0 EUR	200 PC	0 PC
		Cancellation required by customer	1	1	2,500 EUR	1,200 EUR	200 PC	80 PC
		Not assigned	6	3	9,800 EUR	4,800 EUR	800 PC	400 PC
		Result	9	4	15,100 EUR	6,000 EUR	1,200 PC	480 PC
Overall Result			27	11	115,662 EUR	95,106 EUR	2,295 PC	730 PC

Figure 5.15 Quotations per Reason for Rejection

Figure 5.15 shows that some of the quotations have a reason for rejection, so they are rejected while some of them are displayed without reason for rejection (NOT ASSIGNED). Based on the information displayed here, you can specify *restricted key figures* and formulas in the query definition to analyze the totals of rejected quotations. In general, a restricted key figure is a key figure restricted to one or more characteristic values. In our example, we need, for example, a quotation quantity that is restricted to documents with a reason for rejection, which is a reason for rejection not equal to "#". In the query definition, this exclusion is indicated by a red equal's symbol ("="). Figure 5.16 shows such a definition.

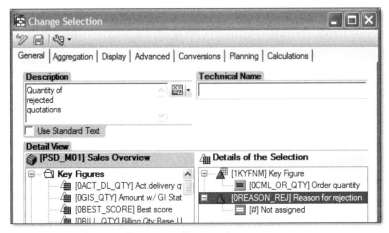

Figure 5.16 Definition of Quantity of Rejected Quotations

Figure 5.17 shows the results with the quotation quantities as examples. Quotation quantities without reasons for rejection are no longer displayed. If you want to, you can also completely hide the resulting blank lines or the customers without rejections.

Sold-to party		Reason for rejection	Rejected quotation quantity	Quantity of rejected quotations	Accepted quantity of rejected quotations
1000	Becker Berlin	Delivery date too late	25 PC	25 PC	0 PC
		Poor quality	5 PC	10 PC	5 PC
		Not assigned			
		Result	30 PC	35 PC	5 PC
1018	Miller's Drugstore	Not assigned			
		Result			
1040	DROBEDA Drugstore	Guarantee	200 PC	200 PC	0 PC
		Cancellation required by customer	120 PC	200 PC	80 PC
		Not assigned			
		Result	320 PC	400 PC	80 PC
Overall Result			350 PC	435 PC	85 PC

Figure 5.17 Rejected Quotation Quantities

This topic is so complex because the items that were already partly accepted can still be rejected retroactively (see Section 4.2.5, Rejected Quotations). Technically, the item then has a reason for rejection. However, it isn't correct to display the entire quantity as rejected. You can calculate the quantities correctly based on the rules listed in the following box.

Rules for Determining Rejected Quotations Correctly

▶ Rejected Quotation Quantity
= Total Quantity of Rejected Quotation Items – Accepted Quantity of Rejected Quotation Items

▶ Total Quantity of Rejected Quotation Items
= Total – Quotation Quantity with Reason for Rejection

▶ Accepted Quantity of Rejected Quotation Items
= Accepted Quotation Quantity with Reason for Rejection

Let's now take a look at the open quotations, that is, the quotations for which no order has been placed yet or that haven't been rejected yet. They can be determined as listed in the following box.

Rules for Determining Open Quotations Correctly

▸ *Number of Open Quotation Items*
   = Total Number of Items – Rejected Items – Number of Accepted Items
▸ *Open Quotation Quantity*
   = Total Quantity – Rejected Quantity – Accepted Quantity
▸ *Open Quotation Value*
   = Total Value – Rejected Value – Accepted Value

Figure 5.18 shows the *number of open quotation items, open quotation value,* and *open quotation quantity* key figures per customer, which were calculated according to these rules.

Table

Sold-to party		Number of open quotation items	Open quotation value	Open quotation quantity	Total quotation quantity	Rejected quotation quantity	Accepted quotation quantity
1000	Becker Berlin	1	171 EUR	15 PC	95 PC	30 PC	50 PC
1018	Miller's Drugstore	8	10,900 EUR	800 PC	1,000 PC		200 PC
1040	DROBEDA Drugstore	3	5,000 EUR	400 PC	1,200 PC	320 PC	480 PC
Overall Result		12	16,071 EUR	1,215 PC	2,295 PC	350 PC	730 PC

Figure 5.18   Open Quotations

This figure also illustrates the option to expand the key figures so that you can display, for example, the already-mentioned quantity key figures as additional information on the open quotation quantity. To achieve this functionality, the key figures were hierarchically structured through drag and drop in the query definition.

5.1.4   Success Quota and Rejection Quota

The relative key figures, *success quota* and *rejection quota*, can be easily determined using the key figures described in Section 5.1.3, Open, Rejected and Accepted Quotations, as a basis. Figure 5.19 puts the rejected quotations into relation to the total number of the quotations. Technically speaking, within the Query Designer we used a formula with the predefined element %A (percentage).

Table

Sold-to party		Rejection quota (number)	Total number of quotation items	Number of rejected quotation items	Rejection quota (value)	Total quotation value	Rejected quotation value	Rejected quota (quantity)	Total quotation quantity	Rejected quotation quantity
1000	Becker Berlin	25.0 %	8	2	0.4 %	86,862 EUR	385 EUR	31.6 %	95 PC	30 PC
1018	Miller's Drugstore		10			13,700 EUR			1,000 PC	
1040	DROBEDA Drugstore	22.2 %	9	2	27.2 %	15,100 EUR	4,100 EUR	26.7 %	1,200 PC	320 PC
Overall Result		14.8 %	27	4	3.9 %	115,662 EUR	4,485 EUR	15.3 %	2,295 PC	350 PC

Figure 5.19   Rejection Quota

Similarly, you can determine the success quota from the relation of accepted quotations to the total number of quotations (see Figure 5.20).

	Sold-to party	Success quota (number)	Total number of quotation items	Number of accepted quotation items	Success quota (value)	Total quotation value	Accepted quotation value	Success quota (quantity)	Total quotation quantity	Accepted quotation quantity
1000	Becker Berlin	62.5 %	8	5	99.4 %	86,862 EUR	86,306 EUR	52.6 %	95 PC	50 PC
1018	Miller's Drugstore	20.0 %	10	2	20.4 %	13,700 EUR	2,800 EUR	20.0 %	1,000 PC	200 PC
1040	DROBEDA Drugstore	44.4 %	9	4	39.7 %	15,100 EUR	6,000 EUR	40.0 %	1,200 PC	480 PC
	Overall Result	40.7 %	27	11	82.2 %	115,662 EUR	95,106 EUR	31.8 %	2,295 PC	730 PC

Figure 5.20 Success Quota

Of course, you can also combine all described key figures into an evaluation.

5.1.5 Expired Quotations

In all previously introduced quotation evaluations, the *valid to* characteristic was provided for navigational purposes. This enables you to flexibly restrict the validity of the open quotations and only display expired quotations, if required. Figure 5.21 shows an example of expired quotations.

You can also use pre-assigned variables to have the report display only quotations that expire on the current date or within a short time. This can be useful information for field sales representatives. You can determine the quota of expired quotations using a similar approach to determining the rejection or success quota.

Filter		Table						
			Sold-to party		Sales document	Valid to	Number of open quotation items	Open quotations value	Open quotations quantity
Calendar Year/Month									
Distribution Channel	Final customer sales	1000	Becker Berlin	20000047	03/31/2008	1	171 EUR	15 PC
Key Figures	,Number of open quo			Result		1	171 EUR	15 PC
Material		1018	Miller's Drugstore	20000015	01/31/2008	1	1,550 EUR	100 PC
Reason for order				20000016	01/31/2008	2	2,950 EUR	200 PC
Reason for rejection				20000018	05/1/2008	1	1,200 EUR	100 PC
Sales document				20000019	05/1/2008	2	2,600 EUR	200 PC
Sales group				20000020	05/1/2008	2	2,600 EUR	200 PC
Sales Office				Result		8	10,900 EUR	800 PC
Sales Organization	Germany Frankfurt		Overall Result			9	11,071 EUR	815 PC
Sold-to party	1000 Becker Berlin,							
Valid to	<= 05/01/2008							

Figure 5.21 Expired Quotations

5.1.6 Sales Cycle

The *sales cycle* is another important key figure for analyzing and evaluating quotations and customers. As described previously, the system enables you to evaluate the order probability. Now, you want to indicate the average time needed until an order is placed. You can determine this for each quotation item as shown in the following box.

Average Time Needed until an Order is Placed

Sales Cycle
= *Creation Date of the First Order Item for a Quotation Item – Creation Date of this Quotation Item*

It's considerably difficult to determine such a key figure within reporting, particularly, because you're only supposed to consider the first assigned sales order item. Because the data model has already established a relationship between the quotation and the order, it makes sense to also add the required creation date of the first sales order item to the quotation item in this context.

Similar to what was described in Section 5.1.2, Order Probability and Expected Order value, there are three options to implement this:

▶ **The DataProvider provides the date information as characteristics**
In reporting, you can use a formula variable to access this information and calculate the difference.

▶ **The DataProvider provides the date information as key figures**
They can be directly used in the formulas.

▶ **The DataProvider stores the sales cycle as a key figure**
The difference is already calculated when the quotations are updated into an InfoCube and stored as the separate *sales cycle* key figure.

In this context, you must ensure that the determination is always implemented at the details level, that is, per quotation item, because the *total* or *average* aggregation doesn't provide a useful result when it's referred to a date field. In our example, we decided to use the third option, that is, to determine a separate key figure within data modeling (see Figure 5.22). For the results rows, you should use the *average of all values* presentation option here.

Table						
Sold-to party		Sales document	Sales document item	Accepted quotation value	Accepted quotation quantity	Sales Cycle
1000	Becker Berlin	20000051	10	57 EUR	5 PC	2
		20000046	10	114 EUR	10 PC	2
		20000032	10	375 EUR	5 PC	1
		20000031	10	375 EUR	5 PC	1
		20000017	10	85,385 EUR	25 PC	5
		Result		86,306 EUR	50 PC	2
1018	Miller's Drugstore	20000018	10	1,400 EUR	100 PC	23
		20000015	10	1,400 EUR	100 PC	23
		Result		2,800 EUR	200 PC	23
1040	DROBEDA Drugstore	20000065	10	600 EUR	50 PC	32
		20000063	10	2,400 EUR	200 PC	46
		20000062	10	1,800 EUR	150 PC	1
			20	1,200 EUR	80 PC	1
		Result		6,000 EUR	480 PC	20
Overall Result				95,106 EUR	730 PC	12

Figure 5.22 Sales Cycle per Quotation Item

A sales cycle for each customer can now easily be implemented using the formula in the following box.

Average Sales Cycle per Customer

Sales Cycle per Customer
= Sales Cycle/Number of Accepted Quotation Items

This formula can be created in the query definition. Figure 5.23 shows the corresponding result.

Table				
Sold-to party		Accepted quotation value	Accepted quotation quantity	Sales Cycle Ø
1000	Becker Berlin	86,306 EUR	50 PC	2
1018	Miller's Drugstore	2,800 EUR	200 PC	23
1040	DROBEDA Drugstore	6,000 EUR	480 PC	20
Overall Result		95,106 EUR	730 PC	12

Figure 5.23 Average Sales Cycle per Customer

Of course, you can now implement this average sales cycle for all characteristics that are available for a quotation item.

179

5.2   Order Key Figures

Within the S&D process, quotations are followed by orders, which are discussed in the following sections.

5.2.1   General Order Key Figures

There are specific general key figures that are also interesting for orders, such as *order value, order quantity, number of documents*, or *number of items*. Similar to the implementation of quotations in evaluations with SAP NetWeaver BI, you can map these general key figures also for orders.

The following evaluations generally have a filter for the *sales and distribution: sales documents* InfoProvider, which contains all quotations and orders. This way, you can keep data from other InfoProviders from being included in the evaluation. In the evaluations, an additional filter is set for the document category, for example, to exclude quotations from the reports. Note that there isn't just one cross-sectional document category for orders but several. The following document categories are introduced as examples for the generic term *order*:

▶ C for "orders"

▶ E for "scheduling agreement"

▶ G for "contract"

▶ H for "returns"

▶ I for "free order"

▶ K for "credit memo request"

▶ L for "debit memo request"

Depending on the Customizing settings in the SD component, additional categories are possible.

You can select which document categories you want to include for each evaluation that is created with SAP NetWeaver BI. These are then restricted via the filter in the report definition. You can also include the *document category* characteristic for the free navigation in the report, which enables you later to freely select which document categories you want to consider in a specific case. We restrict our first example to the categories listed previously and set the corresponding filter in the report definition.

Similar to the evaluations described in Section 5.1, Quotation Key Figures, you can flexibly map different information for orders. For example, you can evaluate general key figures, such as the order value, per material, per customer, per distribution channel, and so on. In this case, the required key figures and characteristics correspond to those of the quotation because quotations and orders are usually stored in the SAP BW system in the same structures similar to the SAP ERP application. It's only the document category that makes the difference. Figure 5.24 shows a corresponding example.

Filter		Table			Order value	Order quantity	Number of orders	Number of order items
			Sold-to party					
Calendar Year/Month	03/2008							
Distribution Channel	Final customer	1172	CBD Computer Based Design		143,138 EUR	783 PC	3	9
Key Figures		1320	Becker Koeln		92,216 EUR	27 PC	1	1
Material		1321	Becker Stuttgart		520,818 EUR	170 PC	1	4
Material		1360	Amadeus		132,537 EUR	707 PC	2	8
Reason for order		1460	C.A.S. Computer Application Systems		158,365 EUR	1,093 PC	4	7
Reason for rejection		Overall Result			1,047,073 EUR	2,780 PC	11	29
Sales doc. type								
Sales document item								
Sales document								
Sales group								
Sales Office								
Sales Organization	Germany Frankf							
SD Document Category								
Sold-to party	1000 Becker Be							

Figure 5.24 Order: General Order Key Figures

This evaluation implements the key figures at the level of the individual sold-to parties. Additional characteristics that you can integrate into the drilldown of the report are optionally available in the filter pane. For example, if you want to view which orders belong to the key figures, you must add a drilldown by sales document (see Figure 5.25).

Sold-to party		Sales document	Order value	Order quantity	Number of orders	Number of order items
1172	CBD Computer Based Design	9871	97,601 EUR	736 PC	1	4
		9897	15,545 EUR	18 PC	1	1
		9907	29,992 EUR	29 PC	1	4
		Result	143,138 EUR	783 PC	3	9
1320	Becker Koeln	9917	92,216 EUR	27 PC	1	1
		Result	92,216 EUR	27 PC	1	1
1321	Becker Stuttgart	9916	520,818 EUR	170 PC	1	4
		Result	520,818 EUR	170 PC	1	4
1360	Amadeus	9874	43,670 EUR	44 PC	1	4
		9893	88,867 EUR	663 PC	1	4
		Result	132,537 EUR	707 PC	2	8
1460	C.A.S. Computer Application Systems	9869	119,802 EUR	1,044 PC	1	4
		9881	1,121 EUR	15 PC	1	1
		9908	11,566 EUR	13 PC	1	1
		9932	25,876 EUR	21 PC	1	1
		Result	158,365 EUR	1,093 PC	4	7
Overall Result			1,047,073 EUR	2,780 PC	11	29

Figure 5.25 Order: General Key Figures — Sales Document

Furthermore, instead of the sales document, you could consider the sold material via the product hierarchy. For this purpose, swap the *sales document* characteristic with the *material* characteristic for which the product hierarchy was activated in the report definition. Figure 5.26 shows the result.

Sold-to party		Material	Order value	Order quantity	Number of orders	Number of order items
1172	CBD Computer Based Design	Result	143,138 EUR	783 PC	3	9
		▼ Product hierarchy	143,138 EUR	783 PC	0	9
		▼ Hardware	143,138 EUR	783 PC	0	9
		▼ PC	143,138 EUR	783 PC	0	9
		▶ Monitor	45,537 EUR	47 PC	0	5
		▶ Processor	18,775 EUR	68 PC	0	1
		▶ Memory	9,024 EUR	120 PC	0	1
		▶ Drive	48,877 EUR	174 PC	0	1
		▶ Input device	20,925 EUR	374 PC	0	1
		▶ Not Assigned Material (s)	0 EUR	0	3	0
1320	Becker Koeln	Result	92,216 EUR	27 PC	1	1
		▼ Product hierarchy	92,216 EUR	27 PC	0	1
		▶ Machines	92,216 EUR	27 PC	0	1
		▶ Not Assigned Material (s)	0 EUR	0	1	0
1321	Becker Stuttgart	Result	520,818 EUR	170 PC	1	4
		▼ Product hierarchy	520,818 EUR	170 PC	0	4
		▶ Machines	520,818 EUR	170 PC	0	4
		▶ Not Assigned Material (s)	0 EUR	0	1	0
1360	Amadeus	Result	132,537 EUR	707 PC	2	8

Figure 5.26 Order: General Key Figures — Product Hierarchy

Figure 5.26 illustrates the same issue that was already described in Section 5.1.1, Quotation Value, Quotation Quantity, Number of Quotations, with regard to the quotations. The *number of orders* key figure is provided at the document header level, whereas the *order value*, *order quantity*, and *number of ordered items* key figures are available at the item level. Consequently, the *number of order* key figure is displayed in a separate row without being assigned to a material. Similar to *quotations*, you also have various options to implement the key figures for different purposes in an optimized way.

You can also implement rejected orders in a similar way to quotations. The Info-Provider contains the reason for rejection as a characteristic and it can be included in the report definition. Figure 5.27 shows an example overview of reasons for rejection in orders created during a particular month.

Table				Order value	Order quantity	Number of orders	Number of order items
Reason for rejection		Sold-to party					
01	Delivery date too late	1321	Becker Stuttgart	578,249 EUR	189 PC	0	3
		Result		578,249 EUR	189 PC	0	3
20	Rejected due to credit check	4999	Hallmann Engineering & Construction L	28,000 EUR	8 PC	0	1
		Result		28,000 EUR	8 PC	0	1
W2	Cancellation required by customer	1172	CBD Computer Based Design	12,956 EUR	10 PC	0	1
		Result		12,956 EUR	10 PC	0	1
#	Not assigned	1000	Becker Berlin	24,000 EUR	4 EA	1	1
		1001	Lamp Market Llc	26 EUR	70 PC	1	1
		1002	Omega Soft-Hardware Outlet	31 EUR	80 PC	1	1
		1033	Karsson High Tech Market	447,862 EUR	452 PC	3	9
		1172	CBD Computer Based Design	124,416 EUR	820 PC	2	4
		1174	Moto Trade Stuttgart	34,965 EUR	1,220 PC	3	4
		1175	Electronic store Bamby	47,120 EUR	45 PC	2	2
		1300	Christal Clear	20 EUR	50 PC	1	1
		1321	Becker Stuttgart	306,857 EUR	94 PC	3	3
		1360	Amadeus	260,859 EUR	1,293 PC	4	13
		1460	C.A.S. Computer Application Systems	212,188 EUR	1,849 PC	2	8
		1900	J & P	31,728 EUR	1,804 PC	2	3
		2004	SudaTech Llc	184,463 EUR	189 PC	1	4
		2007	Software Systems Llc	185,815 EUR	1,309 PC	2	6
		2130	COMPU Tech. Plc	57,173 EUR	63 PC	1	4
		2140	N.I.C. High Tech	179,120 EUR	216 PC	1	4
		2200	HTG Components Llc	186,803 EUR	233 PC	1	4
		2300	Motor store Heidelberg Llc	1,530,000 EUR	102 PC	1	1
		4999	Hallmann Engineering & Construction L	0 EUR	0	1	0
		Result		3,813,446 EUR	*	33	73
Overall Result				4,432,652 EUR	*	33	78

Figure 5.27 Detailed Reasons for Rejection of an Order

Figure 5.27 illustrates the rejected orders categorized under three different reasons for rejection provided by the sold-to parties. The system displays NOT ASSIGNED as a reason for rejection for all orders without a rejection reason. Of course, you can further detail this evaluation, for example, by having the system display the corresponding sales documents. As described in Section 5.1.4, Success Quota and Rejection Quota, you can determine quotas, such as the rejection quota.

5.2.2 Incoming Orders/Orders on Hand

As already detailed in Chapter 4, Key Figures in the Sales and Distribution Process, the two key figures, *incoming orders* and *orders on hand*, are very important control figures in the S&D process. These two values must be provided in SAP NetWeaver BI for evaluations. In this context, the *revenue* key figure is frequently considered because it affects or decreases the orders on hand key figure.

Chapter 4, Key Figures in the Sales and Distribution Process, has already explained that *incoming orders* and *orders on hand* in SAP ERP can be evaluated via a SIS structure. To transfer data to the SAP BW system, you can retrieve it from the SIS structures or implement the required logic in SAP BW. This can be achieved by extracting the underlying documents from SAP ERP and implementing the respective logic during the update of the documents, or within the report definition. At this point, the description is restricted to the options of document extraction. The following paragraphs explain how you can implement the key figures in SAP NetWeaver BI using this variant.

The first step is to implement useful modeling within the SAP BW system. To map the two figures, you need a specific logic because the Business Content doesn't provide an appropriate solution for this. You must implement this logic according to the respective requirements in SAP NetWeaver BI. For this purpose, the *incoming orders* and *orders on hand* key figures are stored in a separate InfoProvider. The respective modeling of the objects in SAP BW and the update logic of the data were discussed in Section 3.6.1, Incoming Orders/Orders on Hand, in detail. If required, you can track these processes there.

The following sections deal with the creation of evaluations for incoming orders and orders on hand. First, you must set a filter for the *sales and distribution: IO/OH/ revenue* InfoCube in the query to keep the system from displaying data twice in the query. This is required because in this InfoProvider — in addition to the already-mentioned InfoProviders providing the mere documents (e.g., *sales and distribution: sales documents* InfoProvider) — calculated and formatted data is stored.

A query that displays the orders on hand at the end of the prior period, the incoming orders and the revenue of the current period, and the orders on hand at the end of this period can be structured as described in the following paragraphs.

To implement the incoming orders and revenue of the current period, you must restrict the two corresponding key figures to the *calendar year/month* characteristic, respectively. In addition, you restrict this characteristic with a variable. In our example, we used a mandatory variable with manual input, requiring a single value entered by the user. Of course, you can also define a user exit variable here that can be derived from the current month of the system date and is filled automatically.

To display the *orders on hand* key figure for the previous month you must restrict the corresponding key figure to the variable mentioned above and additionally set an offset of "-1" to avoid the current month being used. Furthermore, you must select the value range "Less than" the variable for the restriction. The reason is that the *orders on hand* key figure isn't updated as a balance but is continuously determined from the *incoming orders* and *revenue* key figures at document level. Set this restriction for the variable as shown in Figure 5.28.

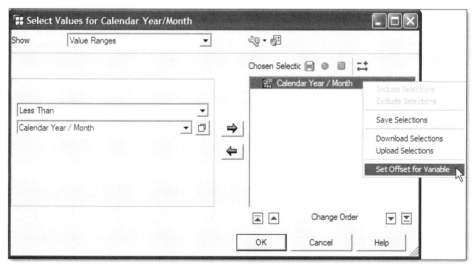

Figure 5.28 Defining the Value Range for the Variable

You define the *orders on hand* key figure at the end of the current period in a similar way. The only difference is that you don't require an offset for the variable of the *calendar year/month* characteristic.

In this case, the key figures were selected based on the amount. Of course, you can map the corresponding quantities in the same way. For our sample report, the system initially displays a selection screen in which you can filter for specific values, for example, on a specific sales organization or a particular distribution channel. This might look like the one displayed in Figure 5.29.

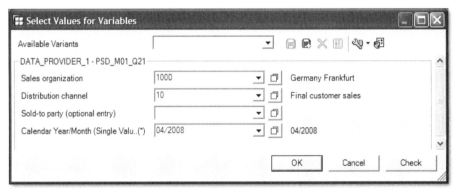

Figure 5.29 Selection of the Incoming Orders/Orders on Hand Query

After you've made the selections and the query has been executed, the system presents the key figures across all order types; that is, it indicates that credit memo requests were also included, for example (see Figure 5.30). Section 5.2.3, Implementing Different Standard Processes, describes how you can present these figures in evaluations separately.

Table			
Orders on hand value Month 03/2008	Incoming orders value Month 04/2008	Revenue Month 04.2008	Orders on hand value Month 04/2008
7,277,822.98 EUR	1,529,814.80 EUR	1,297,387.65 EUR	7,510,250.13 EUR

Figure 5.30 Result of the Incoming Orders/Orders on Hand Query

Figure 5.30 illustrates that the key figures are displayed at a highly aggregated level. If required, you can add more useful characteristics to drilldown into the query using the filter pane. For example, if you want to evaluate the key figures using the product hierarchy, you must include the *material* characteristic with the assigned product hierarchy in the drilldown of the query. The result is shown in Figure 5.31.

Table					
Material		Orders on hand value Month 03/2008	Incoming orders value Month 04/2008	Revenue Month 04/2008	Orders on hand value Month 04/2008
Overall Result		7,277,822.98 EUR	1,529,814.80 EUR	1,297,387.65 EUR	7,510,250.13 EUR
00100	Machines	1,530,848.35 EUR	697,465.35 EUR	618,898.20 EUR	1,609,415.50 EUR
00125	Hardware	5,686,974.63 EUR	832,349.45 EUR	678,489.45 EUR	5,840,834.63 EUR
0012500100	PC	5,662,535.78 EUR	814,770.35 EUR	660,910.35 EUR	5,816,395.78 EUR
0012500105	Work station	24,438.85 EUR	17,579.10 EUR	17,579.10 EUR	24,438.85 EUR
00140	Services	60,000.00 EUR			60,000.00 EUR

Figure 5.31 Incoming Orders/Orders on Hand by Product Hierarchy

5.2.3 Implementing Different Standard Processes

Chapter 4, Key Figures in the Sales and Distribution Process, introduced some standard S&D processes and explained in detail which documents were created with which information at what time in SAP ERP. All these documents are periodically transferred to the SAP BW system and can be evaluated there. By means of the order types or item categories involved in the processes, the following paragraphs can now further detail the standard key figures, *number of documents*, *order value*, or *order quantity*. This enables you to map, for example, the order value of all standard orders or all credit and debit memos. To only display the order value of the standard orders, you must restrict the underlying key figure to the "TA" order type, which refers to standard orders by default.

The following sample queries are defined in the same way as all previously described queries, that is, using the *sales overview* MultiProvider, with restrictions to the *sales and distribution: sales documents* InfoProvider. Figure 5.32 shows a query whose drilldown includes the sales document type, the item category, and the sold-to party; it also displays the *order value, order quantity, number of orders,* and *number of ordered items* key figures.

Table						Order value	Order quantity	Number of orders	Number of ordered items
Sales doc. type		Item category		Sold-to party					
KB	Consignment Fill-up	KBN	Consignment Fill-up	1000	Becker Berlin	0 EUR	1,600 PC	0	7
		#	Not assigned	1000	Becker Berlin	0 EUR	0	2	0
		Result				0 EUR	1,600 PC	2	7
LP	Scheduling agreement	LPN	Sched.Agreement Item	1000	Becker Berlin	54,340 EUR	22 PC	0	1
		#	Not assigned	1000	Becker Berlin	0 EUR	0	1	0
		Result				54,340 EUR	22 PC	1	1
LZ	SchedAg. w/ del.schd	LZN	Sched.Agreement Item	1000	Becker Berlin	61,750 EUR	25 PC	0	1
		#	Not assigned	1000	Becker Berlin	0 EUR	0	1	0
		Result				61,750 EUR	25 PC	1	1
PS1	PS: order	TPC1	Elevator	1000	Becker Berlin	100,000 EUR	1 PC	0	1
		#	Not assigned	1000	Becker Berlin	0 EUR	0	1	0
		Result				100,000 EUR	1 PC	1	1
RE	Returns	REN	Standard Item	1017	Health clinic Ltd.	-10 EUR	-5 PC	0	-1
		#	Not assigned	1017	Health clinic Ltd.	0 EUR	0	-1	0
		Result				-10 EUR	-5 PC	-1	-1
TA	Standard Order	TAB	Indiv.Purchase Order	1000	Becker Berlin	2,005 EUR	20 PC	0	2
		TAN	Standard Item	1000	Becker Berlin	2,470 EUR	1 PC	0	1
				1017	Health clinic Ltd.	10 EUR	5 PC	0	1
				1040	DROBEDA Drugstore	600 EUR	50 PC	0	1
				CUSTOMER01	Becker	214,824 EUR	103,070 PC	0	7
		TAO	Milestone billing	1171	Hitech Ltd.	300,000 EUR	1 PC	0	1
				51171	FRIMO	19,800,000 EUR	66 PC	0	6
		#	Not assigned	1000	Becker Berlin	0 EUR	0	6	0
				1017	Health clinic Ltd.	0 EUR	0	1	0
				1040	DROBEDA Drugstore	0 EUR	0	1	0
				1171	Hitech Ltd.	0 EUR	0	1	0
				51171	FRIMO	0 EUR	0	6	0
				CUSTOMER01	Becker	0 EUR	0	4	0
				T-L67B02	COMPU Tech. Ltd.	0 EUR	0	1	0
		Result				20,319,908 EUR	103,213 PC	20	19
Overall Result						20,535,988 EUR	104,856 PC	24	28

Figure 5.32 Order Types and Item Categories in Detail

This figure once again shows that certain key figures aren't available at the drill-down level. In this case, it's the *number of orders* key figure that can be found at the header level of the order, so it doesn't contain information on the item categories of the order. This key figure is now mapped with an item category that isn't assigned ("#"). If you want to avoid this, you can use the options that were described in Section 5.1, Quotation Key Figures, in detail.

Another option that should be mentioned is to use *constant selections*. You can restrict a key figure of the query to a constant selection through a specific characteristic, in this case, the item category. When the underlying data is accessed in the InfoProvider, the system ignores the constant characteristic for the determination of this key figure value; that is, the system displays the key figure value independently of the concrete attributes of this characteristic.

Figure 5.33 illustrates how you can restrict the *number of orders* key figure in the query mentioned previously.

Figure 5.33 Constant Selection Key Figure

Figure 5.34 shows the corresponding result. The result displays the number of orders and item values in the same row. However, in those cases when there are multiple item categories in one order, the system consequently creates multiple rows in the query result for each order, the number of orders is also displayed several times, and the evaluation becomes inaccurate.

Sales doc. type		Item category		Sold-to party		Order value	Order quantity	Number of orders	Number of ordered items
KB	Consignment Fill-up	KBN	Consignment Fill-up	1000	Becker Berlin	0 EUR	1,600 PC	2	7
		Result				0 EUR	1,600 PC	2	7
LP	Scheduling agreement	LPN	Sched.Agreement Item	1000	Becker Berlin	54,340 EUR	22 PC	1	1
		Result				54,340 EUR	22 PC	1	1
LZ	SchedAg. w/ del.schd	LZN	Sched.Agreement Item	1000	Becker Berlin	61,750 EUR	25 PC	1	1
		Result				61,750 EUR	25 PC	1	1
PS1	PS: order	TPC1	Elevator	1000	Becker Berlin	100,000 EUR	1 PC	1	1
		Result				100,000 EUR	1 PC	1	1
RE	Returns	REN	Standard Item	1017	Health clinic Ltd.	-10 EUR	-5 PC	-1	-1
		Result				-10 EUR	-5 PC	-1	-1
TA	Standard Order	TAB	Indiv.Purchase Order	1000	Becker Berlin	2,005 EUR	20 PC	6	2
		TAN	Standard Item	1000	Becker Berlin	2,470 EUR	1 PC	6	1
				1017	Health clinic Ltd.	10 EUR	5 PC	1	1
				1040	DROBEDA Drugstore	600 EUR	50 PC	1	1
				CUSTOMER01	Becker	214,824 EUR	103,070 PC	4	7
		TAO	Milestone billing	1171	Hitech Ltd.	300,000 EUR	1 PC	1	1
				51171	FRIMO	19,800,000 EUR	66 PC	6	6
		Result				20,319,908 EUR	103,213 PC	20	19
Overall Result						20,535,988 EUR	104,856 PC	24	28

Figure 5.34 Orders Types and Item Categories with a Constant Selection

Of course, you can also add further available characteristics, such as *material number, sales document number*, and so on, to this evaluation, if required.

Another option to evaluate the order types or item categories in detail is to create separate key figures in the query, for example, *order value standard order* or *order value credit memo requests*. For this purpose, you must restrict the corresponding basic key figures to the respective order type or item category in the query. Of course, you can also restrict a key figure to multiple characteristic attributes. This is required, for example, if there are several order types for standard orders. Figure 5.35 shows a possible result of this evaluation.

Table					Order value credit memo requests	Order value consignment issue
	Sales doc. type		Sold-to party	Order value standard order		
G2	Credit Memo Request	1040	DROBEDA Drugstore		-570 EUR	
KE	Consignment Issue	1018	Miller's Drugstore			600 EUR
TA	Standard Order	1000	Becker Berlin	230,251 EUR		
		1018	Miller's Drugstore	6,800 EUR		
		1025	Karl Miller LLC.	27,940 EUR		
		1040	DROBEDA Drugstore	1,260 EUR		
		1400	A.I.T. LLC.	796 EUR		
		12121	Smith Sports	159 EUR		
		95000	William's Food Trade	15,500 EUR		
		T-L64B01	SudaTech LLC.	24,600 EUR		
	Overall Result			307,306 EUR	-570 EUR	600 EUR

Figure 5.35 Key Figures per Order Type — Result

This figure illustrates that the drilldown of the query additionally includes the *sales document type* characteristic. It was added for illustration purposes only and can be removed at anytime.

Such a query enables you to easily calculate quotas (e.g., the percentage of standard orders to the total orders). The quota is defined as a formula and calculates the percentage of the order values of a specific order type in the total order value. Figure 5.36 shows an example for the result.

Table

Sold-to party		Total order value	Order value Standard order	Percent of standard orders	Order value consignment issue	Percent of consignment issue	Order value miscellaneous	Percent of miscellaneous
1000	Becker Berlin	230,251 EUR	230,251 EUR	100.0 %			0 EUR	0.0 %
1018	Miller's Drugstore	7,400 EUR	6,800 EUR	91.9 %	600 EUR	8.1 %	0 EUR	0.0 %
1025	Karl Miller LLC.	27,940 EUR	27,940 EUR	100.0 %				
1040	DROBEDA Drugstore	690 EUR	1,260 EUR	182.6 %			-570 EUR	-82.6 %
1400	A.I.T. LLC.	796 EUR	796 EUR	100.0 %				
12121	Smith Sports	159 EUR	159 EUR	100.0 %				
95000	William's Food Trade	175,500 EUR	15,500 EUR	8.8 %			160,000 EUR	91.2 %
T-L64B01	SudaTech LLC.	24,600 EUR	24,600 EUR	100.0 %				

Figure 5.36 Quotas per Order Type

In addition to the standard key figures described, you can also further detail the *incoming orders* and *orders on hand* key figures using order types or item categories. For example, you can define separate key figures for the respective processes in an evaluation to have the system display the incoming standard orders and the incoming credit memo requests of a period. By defining your own queries, you can decide whether certain processes are supposed to be directly included in incoming orders or orders on hand, or whether you want to completely exclude them or display them separately. Such a procedure is possible for credit memo requests, for example (see Section 4.3.1, Incoming Orders and Orders on Hand). In this case, an evaluation can display the incoming orders or orders on hand and the revenue for all processes except for the credit memo request, on the one hand, and these key figures additionally for credit memos only, on the other hand. This enables you to view all figures separately. Figure 5.37 shows an example for this.

Table

Orders on hand value Month 03/2008	Incoming orders value Month 04/2008	Revenue Month 04/2008	Orders on hand value Month 04/2008	Credit memos on hand value Month 03/2008	Incoming credit memos value Month 04/2008	Billed credits value Month 04/2008	Credit memos on hand value Month 04/2008
7,277,822.98 EUR	1,529,814.80 EUR	1,297,387.65 EUR	7,510,250.13 EUR	-347,600.00 EUR			-347,600.00 EUR

Figure 5.37 Incoming Orders/Orders on Hand by Processes

In the definition of this evaluation, the respective key figures were already restricted to the corresponding order types as previously described. The order type "G2" was excluded in the key figures without a credit memo request. In the other key figures, only this order type was included.

If you also want to view the total values for the *incoming orders, orders on hand*, and *revenue* key figures, you can implement this via simple formulas in the report definition by adding up the respective key figures. To display the totals only if required, you can configure the properties of these key figures accordingly. Figure 5.38 shows the properties of one of these key figures.

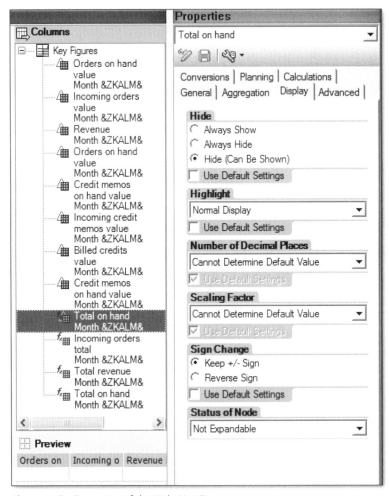

Figure 5.38 Properties of the Hide Key Figure

You can have the system additionally display or swap the key figures via the filter block in the executed query. In Figure 5.39, the totals key figures are displayed while all other key figures are hidden.

Table			
Total on hand Month 03/2008	Incoming orders total Month 04/2008	Total revenue Month 04/2008	Total on hand Month 04/2008
6,930,222.98 EUR	1,529,814.80 EUR	1,297,387.65 EUR	7,162,650.13 EUR

Figure 5.39 Totals Key Figures for Incoming Orders/Orders on Hand

5.2.4 "Consignment" as an Example of Standard Processes

This section uses the consignment process as an example to describe the standard S&D processes. This context is used to explain how you can implement such processes in a detailed evaluation. The following list introduces the various consignment order types.

▶ **"KB" order type — consignment fill-up**
In the consignment process, the customer is initially provided with the goods through the consignment fill-up. The order key figures can later be evaluated via the "KB" order type.

▶ **"KE" order type — consignment issue**
The customer registers an issue with a consignment issue. This process also involves a specific order type, namely, the "KE" order type.

▶ **"KA" order type — consignment pick-up**
A consignment pick-up (order with "KA" order type) is the reverse of the fill-up; that is, the customer returns goods that have not been sold.

▶ **"KR" order type — consignment returns**
Consignment returns ("KR" order type), however, map returns in the consignment stock of the vendor.

These different order types enable you to configure these processes in evaluations in detail. As described in Section 5.2.3, Implementing Different Standard Processes, this can be implemented by including the *order type* characteristic in the drilldown of the query or by defining separate key figures.

In the first variant (*order type* characteristic in the drilldown), you should either restrict the *order type* characteristic to the relevant attributes, or you should define an entry variable for this characteristic to allow the users to select the order types that they want to display. The second variant, the definition of restricted key figures, is illustrated in Figure 5.40.

Table												
Sold-to party		Sales document	Order value fill-up	Order quantity fill-up	Net value withdrawal	Order quantity withdrawal	Order value issue	Order quantity issue	Order value returns	Order quantity returns
1000	Becker Berlin	11966	0 EUR	8 PC						
		11967			72 EUR	6 PC				
		12745	0 EUR	1,250 PC						
		12746	0 EUR	350 PC						
		60000083							-12 EUR	-1 PC
		60000084					0 EUR	-3 PC		
		Result	0 EUR	1,608 PC	72 EUR	6 PC	0 EUR	-3 PC	-12 EUR	-1 PC
1018	Miller's Drugstore	11973	0 EUR	52 PC						
		11974			324 EUR	27 PC				
		12223	0 EUR	10 PC						
		12224	0 EUR	10 L						
		12641	0 EUR	100 PC						
		12642			600 EUR	50 PC				
		60000094					0 EUR	-25 PC		
		Result	0 EUR	*	924 EUR	77 PC	0 EUR	-25 PC		
1118	Drugstore UK	12133	0 EUR	52 PC						
		12134			324 EUR	27 PC				
		Result	0 EUR	52 PC	324 EUR	27 PC				
99500	Electron Commerce Company Llc	12225	0 EUR	5 L						
		Result	0 EUR	5 L						

Figure 5.40 Evaluation for the Consignment Process

In this evaluation, *order value* and *order quantity* are defined for each order type (one for the consignment fill-up, issue, pick-up, and returns, respectively) separately and analyzed at the sold-to party and the sales document level. Consequently, you can track which sales documents were used to implement the respective processes and which quantities or amounts originate from the individual documents. This also illustrates that the consignment fill-up and pick-up processes aren't managed on the basis of values in the order but on the basis of quantities. The consignment issue and returns processes, however, are managed on the basis of values. If the evaluation requires additional information, such as the material number or the creation date of the order, you can integrate them into the drilldown at anytime.

Chapter 6, Cross-Sectional Evaluations, contains examples of additional evaluations for the consignment process, for example, mapping of consignment stock.

5.2.5 Evaluations for Outline Agreements

The following contracts and scheduling agreements are described in the context of outline agreements:

▶ **Contracts**
Contracts define purchase quantities and prices over a specific validity period. Release orders are placed with reference to a contract. The system implements

both processes through orders. Here, you can benefit from comparing the contract value with the release orders in an evaluation. The validity period of the contract may also be used to identify current or already expired contracts.

▶ **Scheduling agreements**
Scheduling agreements, however, affect the release orders through an entry of schedule lines with a specific delivery date for the respective order item. Here, you can compare the target value or target quantity of the scheduling agreement with the release order value or release order quantity.

Let's first take a closer look at the evaluation of contracts.

Contracts

In this context, we want to compare the contract value with the value of the previously placed release orders. This process is complex because the documents that are supposed to be compared are stored in the SAP BW system in different ways. For the contract itself, the contract number is provided in the SALES DOCUMENT field. For release orders, however, this field contains the document number of the release order. The corresponding contract is displayed in the REFERENCE DOCUMENT field. Consequently, the corresponding release orders for the contract can't be mapped in one evaluation without problems. Due to this restriction, we included an additional characteristic, *contract number* (and similar to it the *contract item*), in the data model of our sample scenario. This characteristic is filled as follows during the update of the data within the SAP BW system:

▶ **Contract**
If the incoming data record is a contract (indicated by *document category = G*), the system fills the CONTRACT and CONTRACT ITEM characteristic fields with the sales document number and sales document item.

▶ **Release order**
If the incoming data record is a release order (indicated by *document category of the reference document = G*), the system fills the CONTRACT and CONTRACT ITEM characteristic fields with the reference document number and reference document item.

These two central characteristics enable you to compare contracts and release orders referencing the contracts.

In the definition of the evaluation, you create two key figures. The contract value is restricted to the *document category = G* characteristic, and the release order value is restricted to the *document category of the reference document = G* characteristic. The *contract quantity* and *release order quantity* key figures can be defined in the same way. However, a contract quantity is only filled if the contracts are quantity contracts.

In addition to further required characteristics (e.g., sold-to party), the *contract* characteristic is included in the drilldown of the report. You can provide a variable for this characteristic, if required, which enables the user to already preselect one or more contract numbers when the report is executed. You should restrict this characteristic to exclude the "#" attribute in the report definition to ensure the evaluation includes only contracts and corresponding release orders but no other sales documents. Such an evaluation is shown in Figure 5.41.

Filter		Table							
			Sold-to		Contract	Contract value	Contract quantity	Release order value	Release order quantity
Calendar Year/Month									
Contract	]#[		95000	William's Food Trade	0040000201	245,000 EUR	0 CAR		
Distribution Channel					0040000212	100,000 EUR	0 CAR	5,000 EUR	500 CAR
Item category					0040000213	25,000 EUR	0 CAR	3,500 EUR	350 CAR
Item of Princ. Agmt.					0040000216	100,000 EUR	0 CAR	5,000 EUR	500 CAR
Key Figures					Result	470,000 EUR	0 CAR	13,500 EUR	1,350 CAR
Material									

Figure 5.41 Overview of Contracts and Release Orders

Figure 5.41 illustrates that the displayed contracts are value contracts because the *contract quantity* isn't filled. If you only want to evaluate value contracts or if you only use these types of contracts, you don't need to integrate the *contract quantity* key figure into the report.

As already mentioned, the validity period of a contract is very important information. The preceding query was defined in such a way that you can display the validity periods in the evaluation as required. If you add the validity period start and validity period end to the preceding example, you obtain a result as shown in Figure 5.42.

Table								
Sold-to party		Contract	Validity period start	Validity period end	Contract value	Contract quantity	Release order value	Release order quantity
95000	William's Food Trade	0040000201	01/11/2007	#	245,000 EUR	0 CAR		
		0040000212	05/13/2008	05/31/2008	100,000 EUR	0 CAR	5,000 EUR	500 CAR
		0040000213	05/13/2008	#	25,000 EUR	0 CAR	3,500 EUR	350 CAR
		0040000216	10/14/2008	09/30/2009	100,000 EUR	0 CAR	5,000 EUR	500 CAR
		Result			470,000 EUR	0 CAR	13,500 EUR	1,350 CAR

Figure 5.42 Contracts and Validity Periods

This result displays both the validity period start and the validity period end for all key figures. This was implemented by means of a constant selection. The validity periods are only filled in the contract documents but not in the release orders. To avoid displaying the key figures of the release orders in a second row without an assigned validity period, these key figures were restricted to a constant selection, respectively, for the *validity period start* and *validity period end* characteristics.

If you additionally want to view the orders behind these values, you must include the *sales document* characteristic in the drilldown. For a better overview, the validity periods were removed from the drilldown in our example (see Figure 5.43).

Table								
Sold-to party		Contract	Sales document	Contract value	Contract quantity	Release order value	Release order quantity
95000	William's Food Trade	0040000201	40000201	245,000 EUR	0 CAR		
		0040000212	12643			5,000 EUR	500 CAR
			40000212	100,000 EUR	0 CAR		
			Result	100,000 EUR	0 CAR	5,000 EUR	500 CAR
		0040000213	12645			1,000 EUR	100 CAR
			12646			2,500 EUR	250 CAR
			40000213	25,000 EUR	0 CAR		
			Result	25,000 EUR	0 CAR	3,500 EUR	350 CAR
		0040000216	13020			5,000 EUR	500 CAR
			40000216	100,000 EUR	0 CAR		
			Result	100,000 EUR	0 CAR	5,000 EUR	500 CAR
		Result		470,000 EUR	0 CAR	13,500 EUR	1,350 CAR

Figure 5.43 Contracts and Release Orders in Detail

You could also integrate additional information into the evaluation, such as open values (e.g., open contract values). You can easily create them with your own formula in the query definition by subtracting the release order value from the contract value. Here, you must keep in mind that you can only evaluate such key figures at the aggregated level. For example, if the *sales document* characteristic is included in the drilldown, an open contract value can display useful values only at the totals level.

Scheduling Agreements

This section discusses the scheduling agreements and their evaluation in SAP NetWeaver BI. In this context, the information on the target quantity and target value of the scheduling agreement, as well as the information on the already-fixed release orders at schedule line level is particularly interesting.

The schedule line data records provide the key figures of the delivery dates specified so far. In the report definition, you can determine the target value yourself from the target quantity that is available at the item level of the document. In this context, you can't just copy the item's net value as the target value because the item's net value is always derived from the cumulated values of the schedule lines. The net value at item level and the target value vary until the entire target quantity is fixed. Consequently, you must determine the target value. There are various options to do that.

On the one hand, you could use the target quantity, price, and price unit to calculate the target value already during the update. In this case, the target value is available as a separate key figure in the InfoProvider, which means that you could also display this key figure at the aggregated level although the individual sales document items aren't included in the drilldown of the query.

On the other hand, you can determine the target value directly in the query definition using a specific formula. This method is introduced in the following dialog.

Formula for Determining the Target Value in the Query Definition

Target Value
= Net Value of the Item / Cumulated Order Quantity × Target Quantity

The individual figures of this formula are defined as follows:

▶ **Net value of the item**
= cumulated net value that results from the schedule lines specified so far. This value is provided in the document item data records.

▶ **Cumulated order quantity**
= cumulated order quantity that results from the schedule lines specified so far. This value is provided in the document item data records.

▶ **Target quantity**
= target quantity that is entered at document item level

To compare the target value with the schedule lines specified so far, there are again multiple options available. If you only want to compare the target value with the cumulated schedule line values, you can carry out the evaluation at the document item level and use the cumulated key figures available there. However, if you want to evaluate the individual schedule lines and their values in detail, you must access the key figures at the schedule line level in the evaluation and implement them in detail. For this variant, you must first determine the amount key figures at the schedule line level. This should be done during the data update into the InfoProvider. At the schedule line level, only quantities are visible by default.

Now let's consider the first variant in which you can compare the values at the cumulated level. Such an evaluation might look like the one displayed in Figure 5.44.

Table							
Sold-to party		Sales document	Sales document item	Target value	Target quantity	Already fixed value	Already fixed quantity
95000	William's Food Trade	30000061	10	100,000.00 EUR	10,000 CAR	35,000 EUR	3,500 CAR

Figure 5.44 Scheduling Agreement Overview

If you also want to evaluate which quantities or amounts are still open, you can map this with a simple formula in the query definition. For this purpose, you subtract the already-fixed values from the target values, respectively. Then, you obtain a result as shown in Figure 5.45.

Table									
Sold-to party		Sales document	Sales document item	Target value	Target quantity	Already fixed value	Already fixed quantity	Open value	Open quantity
95000	William's Food Trade	30000061	10	100,000.00 EUR	10,000 CAR	35,000 EUR	3,500 CAR	65,000.00 EUR	6,500 CAR

Figure 5.45 Extended Scheduling Agreement Overview

To display the details of the already-fixed values, you must work at the schedule line level as described earlier. As an example, we'll map the already-fixed quantities with their delivery date in an evaluation. For this purpose, we use the *target quantity* key figure from the item. This key figure is later mapped as a not assigned schedule line ("#") in the evaluation. We also use the *order quantity* key figure, which is available at the schedule line level. Furthermore, we include the *delivery date* characteristic in the evaluation, which leads to the result shown in Figure 5.46.

Sold-to party		Sales document	Sales document item	Schedule Line	Delivery date	Target quantity	Order quantity
95000	William's Food Trade	30000061	10	1	11/15/2008	0 CAR	2,500 CAR
				2	12/15/2008	0 CAR	1,000 CAR
				#	#	10,000 CAR	0 CAR
				Result		10,000 CAR	3,500 CAR

Figure 5.46 Scheduling Agreements and Delivery Dates

If you want to view the open quantity here, you can include it in the report definition as described previously. However, you'll obtain useful values only at the totals level.

5.2.6 Orders with Billing or Delivery Blocks

You can generally link orders with billing or delivery blocks in SAP NetWeaver BI. The required information is provided in the transaction data via various InfoObjects. The information on billing and delivery blocks is stored in SAP ERP as follows:

- **Billing block at header level**
  This applies to the entire document, which means that it's completely blocked.

- **Billing block at item level**
  This block applies only to a particular item and not to the entire document.

- **Delivery block at header level**
  This applies to the entire document.

- **Delivery block at schedule line level**
  This block applies only to the respective schedule line; there are no delivery blocks at the item level.

The standard extractors also provide the header blocks in the document item and document schedule line transaction data. Consequently, the item block is also filled in the document schedule lines. Therefore all data records contain the required information.

To display blocked key figures, such as order values that are subject to a billing or delivery block, you must consider the different levels at which the blocks are implemented. This must be done in the query definition.

To map order values that are subject to a billing block, for example, proceed as follows:

1. First, restrict the standard key figure, *order value*, to the *billing block header* characteristic *not equal to "#"* so that you obtain all values that are subject to a header block.

2. In addition, define a second key figure in which you restrict the standard key figure, *order value*, to the *billing block header* characteristic *equal to "#"* and *billing block item* characteristic *not equal to "#"* so you obtain all values from the documents that are subject to an item block but not to a header block.

3. In the last step, add the two key figures using a formula to obtain the total order value with a billing block. Finally, you can hide the first two key figures if you don't want to evaluate them in detail.

An example of a result of such an evaluation is shown in Figure 5.47.

Filter		Table			Order value with billing block	Order quantity with billing block
			Sold-to party			
Calendar Year/Month						
Distribution Channel		1000	Becker Berlin		-612.00 EUR	-4 PC
Item category		1017	Health clinic Ltd.		-10.00 EUR	-5 PC
Key Figures	,Order value	1018	Miller's Drugstore		-132.00 EUR	-11 PC
Material		1076	Industry Technology		-1,500.00 EUR	-20 PC
Reason for order		1125	Meier European Logistics		-1,500.00 EUR	-100 PC
Reason for rejection		1172	CBD Computer Based Design		19,878.80 EUR	22 PC
Sales doc. type		95100	Grocery store Klein & Fein Ltd.		-890.00 EUR	-1,000 PC
Sales document		Overall Result			15,234.80 EUR	-1,118 PC
Sales group						
Sales Office						
Sales Organization						
Schedule Line						
SD Document Category						
Sold-to party						

Figure 5.47 Overview of the Evaluation of Billing Blocks

The negative order values indicate that the source documents in SAP ERP are credit memo requests. The system sets the billing block automatically when these documents are created. In this context, it makes sense to evaluate the *order value with billing block* key figure by order types to avoid the order value and credit memo request balancing each other out.

For further detailing, you can use the filter block to display additional characteristics, for example, the document number (see Figure 5.48).

Filter		Table				
		Sold-to party		Sales document	Order value with billing block	Order quantity with billing block
Calendar Year/Month						
Distribution Channel		1000	Becker Berlin	60000090	-199.00 EUR	-1 PC
Item category				60000098	-15.00 EUR	-1 PC
Key Figures	,Order value			60000106	-398.00 EUR	-2 PC
Material				Result	-612.00 EUR	-4 PC
Reason for order		1017	Health clinic Ltd.	60000123	-10.00 EUR	-5 PC
Reason for rejection		1018	Miller's Drugstore	60000105	-120.00 EUR	-10 PC
Sales doc. type				60000107	-12.00 EUR	-1 PC
Sales document				Result	-132.00 EUR	-11 PC
Sales group		1076	Industry Technology	60000113	-1,500.00 EUR	-20 PC
Sales Office		1125	Meier European Logistics	60000097	-1,500.00 EUR	-100 PC
Sales Organization		1172	CBD Computer Based Design	8255	19,878.80 EUR	22 PC
Schedule Line		95100	Grocery store Klein & Fein Ltd.	60000109	-890.00 EUR	-1,000 PC
SD Document Category		Overall Result			15,234.80 EUR	-1,118 PC
Sold-to party						

Figure 5.48 Detailed Evaluation of Billing Blocks

Furthermore, it was previously described (see explanation in Figure 5.38) that the *order value with header block* or *order value with item block* auxiliary key figures were initially hidden but could be displayed again in the executed query. That means if you want to display them, you can additionally include them via the filter block as shown in Figure 5.49.

Sold-to party		Sales document	Order value with billing block	Order quantity with billing block	Order value with header block	Order value with item block	Order quantity with header block	Order quantity with item block
1000	Becker Berlin	60000090	-199.00 EUR	-1 PC	-199.00 EUR		-1 PC	
		60000098	-15.00 EUR	-1 PC	-15.00 EUR		-1 PC	
		60000106	-398.00 EUR	-2 PC	-398.00 EUR		-2 PC	
		Result	-612.00 EUR	-4 PC	-612.00 EUR		-4 PC	
1017	Health clinic Ltd.	60000123	-10.00 EUR	-5 PC	-10.00 EUR		-5 PC	
1018	Miller's Drugstore	60000105	-120.00 EUR	-10 PC	-120.00 EUR		-10 PC	
		60000107	-12.00 EUR	-1 PC	-12.00 EUR		-1 PC	
		Result	-132.00 EUR	-11 PC	-132.00 EUR		-11 PC	
1076	Industry Technology	60000113	-1,500.00 EUR	-20 PC	-1,500.00 EUR		-20 PC	
1125	Meier European Logistics	60000097	-1,500.00 EUR	-100 PC	-1,500.00 EUR		-100 PC	
1172	CBD Computer Based Design	8255	19,878.80 EUR	22 PC	19,878.80 EUR		22 PC	
95100	Grocery store Klein & Fein Ltd.	60000109	-890.00 EUR	-1,000 PC	-890.00 EUR		-1,000 PC	
Overall Result			15,234.80 EUR	-1,118 PC	15,234.80 EUR		-1,118 PC	

Figure 5.49 Evaluation of Billing Block Key Figures

Figure 5.49 illustrates that our selection only contains billing blocks at the document header level.

To map values with delivery blocks, you must perform the same steps. Note that delivery blocks can only be implemented at the header level and the schedule line level but not at the item level. To have a correct overview, you must use key figures from the document schedule line here. If you use only values from the document items, you can't map the amounts with schedule line blocks.

If you additionally want to determine particular quotas in an evaluation, for example, order values with billing block with regard to the total order values, you can do this anytime via specific formulas in the report definition.

5.3   Delivery Key Figures

Having discussed orders, this section now deals with delivery documents. Besides the known *quantity*, *value*, and *number of documents* or *number of items* document key figures, the following delivery key figures are frequently considered:

▶ Delivery volume

▶ Picked quantity/picked value

▶ Goods issue quantity/goods issue value

Additional important, delivery-specific key figures can be derived when considering quantities and dates from order and delivery:

▶ On-time delivery performance

▶ Delivery quantity performance

▶ Delivery time

For this purpose, the SAP Business Content provides three different extractors that enable different views of the respective documents, so we used them to fill separate InfoProvider (see Chapter 3, SD Sample Scenario).

▶ **Adding delivery information to the order data**
For example, the *sales and distribution: sales documents* InfoProvider provides additional delivery key figures, such as delivery quantity and delivery value, per order item, and order schedule line. These key figures are made available by specific DataSources (2LIS_11_V_ITM or 2LIS_11_V_SCL).

▶ **Details per order schedule line and delivery item**
In addition, the *sales and distribution: order delivery* InfoCube provides the details per order schedule line and corresponding delivery items, that is, date and quantity information.

▶ **General information on deliveries**

Regardless of this, the *sales and distribution: delivery* InfoCube also contains the pure delivery information in our SAP NetWeaver BI scenario. This allows for detailed analysis of the delivery documents, including the status information regarding picking and goods issue.

In our scenario, the data of the aforementioned InfoCubes are, of course, linked by means of the MultiProvider. Thus, a cross-sectional evaluation is possible, however, only for those characteristics that are supplied with information in all required InfoCubes (e.g., *customer* and *material*).

5.3.1 Outstanding Deliveries per Order

To proceed with the S&D process, we now want to determine the already-performed deliveries and the open deliveries on the basis of the orders. For this purpose, we previously defined a query that is restricted to the *sales and distribution: sales documents* InfoProvider and document category C for orders in the filter. In the example (see Figure 5.50), simple formulas, such as *order quantity – delivery quantity*, are used to determine the outstanding quantities and values within the query definition.

Table

Sold-to party		Material		Order value	Delivered value	Outstanding delivery value	Order quantity	Delivery quantity	Outstanding delivery quantity
1000	Becker Berlin	100-100	Casing	6,995 EUR	4,537 EUR	2,458 EUR	137 PC	124 PC	13 PC
		P-100	Pump PRECISION 100	81,510 EUR	0 EUR	81,510 EUR	33 PC	0 PC	33 PC
		P-102	Pump PRECISION 102	2,885 EUR	0 EUR	2,885 EUR	1 PC	0 PC	1 PC
		PR4711	wash lotion 150ml gla	513 EUR	114 EUR	399 EUR	345 PC	310 PC	35 PC
		PR4712	wash lotion 150ml pla	1,330 EUR	1,330 EUR	0 EUR	250 PC	250 PC	0 PC
		T-ASC12	Flatscreen MS 1575P	153,860 EUR	0 EUR	153,860 EUR	70 PC	0 PC	70 PC
		Result		247,093 EUR	5,981 EUR	241,112 EUR	836 PC	684 PC	152 PC
1018	Miller's Drugstore	PR4711	wash lotion 150ml gla	3,000 EUR	1,800 EUR	1,200 EUR	350 PC	250 PC	100 PC
		PR4712	wash lotion 150ml pla	1,400 EUR	1,400 EUR	0 EUR	100 PC	100 PC	0 PC
		ST4711	wash lotion 300ml gla	3,000 EUR	0 EUR	3,000 EUR	100 PC	0 PC	100 PC
		Result		7,400 EUR	3,200 EUR	4,200 EUR	550 PC	350 PC	200 PC
1040	DROBEDA Drugstore	PR4711	wash lotion 150ml gla	4,800 EUR	4,200 EUR	600 EUR	400 PC	350 PC	50 PC
		PR4712	wash lotion 150ml pla	2,460 EUR	1,260 EUR	1,200 EUR	190 PC	100 PC	90 PC
		Result		7,260 EUR	5,460 EUR	1,800 EUR	590 PC	450 PC	140 PC
Overall Result				261,753 EUR	14,641 EUR	247,112 EUR	1,976 PC	1,484 PC	492 PC

Figure 5.50 Order and Delivery Key Figures

Because this evaluation is based on the order, the system can provide all corresponding characteristics for navigation. Now, we want to view which orders haven't yet been completely delivered. For this purpose, you must use a condition to restrict the evaluation to data with an outstanding delivery quantity "<> 0", that is, to documents that must still be supplied. Figure 5.51 shows the definition of this condition.

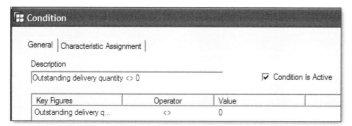

Figure 5.51 Condition: Outstanding Delivery Quantity "<> 0"

In Figure 5.52, the example is filtered to MATERIAL PR4711 per order number.

Table								
		Material	PR4711					
			wash lotion 150ml glass bottle					
Sold-to party		Sales document	Order value	Delivered value	Outstanding delivery value	Order quantity	Delivery quantity	Outstanding delivery quantity
1000	Becker Berlin	12530	57 EUR	0 EUR	57 EUR	5 PC	0 PC	5 PC
		12531	57 EUR	0 EUR	57 EUR	5 PC	0 PC	5 PC
		12540	57 EUR	0 EUR	57 EUR	5 PC	0 PC	5 PC
		12762	228 EUR	0 EUR	228 EUR	20 PC	0 PC	20 PC
		Result	513 EUR	114 EUR	399 EUR	345 PC	310 PC	35 PC
1018	Miller's Drugstore	12647	1,200 EUR	0 EUR	1,200 EUR	100 PC	0 PC	100 PC
		Result	3,000 EUR	1,800 EUR	1,200 EUR	350 PC	250 PC	100 PC
1040	DROBEDA Drugstore	12741	600 EUR	0 EUR	600 EUR	50 PC	0 PC	50 PC
		Result	4,800 EUR	4,200 EUR	600 EUR	400 PC	350 PC	50 PC
Overall Result			8,313 EUR	6,114 EUR	2,199 EUR	1,095 PC	910 PC	185 PC

Figure 5.52 Outstanding Deliveries with Regard to Material PR4711

In this context, we decided to display the material in the columns of the report. This enables us to slightly vary the presentation of the evaluation depending on the objective and target group.

5.3.2 Delivery Quantity, Volume, Number of Deliveries

Let's now turn to the analysis of the already created deliveries. To output the basic key figures (*delivery quantity*, *number of deliveries*, *number of items in delivery*) and specific characteristics of the delivery document, we defined an additional query that is restricted to the *sales and distribution: delivery* InfoCube in the filter. Additional delivery key figures, such as *number of packages*, *weight*, or *delivery volume*, may also be of interest. Of course, they can be implemented, too. Figure 5.53 illustrates our example with data formatting via the product hierarchy.

Material		Delivery quantity	Number of deliveries	Number of items in delivery
Overall Result		9,907 PC	167	245
▼ Machines		5,715 PC	99	170
▶ Pumps		5,437 PC	65	132
▶ Components (Pumps)		278 PC	42	38
▼ Hardware		889 PC	20	30
▶ PC		839 PC	14	26
▶ Work station		50 PC	6	4
▼ Shipping units		5 PC	4	4
▶ Transport equipment		5 PC	4	4
▼ Personal Hygiene		3,298 PC	48	41
▼ Skin Care		3,298 PC	48	41
▼ Normal skin		3,298 PC	48	41
wash lotion 150ml glass bottle	PR4711	1,199 PC	21	15
wash lotion 150ml plastic bottle	PR4712	2,099 PC	28	26

Figure 5.53 Delivery Key Figures by Product Hierarchy

Similar to the documents mentioned, the InfoCube doesn't provide the *number of delivery* key figure per material, so it was directly determined via an exception aggregation in the query, as described earlier in this chapter in the explanation for Figure 5.6.

The *delivery value* key figure is also initially not available in this InfoCube because it isn't defined in the delivery document in SAP ERP. If required, you can add the delivery value in the data model and determine it, for example, from the data of the DataProvider mentioned in Section 5.3.1, Outstanding Deliveries per Order. The following paragraphs, however, primarily focus on the delivery quantity.

The evaluation that was used for Figure 5.53 enables you to also map the status of the deliveries regarding picking and goods issue posting, which makes it possible to display the open deliveries. Figure 5.54 shows an example that can be drilled down to the delivery item level, if required.

Ship-To Party		Picking status	Goods movement status	Delivery quantity
1000	Becker Berlin	A	A	31 PC
		C	A	6 PC
			C	2,521 PC
		#	C	-8 PC
1018	Miller's Drugstore	C	A	112 PC
			C	1,327 PC
		#	C	-85 PC
1020	Becker Berlin (Lagerung)	C	C	520 PC
1040	DROBEDA Drugstore	C	C	550 PC
Overall Result				4,974 PC

Figure 5.54 Delivery Status per Ship-to Party

Unfortunately, the layout for this information is neither appealing nor user friendly. A better solution is to use additional restricted key figures within the query definition to format the data for the report's recipient (see Figure 5.55).

Table		Delivery quantity	Open delivery quantity	Picking quantity	Picking quantity excluding GI	Goods issue quantity
1000	Becker Berlin	2,550 PC	31 PC	2,519 PC	6 PC	2,513 PC
1018	Miller's Drugstore	1,354 PC		1,354 PC	112 PC	1,242 PC
1020	Becker Berlin (Lagerung)	520 PC		520 PC		520 PC
1040	DROBEDA Drugstore	550 PC		550 PC		550 PC
Overall Result		4,974 PC	31 PC	4,943 PC	118 PC	4,825 PC

Figure 5.55 Comparison of the Delivery Quantities (Open, Picked, Goods Issue)

In contrast to the status information used here, you can't evaluate the billing status of the delivery without problems; and this option isn't provided in the SAP standard anyway because it's only an indirect change of the delivery document (see Section 5.1.3, Open, Rejected, and Accepted Quotations).

5.3.3 Delivery Performance (On-Time Delivery Performance, Delivery Time)

The determination of the on-time delivery performance, that is, the comparison of the requested delivery date or the confirmed date of the order and the actual delivery date, is a bit more complicated. Because the comparison of the dates at the aggregated level don't provide a useful result (see Section 5.1.6, Sales Cycle), you must implement the calculations given in the following box separately for each order schedule line and the corresponding delivery items.

> **Determination of the On-Time Delivery Performance**
>
> ► *On-Time Delivery Performance in Days (Requested Delivery Date)*
> *= Actual Delivery Date – Requested Delivery Date*
>
> ► *On-Time Delivery Performance in Days (Confirmation)*
> *= Actual Delivery Date – Confirmed Date*

Figure 5.56 shows the determined key figures also for individual documents here.

Table

Sales document	Sales document item	Schedule line	Delivery	Item	Requested deliv.date	Confirmed deliv.date	Actual deliv.date	Delivery quantity	On-time delivery performance (requested date)	On-time delivery performance (confirmed date)
5673	10	2	80004572	10	12/23/2002	12/29/2002	03/4/2003	220 PC	71	65
	20	1	80004572	20	12/23/2002	12/23/2002	03/4/2003	24 PC	71	71
	30	1	80004572	30	12/23/2002	12/23/2002	03/4/2003	21 PC	71	71
6429	10	2	80007584	10	08/17/2004	08/30/2004	08/26/2004	36 PC	9	-4
		3	80007581	10	08/17/2004	08/21/2004	08/28/2004	10 PC	11	7
	20	2	80007584	20	08/17/2004	08/30/2004	08/26/2004	27 PC	9	-4
		3	80007581	20	08/17/2004	08/21/2004	08/28/2004	19 PC	11	7
	30	1	80007581	30	08/17/2004	08/17/2004	08/28/2004	10 PC	11	11
			80007584	30	08/17/2004	08/17/2004	08/26/2004	20 PC	9	9
	40	2	80007584	40	08/17/2004	08/30/2004	08/26/2004	66 PC	9	-4
		3	80007581	40	08/17/2004	08/21/2004	08/28/2004	2 PC	11	7
12629	10	2	80015593	10	04/29/2008	05/5/2008	05/13/2008	200 PC	14	8
12642	10	1	80015590	10	05/7/2008	05/7/2008	05/7/2008	50 PC	0	0

Figure 5.56 On-Time Delivery Performance per Delivery Item

Besides the actual determination of these key figures that can be implemented directly in the query at the level shown in Figure 5.56, some general questions arise for reporting, for example, how negative values are supposed to affect the on-time delivery performance. This problem was already dealt with in detail in Section 4.3.2, Orders with Delivery or Billing Blocks. Depending on the complexity of the determination that you want to use, it's absolutely necessary to already implement this in the data model by means of source code. However, this should be generally carried out for determining the on-time delivery performance, because the reporting usually doesn't require a detailed mapping per order schedule line and delivery item.

The following sections describe the implementation of the scoring system that was introduced in Section 4.3.2, Orders with Delivery or Billing Blocks. You can even determine the respective score at the detailed level in the query design through formulas (see Figure 5.57).

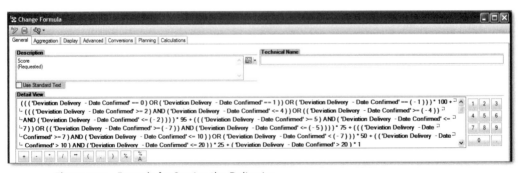

Figure 5.57 Formula for Scoring the Deliveries

For reasons of clarity, you can also divide this formula into several smaller formulas or map one column per score, if required. Figure 5.58 shows the result of the formula from Figure 5.57.

Sales document	Sales document item	Schedule Line	Delivery	Item	On-time delivery performance (Requested)	Score (Requested)	On-time delivery performance (Confirmed)	Score (Confirmed)
5673	10	2	80004572	10	71	1	65	1
	20	1	80004572	20	71	1	71	1
	30	1	80004572	30	71	1	71	1
6429	10	2	80007584	10	9	50	-4	95
		3	80007581	10	11	25	7	125
	20	2	80007584	20	9	50	-4	95
		3	80007581	20	11	25	7	125
	30	1	80007584	30	9	50	9	50
			80007581	30	11	25	11	25
	40	2	80007584	40	9	50	-4	95
		3	80007581	40	11	25	7	125
12629	10	2	80015593	10	14	25	8	50
12642	10	1	80015590	10	0	100	0	100

Figure 5.58 On-Time Delivery Performance and Scores per Delivery Item

To avoid complexity within the query and to enhance flexibility in reporting, we used source code to determine separate key figures in the data model that included these scores. Consequently, you can display average scores at the aggregated level (see Figure 5.59).

Sold-to party		Material		Ø Score (Requested)	Ø Score (Confirmed)	Delivery quantity
Overall Result				37	47	10,223 PC
1000	Becker Berlin	Machines		23	37	5,921 PC
		Pumps		16	34	5,651 PC
		Components (Pumps)		54	54	270 PC
		PC		63	70	718 PC
		PC ensemble		58	58	12 PC
		Monitor		65	64	140 PC
		Processor		63	63	11 PC
		Input device		64	95	555 PC
		Skin Care		87	76	918 PC
1018	Miller's Drugstore	Work station		67	67	141 PC
		Skin Care		72	65	1,625 PC
1040	DROBEDA Drugstore Trade ltd.	Skin Care		62	69	900 PC
		Normal skin		62	69	900 PC
			wash lotion 150ml glass bottle	68	79	700 PC
			wash lotion 150ml plastic bottle	50	50	200 PC

Figure 5.59 On-Time Delivery Performance — Average Score

As already mentioned in Section 4.5.2, On-Time Delivery Performance, it may also be useful to weight these scores by quantities or values. An option in this context is to again determine separate key figures within data modeling. In our example, we multiplied the score of the delivery item that was determined for Figure 5.59 by the delivery quantity. We then stored the result as a key figure. Within the query definition, we can now divide the key figure weighted with the quantity by the delivery quantity. The final formula is shown in the following box.

Determination of a Weighted Average Score

Weighted Average Score
= Score of the Delivery Item × Quantity of the Delivery Item/Cumulated Delivery Quantity according to Query Drilldown

---

In Figure 5.60, this result is compared to the pure average scores.

Table

Sold-to party		Material		Ø Score (Requested)	Ø Score weighted (Requested)	Ø Score (Confirmed)	Ø Score weighted (Confirmed)	Delivery quantity
Overall Result				37	40	47	57	10,223 PC
1000	Becker Berlin	▼ Machines		23	19	37	46	5,921 PC
		▶ Pumps		16	17	34	46	5,651 PC
		▶ Components (Pumps)		54	52	54	52	270 PC
		▼ PC		63	52	70	86	718 PC
		▶ PC ensemble		58	71	58	71	12 PC
		▶ Monitor		65	55	64	55	140 PC
		▶ Processor		63	73	63	73	11 PC
		▶ Input device		64	50	95	95	555 PC
		▶ Skin Care		87	75	76	63	918 PC
1018	Miller's Drugstore	▶ Work station		67	67	67	67	141 PC
		▶ Skin Care		72	79	65	69	1,625 PC
1040	DROBEDA Drugstore Trade ltd.	▼ Skin Care		62	60	69	71	900 PC
		▼ Normal skin		62	60	69	71	900 PC
			wash lotion 150ml glass bottle	68	63	79	76	700 PC
			wash lotion 150ml plastic bottle	50	50	50	50	200 PC

Figure 5.60 On-Time Delivery Performance — Weighted Average Score

As you can see in Figure 5.60, the weighted score sometimes considerably deviates from the pure average score. This example is supposed to show that you can implement the on-time delivery performance in SAP NetWeaver BI in many different ways. The result and the information value of this key figure largely depend on the detailed definition that you specified previously.

At this point, we don't want to further discuss the figure of the delivery time introduced in Section 4.5.3, Delivery Time, because this key figure can be implemented similar to the on-time delivery performance.

5.4 Billing Key Figures

Billing documents represent the final stage in the S&D process. The following sections discuss the implementation of the resulting key figures in detail. All evaluations mentioned in the following sections are based on data of the *sales and distribution: billing documents* InfoProvider. Therefore, we set a filter for this Info-Provider in all evaluations.

5.4.1 General Billing Key Figures

Some key figures, such as the *revenue*, the *sales quantity*, and the *number of billing documents,* or *billing items*, are always interesting in this context. These are key figures provided by the standard extractors and are available without having to use a specific logic in SAP NetWeaver BI. Depending on the content and level of details required, you can map these key figures for different characteristics. For example, you can analyze the revenue per sales organization and distribution channel, per customer, or per material. If you want to further detail this, you can also include the billing number and item in the report definition to carry out the evaluation at the document level. Because these quite simple evaluations were already introduced several times, we only describe a brief, simple example here. Figure 5.61 shows the selection screen.

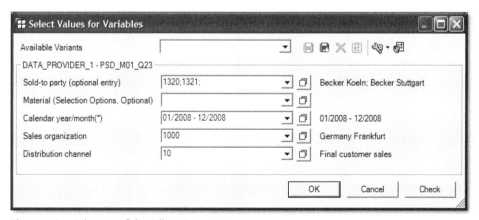

Figure 5.61 Selection of the Billing Documents

These selections lead to the result shown in Figure 5.62.

Table

Sold-to party		Material		Net value	Billing quantity in base unit	Number of billing items	Number of billing docs
1320	Becker Koeln	P-101	Pump PRECISION 101	99,130.40 EUR	37 PC	1	0
		P-102	Pump PRECISION 102	151,855.00 EUR	50 PC	2	0
		P-103	Pump PRECISION 103	106,348.80 EUR	32 PC	1	0
		P-104	Pump PRECISION 104	184,431.60 EUR	54 PC	2	0
		P-402	Pump standard IDESNO	455,512.20 EUR	143 PC	2	0
		#	Not assigned	0.00	0.000	0	5
		Result		997,278.00 EUR	316 PC	8	5
1321	Becker Stuttgart	P-101	Pump PRECISION 101	675,158.40 EUR	252 PC	6	0
		P-102	Pump PRECISION 102	300,672.90 EUR	99 PC	4	0
		P-103	Pump PRECISION 103	501,833.40 EUR	151 PC	5	0
		P-104	Pump PRECISION 104	262,985.80 EUR	77 PC	3	0
		P-402	Pump standard IDESNO	831,389.40 EUR	261 PC	4	0
		#	Not assigned	0.00	0.000	0	7
		Result		2,572,039.90 EUR	840 PC	22	7
Overall Result				3,569,317.90 EUR	1,156 PC	30	12

Figure 5.62 General Billing Key Figures

This figure shows that the already-known problem occurs here, too, which is that the *number of billing documents* key figure isn't contained at the item level. This problem can be solved in the same way as described for quotations and orders.

For example, if you swap the material number with the billing number in this evaluation so that the drilldown no longer includes item characteristics, you obtain the result displayed in Figure 5.63.

Table

Sold-to party		Billing document	Net value	Billing quantity in base unit	Number of billing items	Number of billing docs
1320	Becker Koeln	90034527	92,215.80 EUR	27 PC	1	1
		90034755	72,890.40 EUR	24 PC	1	1
		90034964	229,348.80 EUR	72 PC	1	1
		90035117	503,692.60 EUR	156 PC	4	1
		90035207	99,130.40 EUR	37 PC	1	1
		Result	997,278.00 EUR	316 PC	8	5
1321	Becker Stuttgart	90034370	499,306.00 EUR	160 PC	4	1
		90034455	480,808.80 EUR	157 PC	4	1
		90034526	520,817.80 EUR	170 PC	4	1
		90034609	115,205.60 EUR	43 PC	1	1
		90034670	115,205.60 EUR	43 PC	1	1
		90035039	411,284.50 EUR	134 PC	4	1
		90035206	429,411.60 EUR	133 PC	4	1
		Result	2,572,039.90 EUR	840 PC	22	7
Overall Result			3,569,317.90 EUR	1,156 PC	30	12

Figure 5.63 Variant of the General Billing Key Figures

5.4.2 Key Figures from Billing Conditions

In the context of evaluations of billing documents, the conditions of the documents are interesting as well. From conditions, you can derive further important information, for example, the amount of customer discounts, cash discounts, rebates, or surcharges. This information is stored as separate key figures in SAP BW, which can then be evaluated at the document level in detail or at the aggregated level as required.

The standard extractor for the billing item data only provides a part of the relevant amounts, such as net value or subtotal, for the SAP BW system. If you want to additionally map specific conditions in evaluations, you must determine and update these key figures yourself with your own logic in SAP BW. In this case, the corresponding conditions, which are stored in a separate DataStore, are read during the update of the billing item data and stored as separate key figures in the billing InfoCube. They are then available for evaluations in this InfoCube.

Figure 5.64 shows an evaluation of customer discounts and cash discounts per sales organization, distribution channel, and month at the aggregated level.

| Table | | | | | |
Sales Organization	Distribution Channel	Calendar Year/Month	Revenue	Customer Discount	Cash Discount
Germany Frankfurt	Final customer sales	01/2008	1,205,734.85 EUR	-4,993.06 EUR	-39,211.58 EUR
		02/2008	1,257,718.35 EUR	-4,808.09 EUR	-40,943.69 EUR
		03/2008	1,196,520.15 EUR	-6,130.34 EUR	-38,538.61 EUR
		04/2008	1,297,387.65 EUR	-1,152.06 EUR	-42,292.60 EUR
		05/2008	1,123,868.20 EUR	-1,152.06 EUR	-36,728.70 EUR
		06/2008	1,242,536.45 EUR	-728.90 EUR	-38,650.32 EUR
		Result	7,323,765.65 EUR	-18,964.51 EUR	-236,365.50 EUR
	Sold for resale	01/2008	*	0.00 EUR	-.*
		02/2008	*	0.00 EUR	-.*
		03/2008	2,380,628.91 EUR	0.00 EUR	-75,365.55 EUR
		04/2008	*	0.00 EUR	-.*
		05/2008	*	0.00 EUR	-.*
		06/2008	*	0.00 EUR	-.*
		Result	*	0.00 EUR	-.*
	Service	01/2008	536.91 EUR	0.00 EUR	-17.46 EUR
		02/2008	536.91 EUR	0.00 EUR	-17.46 EUR
		03/2008	536.91 EUR	0.00 EUR	-17.46 EUR
		04/2008	536.91 EUR	0.00 EUR	-17.46 EUR
		05/2008	536.91 EUR	0.00 EUR	-17.46 EUR
		06/2008	536.91 EUR	0.00 EUR	-17.46 EUR
		Result	3,221.46 EUR	0.00 EUR	-104.76 EUR
	Result		*	-18,964.51 EUR	-.*

Figure 5.64 Evaluation of Customer Discounts and Cash Discounts at the Aggregated Level

Figure 5.64 illustrates that the key figures can be provided in different currencies in the DataStore. For example, the *cash discount* key figure is provided in different currencies in the *sold for resale* distribution channel and is displayed as "*". There are different options to solve this presentation problem. One approach is to integrate the *document currency* characteristic into the drilldown of the report. As a result, the system displays all key figures per existing currency. An alternative is to include a currency translation for the key figures. This can be configured in the properties of the key figures in the query definition. Here you define which *currency translation type* you want to use. First, however, this currency translation type must be defined in SAP BW and created (Transaction RSCUR). Figure 5.65 shows the integration of the currency translation with the properties of the key figures in the query.

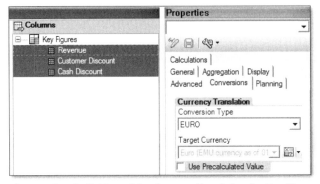

Figure 5.65 Definition of the Currency Translation for Key Figures

Figure 5.66 shows the corresponding result.

Sales Organization	Distribution Channel	Calendar Year/Month	Revenue	Customer Discount	Cash Discount
Germany Frankfurt	Final customer sales	01/2008	1,205,734.85 EUR	-4,993.06 EUR	-39,211.58 EUR
		02/2008	1,257,718.35 EUR	-4,808.09 EUR	-40,943.69 EUR
		03/2008	1,196,520.15 EUR	-6,130.34 EUR	-38,538.61 EUR
		04/2008	1,297,387.65 EUR	-1,152.06 EUR	-42,292.60 EUR
		05/2008	1,123,868.20 EUR	-1,152.06 EUR	-36,728.70 EUR
		06/2008	1,242,536.45 EUR	-728.90 EUR	-38,650.32 EUR
		Result	7,323,765.65 EUR	-18,964.51 EUR	-236,365.50 EUR
	Sold for resale	01/2008	2,222,843.18 EUR	0.00 EUR	-70,406.53 EUR
		02/2008	2,431,390.25 EUR	0.00 EUR	-79,522.59 EUR
		03/2008	2,380,628.91 EUR	0.00 EUR	-75,365.55 EUR
		04/2008	3,243,056.18 EUR	0.00 EUR	-109,495.30 EUR
		05/2008	3,365,582.40 EUR	0.00 EUR	-99,383.11 EUR
		06/2008	3,409,507.71 EUR	0.00 EUR	-111,239.95 EUR
		Result	17,053,008.62 EUR	0.00 EUR	-545,413.02 EUR
	Service	01/2008	536.91 EUR	0.00 EUR	-17.46 EUR
		02/2008	536.91 EUR	0.00 EUR	-17.46 EUR
		03/2008	536.91 EUR	0.00 EUR	-17.46 EUR
		04/2008	536.91 EUR	0.00 EUR	-17.46 EUR
		05/2008	536.91 EUR	0.00 EUR	-17.46 EUR
		06/2008	536.91 EUR	0.00 EUR	-17.46 EUR
		Result	3,221.46 EUR	0.00 EUR	-104.76 EUR
	Result		24,379,995.73 EUR	-18,964.51 EUR	-781,883.28 EUR

Figure 5.66 Condition Key Figures After a Currency Translation

Because the condition key figures were integrated into the data model and are consequently available at the billing item level, you can add further characteristics in the report definition, if necessary. This enables you to generate detailed views that can be drilled down to the individual billing documents and items as required.

Similar to the mapping of different currencies, problems regarding the "*" display may also occur for analyses of quantities if the units of measure differ. This problem can be solved in a similar way by using specific *quantity conversion types* so that all quantities are converted in base units of measure, for example. However, for cross-material evaluations, it usually makes sense to display each unit of measure separately.

5.4.3 Margin Analysis

The margin analysis is a special example for the use of key figures from billing conditions.

The *margin* is determined via the relation of the contribution margin to the revenue. Consequently, the contribution margin is required to determine the margin. You can calculate the contribution margin by subtracting the cost of goods manufactured of the material from the net value of the item. You can derive the cost of goods manufactured of the material via the *cost of goods sold* from the VPRS condition.

The used InfoProvider in SAP BW contains all figures that you require to determine the margin. A standard extractor provides the revenue as a *net value*. The cost is a condition value that is also made available by the standard extractor. In SAP BW, it's referred to as the *cost of goods sold in document currency* key figure. To calculate the determined margin in an evaluation, proceed as follows:

1. Integrate the *net value* and *cost of goods sold* in document currency key figures into the query definition.
2. Integrate a formula for the contribution margin with the following logic: *Contribution Margin = Net Value – Cost of Goods Sold*.
3. Integrate a formula for the margin with the following logic: Margin = Percentages of the Contribution Margin in Revenue.
4. Hide the *net value*, *cost of goods sold*, and *contribution margin* key figures, if you don't want to display them in the evaluation.

Such an evaluation might look like the one displayed in Figure 5.67.

Table							
Sold-to party		Billing document	Billing item	Net value	Cost of Goods Sold	Contribution margin	Margin
1032	Institute for Environmental Research	90034754	10	96,378.60 EUR	17,123.92 EUR	79,254.68 EUR	82.23 %
			20	207,051.00 EUR	30,043.00 EUR	177,008.00 EUR	85.49 %
			30	104,488.80 EUR	18,794.49 EUR	85,694.31 EUR	82.01 %
			40	85,385.00 EUR	11,795.50 EUR	73,589.50 EUR	86.19 %
			Result	493,303.40 EUR	77,756.91 EUR	415,546.49 EUR	84.24 %
1172	CBD Computer Based Design	90034699	10	9,324.80 EUR	6,299.20 EUR	3,025.60 EUR	32.45 %
			20	21,540.75 EUR	6,352.50 EUR	15,188.25 EUR	70.51 %
			30	50,281.10 EUR	55,364.70 EUR	-5,083.60 EUR	-10.11 %
			40	19,327.00 EUR	13,804.00 EUR	5,523.00 EUR	28.58 %
			Result	100,473.65 EUR	81,820.40 EUR	18,653.25 EUR	18.57 %
		90034727	10	6,864.90 EUR	4,438.02 EUR	2,426.88 EUR	35.35 %
			20	12,161.80 EUR	7,873.60 EUR	4,288.20 EUR	35.26 %
			30	12,940.20 EUR	16,565.38 EUR	-3,625.18 EUR	-28.01 %
			40	10,308.00 EUR	6,687.60 EUR	3,620.40 EUR	35.12 %
			Result	42,274.90 EUR	35,564.60 EUR	6,710.30 EUR	15.87 %
		90034737	10	8,990.40 EUR	5,849.60 EUR	3,140.80 EUR	34.94 %
			20	9,448.80 EUR	6,135.63 EUR	3,313.17 EUR	35.06 %
			30	11,566.10 EUR	7,511.40 EUR	4,054.70 EUR	35.06 %
			40	1,016.50 EUR	659.60 EUR	356.90 EUR	35.11 %
			Result	31,021.80 EUR	20,156.23 EUR	10,865.57 EUR	35.03 %
		Result		173,770.35 EUR	137,541.23 EUR	36,229.12 EUR	20.85 %
Overall Result				667,073.75 EUR	215,298.14 EUR	451,775.61 EUR	67.72 %

Figure 5.67   Margin per Billing Item

By default, the margin is determined from the cumulated figures for *net value* and *contribution margin* and displayed in the results row. You can configure the properties of the margin key figure in such a way that the results row displays the average of all values, for example. After all, mapping the margin at the aggregated level (see Section 5.1, Quotation Key Figures) is another issue here.

5.5   Key Figures in the Cross-Company Business

The cross-company business is a special case in the S&D process. The distinctive features of this process and the resulting difficulties regarding the evaluation of this business were discussed in detail in Section 4.7, Key Figures in the Cross-Company Business. This section describes the advantages of an evaluation in SAP NetWeaver BI.

Similar to the previous sections, the InfoProvider that provides the respective data should be mentioned here. All evaluations explained in this section are based on data of the *sales and distribution: IO/OH/revenue* InfoProvider. Therefore, a filter was set for this InfoProvider in all evaluations.

5.5.1 Cross-Company Sales

The distinctive aspect of the *cross-company sales* process is the creation of a sales order in the sales area of the selling company code (A). The delivery is made by a plant of an associate company (B), that is, by a different company code in the group. The system generates two billing documents — one that names the end customer as the payer and an internal billing document in which A is the payer.

A can evaluate the process without any problems; incoming orders, order on hand, and revenue are determined and updated. However, for B, there is only a billing document but no order. Consequently, it can't determine the incoming orders or orders on hand. SAP ERP provides no standard solution for this purpose, but SAP NetWeaver BI enables you to solve this problem with your own logic. You can do that with the following procedure:

1. **Check whether the process is a cross-company sales process**
   The system checks during the update of the sales order items into the SAP BW system whether the process is a cross-company sales process. This is the case when the sales organization from the document (A) is assigned to a different company code (otherwise, it would only be a cross-plant sales process) than the sales organization that can be determined from the master data of the plant (B). It must be mentioned for further explanation that the plant in the document item corresponds to the plant from B in such cases. A respective sales organization and distribution channel are generally maintained in the master data of the plant.

2. **Duplicate and further process the document in SAP BW**
   In such cases, the incoming data record is duplicated within SAP BW. As characteristics, it contains the *sales organization* and *distribution channel* that the system derives from the master data of the delivering plant (B). From the determined sales organization (B), in turn, it derives the company code (B) and the local currency, which are contained in the master data. Furthermore, you must fill the *sold-to party*, *ship-to party*, *bill-to party*, and *payer* information in this data record, which in this case is A. You can derive this information from the master data of the sales organization (A) of the original document. You should note in this context that a customer number is generally maintained in the master data of the sales organization. This number is required for these cross-company purposes.

3. **Adapt the net value**

   You can't just copy the net value of the duplicated order. Instead, the net value must correspond to the cost between the two organizational units. For this reason, the conditions of the original order are read. The cost is stored in a specific condition type. This condition type is defined in the Customizing in SAP ERP.

The result of this process is a second sales order for B. This enables B to also output incoming orders and orders on hand so that the corresponding values are included in the general evaluations. Figure 5.68 shows an evaluation of such a cross-company sales process.

Sales Organization	Distribution Channel	Company code	Sold-to party		Sales document	Billing document	Incoming orders value	Revenue	Orders on hand value
UK Heathrow/Hayes	10	2000	12500	Chemical Machines Ltd.	13024	90036997	0.00 EUR	10,000.00 EUR	-10,000.00 EUR
						#	10,000.00 EUR	0.00 EUR	10,000.00 EUR
		Result					10,000.00 EUR	10,000.00 EUR	0.00 EUR
Germany Frankfurt	10	1000	13000	Sales Company UK	13024	90036998	0.00 EUR	7,500.00 EUR	-7,500.00 EUR
						#	7,500.00 EUR	0.00 EUR	7,500.00 EUR
		Result					7,500.00 EUR	7,500.00 EUR	0.00 EUR
Overall Result							17,500.00 EUR	17,500.00 EUR	0.00 EUR

Figure 5.68 Evaluation of a Cross-Company Sales Process

This figure illustrates that the order 13024 exists in two company codes. For the selling company code 2000, the sold-to party is an end customer. However, the delivering company code has "Sales Company UK", "13000" (representing the selling company code), as the sold-to party. This figure also illustrates that, due to the duplication of the order, the *incoming orders* and *orders on hand* key figures are updated in both company codes.

Another aspect that is emphasized here is the relationship among the *incoming orders*, *revenue*, and *orders on hand* key figures. You can see that the order increases the incoming orders and orders on hand, whereas the billing document increases the revenue and decreases the orders on hand. At totals level, you can view the respective current statuses. In our example, there is a total for each company code and an overall result for the two company codes (refer to Figure 5.68). However, it only makes sense to map an overall result if you don't want to consider consolidated information.

5.5.2 Cross-Company Stock Transfer

In contrast to cross-company sales, cross-company stock transfers take place when a company code purchases goods at a different company code. Here, a stock transport order is created in the purchasing company code (C). The delivering company code (D) delivers the goods to C and creates an internal billing document with reference to the delivery.

In this context, the problem is immediately obvious, too. In the delivering company code, neither incoming orders nor orders on hand are updated because there is no order in the system. Within SAP NetWeaver BI, you can solve this problem by proceeding as follows:

1. **Extract the purchase orders from SAP ERP**
   You extract the purchase orders from the SAP ERP MM (materials management) component into the SAP BW system via standard extractors.

2. **Check whether the process is a cross-company stock transfer process**
   When this data is updated, only the stock transport orders are updated into the data target. The system discards all other purchase orders here (if required, they are stored in other DataStores if you generally want to evaluate all purchase orders for other purposes). You recognize stock transport orders because the EKKO-RESWK field is filled. Consequently, the respective information, *plant* and *delivering plant*, of the data record is checked. The company code of the plant mustn't be identical to the company code of the delivering plant. Note that you can derive the company code from the master data of the plant or delivering plant.

3. **Store and further process the transport order as a sales order**
   If a stock transport order is provided, it's stored as an sales order in the delivering company code (D) within SAP BW. Here, the sales order number and item are filled from the purchase order number and item. First, specific characteristics are determined: *sold-to party*, *ship-to party*, *bill-to party*, and *payer*. They can be derived from the master data of the plant (ordering plant [C]) because a customer is maintained for cross-company processes here. Additionally, you need to determine the sales organization and distribution channel. For this purpose, we access the master data of the delivering plant (D).

By means of this procedure, the system artificially generates the missing sales order in the delivering company code in SAP NetWeaver BI. This enables you to map the incoming orders and orders on hand completely. The logic described here enables you to artificially generate an order within SAP NetWeaver BI in the delivering company code, 1000, for the stock transport order shown in Figure 4.54. The corresponding result is shown in Figure 5.69.

Table									
Sales Organization	Distribution Channel	Company code	Sold-to party		Sales document	Billing document	Incoming orders value	Revenue	Orders on hand value
Germany Frankfurt	10	1000	1186	2000 London	4500017676	90036812	0.00 EUR	650.00 EUR	-650.00 EUR
						#	650.00 EUR	0.00 EUR	650.00 EUR
						Result	650.00 EUR	650.00 EUR	0.00 EUR
					4500053802	90036999	0.00 EUR	6,500.00 EUR	-6,500.00 EUR
						#	6,500.00 EUR	0.00 EUR	6,500.00 EUR
						Result	6,500.00 EUR	6,500.00 EUR	0.00 EUR
					Result		7,150.00 EUR	7,150.00 EUR	0.00 EUR

Figure 5.69 Evaluation of Cross-Company Stock Transfers

Now you can also map the *incoming orders* and *orders on hand* key figures for this process, which allows for complete reporting.

5.6   Summary

This chapter introduced the implementation of process-oriented sales key figures using SAP NetWeaver BI. In this context, it referred to the key figures and processes described in Chapter 4, Key Figures in the Sales and Distribution Process, and explained the various options to format this information. In addition to the evaluation of the SAP standard general key figures, this chapter also showed how you can extend and optimize reporting according to your requirements. Although we couldn't cover all functions and options in SAP NetWeaver BI, we introduced the most important and most frequently used methods, and discussed the advantages and disadvantages of individual options. Together with Chapter 3, SD Sample Scenario, this chapter illustrated what comprehensive S&D controlling with SAP NetWeaver BI can look like.

Because this chapter only dealt with detailed analyses in Microsoft Excel, the next chapter uses some examples for cross-sectional evaluations in the web.

6 Cross-Sectional Evaluations

What is an evaluation supposed to look like that provides the required data in an appealing design? This question can be answered with examples from SAP NetWeaver BI Portal applications.

The following chapter introduces you to the options for mapping cross-sectional evaluations. In this context, we use examples of evaluations with regard to a material or sold-to party. You can implement such evaluations with various tools, for example, with the Web Application Designer (introduced in Chapter 2, SAP NetWeaver BI), Visual Composer, or Microsoft Excel workbooks. The evaluations described in this chapter are illustrated with these first two tools.

6.1 Tools

Visual Composer allows you to design applications for *SAP NetWeaver Portal* without any programming. With a model defined in Visual Composer you can map the required key figures and characteristics, as well as custom-developed fields with different display elements. This includes, for example, table views of all data or subareas, statistical charts, and form views of single values. Queries and views previously created in BEx Analyzer form the source of the characteristics and key figures.

Visual Composer also enables you to call *web templates* and transfer characteristic and variable values in order to initiate dynamic evaluations, if applicable without user intervention.

Section 2.4, Web Reporting, already introduced the functions of the *Web Application Designer*. In this context, it's used to illustrate the following:

▶ How you trigger individual analyses from the Visual Composer application and, in addition to displaying statistical data, manually and conveniently navigate within these analyses

▶ How you can map the data initially formatted in Visual Composer with a web template using alternative options

All evaluations described in the following sections can also be created via Excel reporting, a topic explained in detail in Section 2.3, Reporting Options in Microsoft Excel, and can subsequently be saved as workbooks. However, the following sections focus on web reporting.

There is no general answer to the question about which tool is best suited for your requirements. The selection of the appropriate tool also depends on the target group for the created evaluations. Many users like to work with detailed analyses in Excel, whereas others prefer appealing layouts and easy web access to important information or key figures. The following sections explain how you can vary and combine these requirements.

6.2   Evaluation via Visual Composer

Let's first take a look at applications created using Visual Composer. Similar to web applications or web templates (see Section 2.2, The Basic Principles of Data Retrieval), they can be integrated with SAP NetWeaver Portal. For this purpose, we generated a separate portal role and assigned it to the users. Consequently, the portal now contains a new menu entry, SALES AND DISTRIBUTION • OVERVIEW (see Figure 6.1), which provides the two evaluations, MATERIAL DETAILS and CUSTOMER DETAILS.

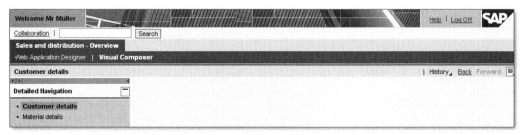

Figure 6.1   New Menu Entry in SAP NetWeaver Portal

6.2.1   Details per Material

This evaluation maps different information about a material. In addition to sales key figures, such as sales per material, or typical material information, such as master data and stock, you can evaluate cross-sectional data. For example, you can find all customers who've purchased a particular material. Figure 6.2 shows the initial screen, which contains the area for the material selection.

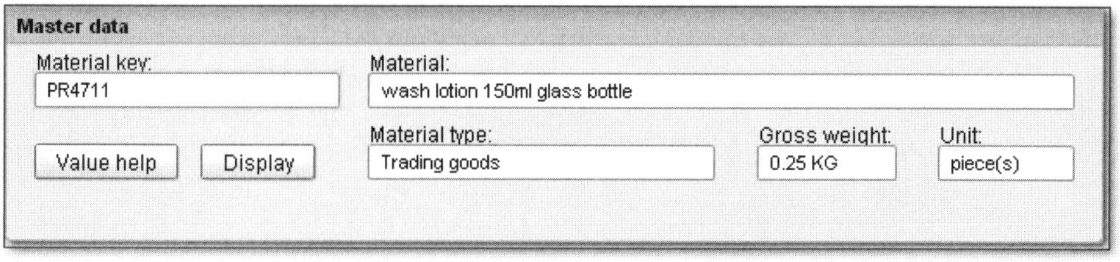

Figure 6.2 Area for the Material Selection and Master Data Display

First of all you enter the required material key in the respective field or select it from a list using value help. Subsequently, the system displays the corresponding master data. The material key is also the basis for the determination of additional data from various queries that can be based on completely different DataProviders. Figure 6.3 shows the entire screen after a material has been selected. Because the top area includes the actual master data, and the bottom area contains the corresponding transaction data, a clear structure is given.

In this view, the transaction data is divided into four categories:

▶ Stocks

▶ Units/prices

▶ Revenues per sold-to party

▶ Order quantities per sold-to party

These categories are described in the following sections in further detail.

When selecting the STOCKS tab, the system maps the consignment stock not assigned to a storage location in our plant (see Consignment in Section 4.3.1) and for the total stock, valuated stock, and quality inspection stock. It does this as an aggregated value (in a base unit of measure) and in the form of a bar chart that assigns the stock to the individual storage locations (see Figure 6.3). By moving the mouse pointer to a value range, you can view the detailed values in the chart. As you can see in Figure 6.3, the system displays a *tool tip* that provides detailed information on this value. The developers can create such tool tips for nearly all elements. They can be helpful for explaining the displayed content, or functionality of buttons and text fields without any length restrictions.

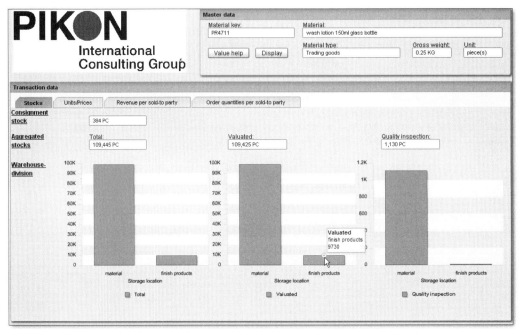

Figure 6.3 Overview After the Material Selection

In addition to the stock quantities, the value of the material is often interesting as well. Of course, you could map it in the same way, but alternatively you could have the system display the current material price. In the material master of SAP ERP there are two prices maintained for our example: a standard price and an average price. The UNITS/PRICES tab in Figure 6.4 displays these prices as well as the PRICE CONTROL indicator. This indicator defines which of these two prices is relevant for the evaluation of stocks.

The right area in Figure 6.4 shows the available quantity units and conversion factors for the selected material. They were also copied from the material master in SAP ERP and constitute the basis for the quantity conversions in SAP BW (see Section 5.4.2, Key Figures from Billing Conditions).

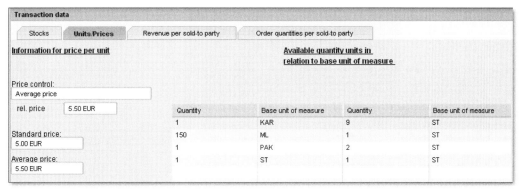

Figure 6.4 Units and Individual Prices

The Revenue per Sold-to Party tab (see Figure 6.5) maps the supplied sold-to parties with quantity, revenue, contribution margin, and margin key figures. This table lists all billing data for the selected material at the sold-to party level. It consequently provides an overview of the revenue and profitability of the material across all customers.

Transaction data

Stocks	Units/prices	Revenue per sold-to party	Order quantity per sold-to party		

Billing documents

Sold-to party	Billing quantity	Billing net value	Cost of goods sold	Contribution margin	Margin
Becker Berlin	10 PC	117.00 EUR	55.00 EUR	62.00 EUR	53.0 %
Miller's Drugstore	182 PC	2,184.00 EUR	901.00 EUR	1,283.00 EUR	58.7 %
Karl Miller LLC.	110 PC	1,320.00 EUR	605.00 EUR	715.00 EUR	54.2 %
DROBEDA Drugstore Trade ltd.	140 PC	1,680.00 EUR	770.00 EUR	910.00 EUR	54.2 %
Drugstore UK	27 PC	324.00 EUR	148.50 EUR	175.50 EUR	54.2 %

Figure 6.5 Revenue per Sold-to Party

In this context, it's also possible to display the number of free deliveries, samples, or credit memos per customer to complement the material overview.

The last tab, Order quantities per sold-to party, is a supplement here. This tab displays the order quantities per sold-to party, for example, for the current year and the previous year (see Figure 6.6). In our example, a pie chart was chosen because it is the best method to indicate that three quarters of the sales volume were made by only two customers in the period selected. Of course, you could use other charts or tables to display the data as you wish.

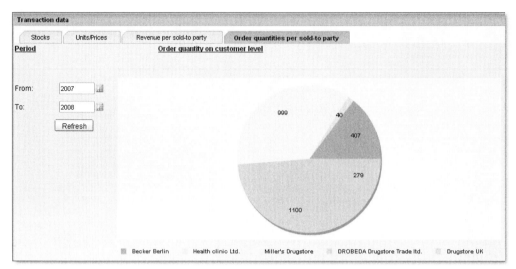

Figure 6.6 Order Quantities per Sold-to Party

As you can see in the left area of Figure 6.6, this application also allows you to select any period and refresh the chart accordingly. In our example, you can only make this selection on an annual basis. Depending on the level of detail from the DataProvider, you could choose any other periodicity, such as quarterly, monthly, weekly, or daily.

As mentioned at the beginning, the data is made available by different InfoProviders. To map the information onto the ORDER QUANTITIES PER SOLD-TO PARTY and REVENUE PER SOLD-TO PARTY tabs, the InfoProviders described in Chapter 3, SD Sample Scenario, were used. However, a separate InfoCube for material stock and movements provided the information for the STOCKS tab. Additional information, such as general master data and the information on the UNITS/PRICES tab is directly supplied from the InfoObject master data. This illustrates how merging information from various sources can be implemented in a clearly structured application. Of course, you could combine the information from various sources on a single page. However, in this application tabs were preferred because they allowed us to group various data for an optimized presentation.

6.2.2 Details per Customer

For an evaluation at the customer level, the customer's information is determined from a selection area relating to the sold-to party. In this area, we provided two methods to determine the sold-to party. Either you can select it from a top 10 list based on their sales volume, or you can make it through the provided value help, which lists all sold-to parties available. From now on, the sold-to party number is the basis for further data determination processes. Figure 6.7 shows the selection area. The top area displays a *wizard* that divides the selection area and customer data area for visual clarity.

Figure 6.7 Selection Screen for Sold-to Party

If you click on the EXECUTE button after the selection, this screen closes and a screen with the required data opens (see Figure 6.8). Here, you can use the BACK button to return to the selection screen at any time. The REFRESH button next to it updates the TRANSACTION DATA, if required.

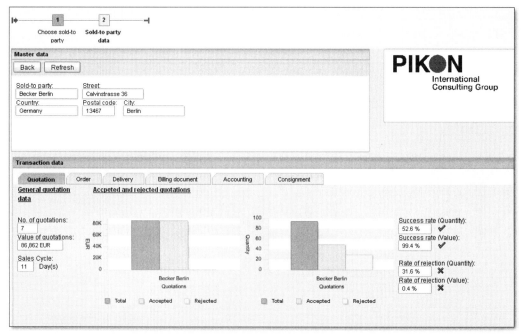

Figure 6.8 Customer Data Area After the Selection of the Sold-to Party

The screen is divided into two areas; the top area contains the master data of the sold-to party, which doesn't have to be restricted to the address data selected in our example. The area below contains the transaction data or business data of the sold-to party. The tabs displayed include all required information, respectively grouped and formatted. They contain the key figures previously described in Chapter 4, Key Figures in the Sales and Distribution Process. In addition, the tabs contain information on the selected sold-to party's not originating from the sales and distribution (SD) component of SAP ERP.

The following sections detail the individual tabs and the information mapped in those tabs.

Quotation Tab

The QUOTATION tab shown in Figure 6.8 displays some of the quotation key figures that you already know from Section 5.1, Quotation Key Figures. This tab has two areas. The General Quotation area includes data such as No. OF QUOTATIONS, VALUE OF QUOTATIONS, and SALES CYCLE IN DAYS. The ACCEPTED AND REJECTED QUOTATIONS area includes accepted and rejected quotations based on their values and quantities displayed in the form of quotation rates, with regard to whether they were successful or rejected.

Order Tab

The ORDER tab (see Figure 6.9), in contrast, provides common information and details about the order.

Transaction data

Quotation	Order	Delivery	Billing document	Accounting	Consignment

Common information

Order value:
52,101,474 EUR

Total:
215

No. of order items:
242

Details

Sales doc. type	Net value	Open orders total
Scheduling agreement	54,350.00 EUR	54,340.00 EUR
SchedAg. w/ del.schd	61,750.00 EUR	24,700.00 EUR
PS: order	640,014.11 EUR	440,014.11 EUR
Returns	-53,196.20 EUR	-597.00 EUR
Invoice correct. req	-98.00 EUR	0.00 EUR
Standard Order	51,352,823.09 EUR	4,917,333.06 EUR
VBV	423.21 EUR	0.00 EUR

Figure 6.9 Information on the Order

This area displays the ORDER VALUE, that is, the overall value of all orders from the sold-to party, the total number of orders and items ordered. The table next to it groups the orders by sales document type. In this example, it also maps the corresponding net value and open order values.

Delivery Tab

The DELIVERY tab illustrated in Figure 6.10 displays the information on the on-time delivery performance. This includes the number of delay in days per delivery process. This key figure is determined as an average value for all deliveries and then mapped in the left area of the screen. The tab also displays statistics on the delay in delivery in the form of a run chart. (We did not map general delivery key figures, but it would of course be possible.)

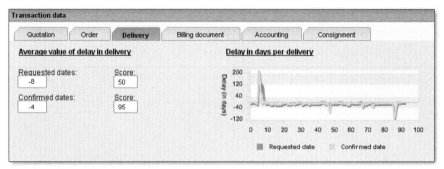

Figure 6.10 Information on the Delivery

You confirm a delivery date to the sold-to party by scheduling the order. The sold-to party may also specify a requested delivery date, which is then stored in the order. According to the respective point of view, different delays may occur (see Figure 6.10). Chapter 4, Key Figures in the Sales and Distribution Process, introduced a scoring scheme where you can assign scores to the delivery processes. This scoring scheme allows for a meaningful evaluation of the on-time delivery performance for a particular sold-to party and enables you to better compare different delivery processes. The resulting score is also displayed in the left area of the screen. For example, a too early delivery of less than eight days would be a score of 50 according to Table 4.2 in Section 4.5.2, On-Time Delivery Performance.

Billing Document Tab

In addition to the billing quantity in the base unit of measure and the corresponding billed net value, the BILLING DOCUMENT tab contains a table with the individual billing values (see Figure 6.11) based on the sales organization, distribution channel, division, and material. This view displays the BILLING NET VALUE, FREIGHT, BONUS, CUSTOMER DISCOUNT, SURCHARGE, and CASH DISCOUNT key figures.

Sales organizatic	Distribution chan	Division	Material	Billing net value	Freight	Bonus	Customer discou	Surcharge	Cash discount
Germany Frankfu	Final customer sa	Cross-division	-Product hierar	1,249,119.10 EUF	0.00 EUR	-73.62 EUR	-32,201.73 EUR	0.00 EUR	-294,692.67 EUF
Germany Frankfu	Final customer sa	Cross-division	+Machines	1,145,806.00 EUF	0.00 EUR	-68.06 EUR	-25,731.68 EUR	0.00 EUR	-246,953.49 EUF
Germany Frankfu	Final customer sa	Cross-division	+Elevators	0.00 EUR	0.00 EUR	0.00 EUR	0.00 EUR	0.00 EUR	-33,288.87 EUF
Germany Frankfu	Final customer sa	Cross-division	+Hardware	103,158.60 EUR	0.00 EUR	-1.28 EUR	-6,461.00 EUR	0.00 EUR	-14,444.79 EUF
Germany Frankfu	Final customer sa	Cross-division	+Shipping unit	154.50 EUR	0.00 EUR	-4.28 EUR	-9.05 EUR	0.00 EUR	-5.52 EUR
Germany Frankfu	Final customer sa	Cross-division	+Not Assigned	85,930.65 EUR	4.00 EUR	-1,493.43 EUR	-6,560.20 EUR	9.05 EUR	-3,091.70 EUR

Figure 6.11 Information on the Billing Document

The user can also navigate to a web template by clicking on the DETAILS button. This web template provides a billing query based on the sold-to party and allows for an individual design of the layout by navigation. The example of the analysis of days overdue in the next section illustrates such navigation.

Accounting Tab

The ACCOUNTING tab maps the payment history of the sold-to party as a chart (see Figure 6.12). The payment delay is displayed in days based on the billing documents with or without cash discount. This tab also provides additional information for accounts receivable, including the revenue and balance of the period, the credit limit, and the number of days sales outstanding key figures. This is the average numbers of days that pass from the issue of a billing document to the receipt of a payment.

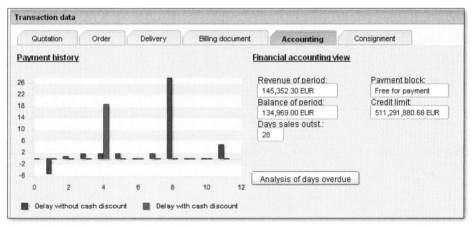

Figure 6.12   Information on Accounting

You can map the analysis of days overdue, which groups the delays into different time frames, in an outsourced web template by clicking on the ANALYSIS OF DAYS OVERDUE button (see Figure 6.13). This also illustrates the close relationship between the various applications.

You can freely navigate within the web template. For example, you can remove the drilldown by document type or call data from a different company code as required. The corresponding result can then be exported to Excel or as a PDF using inbuilt system buttons.

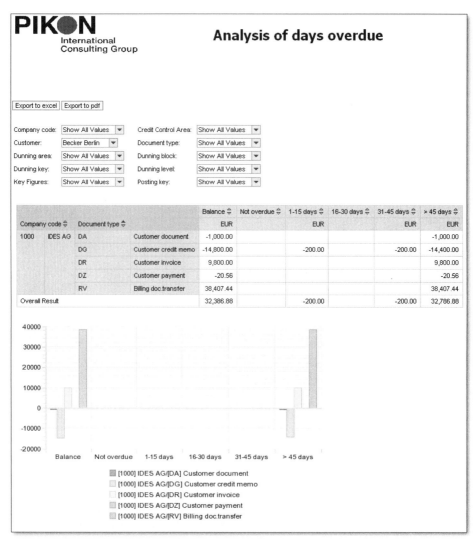

Figure 6.13 Web Template for the Analysis of Days Overdue

Consignment Tab

The last tab, CONSIGNMENT, shown in Figure 6.14 displays a table of the stock still owned by the contractor but is in possession of the selected sold-to party. As well as the quantity, it also maps the material description and the corresponding issue value.

Transaction data			
Quotation	Order	Delivery	Billing document	Accounting	**Consignment**

Material	Issue quantity of consignment stock at i	Issue value	Receipt quantity of consignment stock a
Casing	0 PC	0.00 EUR	300 PC
mineral water 0,2 litre glass bottle	2 PC	0.80 EUR	769 PC
mineral water 0,33 litre glass bottle	6 PC	3.00 EUR	1,527 PC
mineral water 0,5 litre glass bottle	3 PC	1.65 EUR	907 PC
wash lotion 150ml glass bottle	18 PC	99.00 EUR	936 PC
wash lotion 150ml plastic bottle	5 PC	27.50 EUR	465 PC

Figure 6.14 Information on the Customer Consignment

Similar to the material application, data from different enterprise areas was integrated with this application. It focuses on the customer; consequently, some key figures of sales and distribution controlling assume a critical role. However, the view is complemented and optimized by means of additional accounting and consignment data.

6.2.3 Technical Background of the Visual Composer

This section discusses a part of the design area of Visual Composer in detail. In this context, we refer to the CUSTOMER DETAILS application. However, a very detailed look behind the scenes would take far too long, so this section only roughly describes the process from selecting the sold-to party to displaying the data. Figure 6.15 illustrates the entry point to the model.

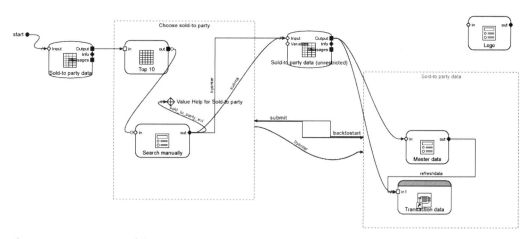

Figure 6.15 Entry Point of the Program with Sold-to Party Selection

This model must be read from left to right. It maps the two most critical elements in the CHOOSE SOLD-TO PARTY layer:

▶ The top 10 table view element

▶ The search manually form view element

They can be used to later search for the sold-to party number. After having confirmed the selection, the system executes the sold-to party data (unrestricted) query with the characteristic restriction to the corresponding sold-to party number. In the SOLD-TO PARTY DATA layer, the master data form view element is then filled with the corresponding values from the result of the query, and the sold-to party number is transferred to the embedded transaction data iView element.

A Nested iView is an element that can include more components, such as form view elements, or table view elements. In this scenario, the Nested iView element contains the transaction data. For modeling, this element provides the option to limit the application to a manageable size and allows for thematic separations. In our example, this structure separates the master data from the transaction data.

Note that a Nested iView element can't directly access data from outside its level (e.g., the sold-to party number of the sold-to party data query). *Signals* are the solution here. The system transfers the sold-to party number in the form of a signal element to the Nested iView element. Consequently, it's available within the iView as an incoming signal. Figure 6.16 shows an excerpt of the Nested iView element.

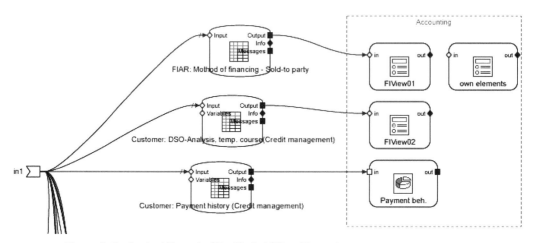

Figure 6.16 Content Excerpt of the Nested iView Element

The IN1 connector symbol that maps the start element of the Nested iView (shown on the left in Figure 6.16) can be considered as the sold-to party number selected at the beginning. This value is now available to be used as the characteristic restriction for other queries. To limit the complexity of this area, it should be mentioned that a similar process takes place for each tab of the application within its own Nested iView. The ACCOUNTING tab is almost predestined to be used as an example of the interaction between multiple applications.

In Figure 6.16, three queries with a characteristic restriction to the sold-to party (indicated by the binding arrows between the IN symbol signal and the query symbols) are triggered. The results are included in two form views and one chart view within the Accounting iView element. This illustrates that the Accounting iView element in the executed application corresponds to the tab with the same name. The single form view element shown on the top right in the figure contains HTML text elements to map the headings and a button that provides the interface for calling a web template with an analysis of days overdue. Within the button definition, the URL of the web template—including the corresponding sold-to party number—is transferred to the web browser. In this regard, no further modeling steps must be performed in the application. The system now starts the web template in the web browser independently of Visual Composer. It provides the functions that were modeled in the Web Application Designer (see Section 2.4, Web Reporting).

6.3 Evaluation via the Web Application Designer — The Sales and Distribution Overview Web Template

Now that you've seen the cross-sectional evaluations with examples from Visual Composer applications, this section moves on to deal with the evaluation options based on web templates. To compare Visual Composer with the Web Application Designer, the same data is used (but not to the full extent).

Like our Visual Composer applications, this template is also divided into DETAILS PER CUSTOMER and DETAILS PER MATERIAL tabs. In contrast to the Visual Composer tool, however, we decided to combine both sub applications in one overall application. This enables you, for example, to design a menu control for both applications. You'll learn more about this later.

We used a design that maps evaluations in the conventional way (DETAILS PER MATERIAL) but also allows for a creative layout of information (DETAILS PER CUSTOMER). This shows the various options that the Web Application Designer provides. Like the applications of Visual Composer, the web template is integrated into SAP NetWeaver Portal by being assigned to our portal role. Consequently, the menu is extended by a web application entry. Figure 6.17 displays the structure of the application, including the portal menu entry.

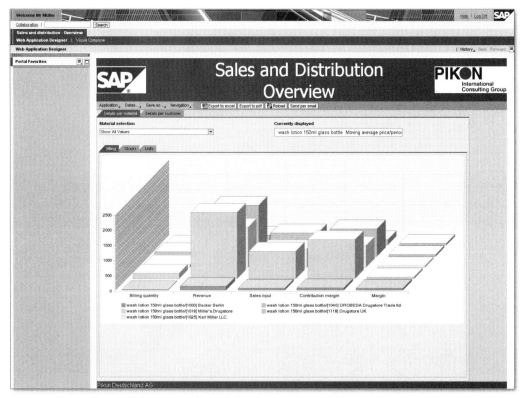

Figure 6.17   Initial Screen of the Web Application

The navigation pane shown in Figure 6.17 results again from the portal integration, as the Visual Composer application previously introduced. The right area of the screen includes the initial view of the actual web application, which is described in further detail in the following paragraphs.

The header area of our web template displays design elements, such as a company logo and title. Below the header, the menu area and tool bar are available within the entire web application and serve to control both sub applications. Currently, our menu area comprises of the following functions:

▶ Closing the application

▶ Reloading data

▶ Exporting to Excel or PDF files

▶ Navigations steps, for example, BACK TO START or BACK ONE NAVIGATION STEP

Such a menu is provided as a web item in the Web Application Designer and can be integrated with any web template, if required. You can freely configure the menu entries. You can also provide specific functions via buttons. For illustration, the web template includes buttons that enable the export of the evaluation to an Excel or PDF file (like the corresponding menu functions). You can also click on the REFRESH button to again import all displayed master data and transaction data of the material or customer from SAP BW. This function is of particular use when the data in SAP BW is updated during the day.

In addition, the SEND PER EMAIL button enables you to send the web template via BEx Broadcaster. You can use the Broadcaster for various purposes, for example, you can regularly send evaluations by email to specific user groups. This function is often used to automatically send the corresponding revenue figures, plan/actual comparisons, or target checks to field sales representatives by email. The Broadcaster can also be used in exception reporting whereby emails to people responsible are triggered when a value exceeds or falls below a certain threshold value. In our example, the function is provided as a button, which means that a user who analyzes the current data can send this evaluation, for example, as a PDF file, or link to other users.

Let's now take a look at the two sub applications in the bottom area of the screen, DETAILS PER MATERIAL and DETAILS PER CUSTOMER. When you start the application, it first displays the DETAILS PER MATERIAL area. You can select the required material via a dropdown field. The mere selection in this web item triggers the loading of material-specific data. The header area displays the material master data as a ticker here and the bottom area maps the transaction data that was previously organized in different subareas using tabs.

Figure 6.17 has already shown that the BILLING DOCUMENT tab displays various billing key figures in a chart. Additional tabs provide information on STOCKS and UNITS/PRICES.

We now turn to the DETAILS PER CUSTOMER tab, which represents the second sub application. This information is mapped entirely differently to show you the various options of this tool. Figure 6.18 displays the web template, which contains different small evaluations for a customer. As a background for this page an appropriate image was used, which considerably changes the look to the site. The master data of the selected customer is located in the center of the web template; in our example it's displayed as a ticker again.

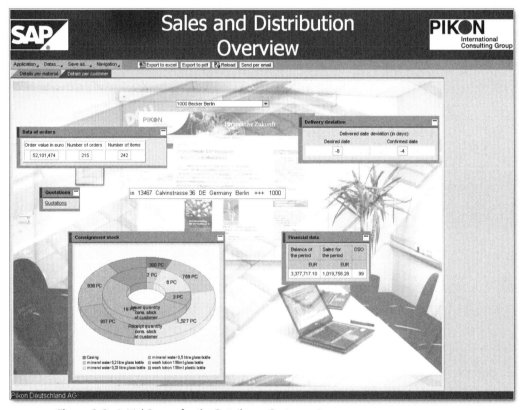

Figure 6.18   Initial Screen for the Details per Customer Area

In the header area, you can select the required customer. The selection immediately affects the evaluations below. They include in the example:

- Data of orders
- Delivery deviation information
- Consignment stocks
- Quotations
- Financial data
- Customer master data

You can open or close the web items that contain the transaction data of the customer as required. When the web item is closed, only the heading, for example, DATA OF ORDERS, is visible. This enables you to map multiple small analysis results in the screen in an appealing design. Of course, you can define the number and types of analyses displayed and their arrangement on the website, according to your needs and those of the target group when you create the web template using Web Application Designer. For the web template shown in Figure 6.18, we used different standard web items.

The FINANCIAL DATA table is based on a simple analysis item; the DATA OF ORDERS and DELIVERY DEVIATION tables, in contrast, were formatted with analysis and text items to display the values in a different design. To map the CONSIGNMENT STOCK, we selected a ring layout from the numerous chart categories available. While all of these evaluation elements directly map their result, the QUOTATIONS area contains a link (URL) to an additional web template. This web template opens in a new window when the currently selected sold-to party number is transferred. As you can see in Figure 6.19, it displays the graphically formatted quotation data.

If you now compare the web templates of Figures 6.13, 6.17, 6.18, and 6.19, you can imagine the creative power you're provided with to create appealing, plain, or even spectacular designs for your evaluations.

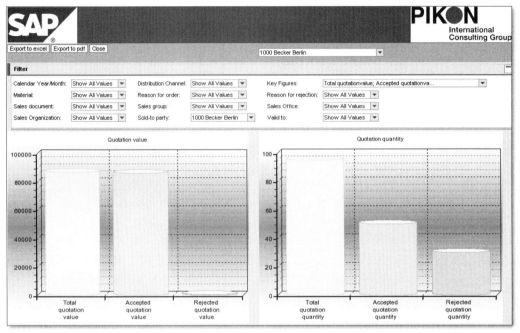

Figure 6.19 Quotation Analysis

6.4 Summary

This chapter introduced the means by which you can carry out cross-sectional evaluations. In this context, it described two methods in more detail: the web-based Visual Composer and Web Application Designer tools. Both enable you to create complex applications to carry out flexible and target group-oriented analyses. You can also link them, which enables the developer to design a comprehensive web application that combines the respective advantages of the tools. You can create plain web applications very quickly via drag and drop but also cover complex requirements with these tools. This ensures maximum flexibility.

7 Summary

This book has showed you how to use *SAP NetWeaver Business Intelligence* (SAP NetWeaver BI)—based on source data of the SAP ERP system—to implement key figures for process-oriented controlling of sales and distribution processes. We identified ways that you can gradually convert raw data created by users in transactional systems on a daily basis, into information for measuring, controlling, and optimizing business processes. We are convinced that using a BI system is a future-oriented and profitable investment that will consequently optimize the processes of your enterprise.

Chapter 1 first outlined the goals and reasons for writing this book. Because we particularly wanted to show the interplay of SAP ERP *and* SAP NetWeaver BI, that is, discuss both the creation of source data and their preparation, it was logical to start with a brief overview of the SAP ERP system in the first chapter. This was followed by a discussion that detailed the significant basics of the SAP NetWeaver BI system.

Chapter 2 delved into these aspects and discussed the elementary components of SAP BW. You learned about the procedures for extracting and preparing data. We showed you which objects are available as modules for modeling data in SAP BW and how you can use these tools properly. Based on this information, the navigation and design options in reporting both in Microsoft Excel and on the web were presented. This part of the book provided the basic information required to understand the subsequent examples.

In Chapter 3, these examples started with a data model for mapping a sales scenario, which was initially based on the data sources of SAP Business Content. This allows you to evaluate information, which is provided as SAP standard. We also extended and enriched this information to show you the options for mapping individual requirements of your enterprise.

Chapter 4 outlined the creation of source data in SAP ERP. Along the sales and distribution process, which we subdivided into the phases of quotation processing, order processing, delivery, and billing document, we provided examples of key figures for the process-oriented sales and distribution controlling. You learned how the raw data develops along the business value chain. Particular attention was paid to the cross-company processes that are used to map inter-company delivery relationships and those that bear specific problems with regard to updating key figures.

Chapter 4 provides examples of the necessary requirements for sales and distribution controlling. Chapters 5 and 6 detailed the options for implementing these requirements in SAP NetWeaver BI. Wherever possible and useful, we provided multiple solutions to familiarize you with the design options available for the various components. This way, we showed the pros and cons of the various solutions so that you can evaluate them accordingly.

Ultimately, business intelligence allows users fast and easy access to important information in both form and content. With regard to content, Chapter 6 focused on cross-module evaluations. In this context, we provided information for an object (e.g., customer, material) from different areas in a compact form. For the optimal design and formatting of reports, we presented the tools SAP NetWeaver Visual Composer and Web Application Designer. They are particularly powerful when used in combination.

We hope that this book provided you with useful suggestions as well as methods and options to design intelligent solutions for process-oriented sales and distribution controlling with SAP NetWeaver BI.

We look forward to receiving your feedback!

The Authors

Susanne Hess has worked at PIKON Deutschland AG since 2002, where she is a Senior Consultant in Business Intelligence. She specializes in projects for the implementation of reporting systems and enterprise planning systems using SAP NetWeaver BI. In her work, Susanne has successfully implemented several requirements in the areas of sales controlling.

Stefanie Lenz has worked at PIKON Deutschland AG since 1998 and is manager of the Business Intelligence department. This department focuses on designing and implementing business intelligence solutions using SAP NetWeaver BI. She specializes in all SAP NetWeaver BI components: data extraction from source systems, modeling in SAP BW, programming of additional requirements, reporting, and implementing planning functions.

Jochen Scheibler is a member of the Board of Management of PIKON Deutschland AG (*www.pikon.com*), a consulting and software company that specializes in SAP. He and his business partner Jörg Hofmann founded the company in 1996. Jochen has worked for several years in the area of process-oriented SAP projects, with a particular emphasis on optimizing the entire business value chain. Jochen Scheibler is an established SAP PRESS author.

Index

Master CTM tools and techniques

Learn advanced planning methods
and special modeling techniques

Find valuable tips and best practices
from real-life projects

Balaji Gaddam

Capable to Match (CTM) with SAP APO

This is the first book that explains and teaches all of the core functions of
SAP's Capable-to-Match (CTM) functionality. This step-by-step guide for
configuring CTM, including CTM Master Data selection, Order Selection,
CTM Profile maintenance, and CTM configuration, educates readers on
the basic aspects of CTM, such as Demand Prioritization, Supply
Categorization, Multilevel Inventory, and Production Planning, as well as
several advanced topics including, CTM planning for Safety Stock, Safety
Days of Supply, and Maximum Earliness.

approx. 260 pp., 85,– Euro / US$ 85
ISBN 978-1-59229-244-8, April 2009

>> www.sap-press.de/1965

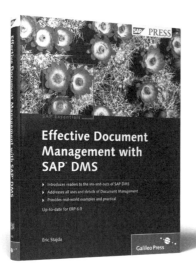

Introduces readers to the ins-and-outs of SAP DMS

Addresses all uses and details of Document Management

Provides real-world examples and practical

Up-to-date for ERP 6.0

Eric Stajda

Effective Document Management with SAP DMS

This essentials guide is a complete and practical resource to SAP Document Management System. It teaches project managers, functional users, and consultants everything they need to know to understand, configure, and use SAP DMS, and provides step-by-step instructions and real-world scenarios. This is a must-have book for anyone interested in learning about and creating an efficient, effective document management system using SAP.

approx. 202 pp., 68,– Euro / US$ 85
ISBN 978-1-59229-240-0

>> www.sap-press.de/1936

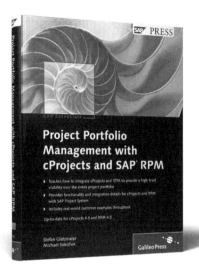

Teaches how to integrate cProjects and RPM
to provide a high-level visibility over the entire
project portfolio

Provides functionality and integration details for
cProjects and RPM with SAP Project System

Includes real-world customer examples
throughout

Up-to-date for cProjects 4.5 and RPM 4.5

Stefan Glatzmaier, Michael Sokollek

Project Portfolio Management with SAP RPM and cProjects

SAP PRESS Essentials 49

This essentials guide introduces and teaches users how to integrate and
use project portfolio management with SAP to support their business
processes. The book focuses on cProjects and SAP RPM, as well as the
integration with SAP Project System. With real-life examples, this book
uses examples to illustrate specific solution options and projects. The
main chapters are based on the actual business processes in an enterprise
and contain industry-specific recommendations. The book is based on
the latest releases, and is a must-have addition to any SAP library.

approx. 356 pp., 68,– Euro / US$ 85
ISBN 978-1-59229-224-0

>> www.sap-press.de/1838

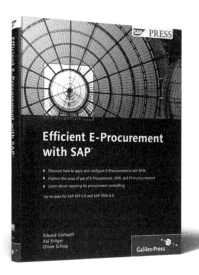

Learn how to use E-Procurement effectively with other SAP components, including MM and Financials

Explore the implementation processes to ensure an effective implementation

Find out how to optimize your procurement processes, reduce ordering costs, decentralize purchase orders, and more

Up-to-date for SAP ERP 6.0

Eduard Gerhardt, Kai Krüger, Oliver Schipp

Efficient E-Procurement with SAP

SAP PRESS Essentials 47

This book describes how to carry out procurement processes and map these processes in the SAP system, using the E-Procurement solution. Readers will learn which SAP tool is best suited for which requirement in purchasing and procurement, and which usage options these tools provide. Above all, readers will get to know how they can use E-Procurement in order to optimize their own procurement processes, reduce ordering costs, decentralize purchase orders, and reduce the Purchasing department workload.

201 pp., 2008, 68,– Euro / US$ 85
ISBN 978-1-59229-209-7

>> www.sap-press.de/1789

SAP PRESS

Master real-life business processes and the structuringof plant maintenance technical systems

Discover tips and tricks for implementing daily operations

Explore interfaces, reporting, and new EAM technologies – MAM, RFID, Enterprise SOA, NetWeaver Portal, and more

Karl Liebstückel

SAP Enterprise Asset Management

This is a must-have guide for anyone interested in learning about the implementation and customization of SAP EAM. Consultants, managers, and administrators will learn about the plant maintenance process, how to evaluate which processes work best for them, and then go on to review the actual configuration steps of these processes. This book includes practical tips and best practices for implementation projects. The companion DVD contains examples, practice tests, presentations, and more. This book is up-to-date for SAP ERP 6.0.

552 pp., 2008, with CD, 69,95 Euro / US$ 69.95
ISBN 978-1-59229-150-2

>> www.sap-press.de/1528

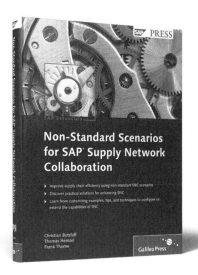

Improve supply chain efficiency using
non-standard SNC scenarios

Discover practical solutions for
enhancing SNC

Learn from customizing examples,
tips, and techniques to configure or
extend the capabilities of SNC

Christian Butzlaff, Thomas Heinzel, Frank Thome

Non-Standard Scenarios for
SAP Supply Network Collaboration

SAP PRESS Essentials 43

This Essentials is a detailed guide for those needing unique and new
scenarios to maximize their SNC solution. Based on SAP SNC 5.1, it
focuses on insightful, new information usually only available from highly
experienced consultants or SAP development, such as enhanced business
scenarios, and notification and authorization enhancements. The book
begins with a concise review of SNC, its architecture, and standard
scenarios, and then quickly moves on to the non-standard scenarios
and other techniques for enhancing and customizing SAP SNC.

approx. 200 pp., 68,– Euro / US$ 85
ISBN 978-1-59229-195-3, Jan 2009

>> www.sap-press.de/1741

Interested in reading more?

Please visit our Web site for all
new book releases from SAP PRESS.

www.sap-press.com